Education Between State, Markets, and Civil Society

Comparative Perspectives

Sociocultural, Political, and Historical Studies in Education
Joel Spring, Editor

Education between State, Markets, and Civil Society

Comparative Perspectives

Edited by

HEINZ-DIETER MEYER
State University of New York at Albany

WILLIAM L. BOYD
The Pennsylvania State University

2001

LAWRENCE ERLBAUM ASSOCIATES, PUBLISHERS
Mahwah, New Jersey   London

Lawrence Erlbaum Associates, Inc., Publishers
10 Industrial Avenue
Mahwah, New Jersey 07430

Cover design by Kathryn Houghtaling Lacey

Library of Congress Cataloging-in-Publication Data

Education between state, markets, and civil society : comparative perspectives / edited
By Heinz-Dieter Meyer and William Lowe Boyd.
    p. cm.
    Includes bibliographical references and index.
    ISBN 0-8058-3195-9 (hardcover : alk. paper)
    1.   Education and state—Cross-cultural studies. 2. Education—Social
Aspects—Cross-cultural studies. 3. Education—Economic aspects—Cross-cultural studies.
I. Meyer, Heinz-Dieter. II. Boyd, William L.

LC71 .E29 2000
379—dc21

                                                      00-042696

Books published by Lawrence Erlbaum Associates are printed on acid-free paper,
and their bindings are chosen for strength and durability.

Printed in the United States of America
10   9   8   7   6   5   4   3   2   1

Contents

Preface

The idea for this book originated in a collaboration of European and American scholars interested in education and civil society, which was sponsored in part by a Trans-Coop grant from the German–American Academic Council (GAAC). The project resulted in two conference in 1997 and 1998, the first in Boston hosted by the Institute for Economic Culture at Boston University, the second in Göttingen, Germany, in 1998 hosted by the Center for Europe- and North-America Studies at the University of Göttingen. We thank Charles Glenn and Peter L. Berger in Boston, and Horst Kern and Peter Loesche in Göttingen for generous support and hospitality. Thanks also to our editors at Lawrence Erlbaum Associates, Naomi Silverman and Lori Hawver, and to Bonnie Johnson and Huaying Zhang (at Penn State and SUNY Albany, respectively) whose skill and patience helped see this project through to the end.

At the center of this book is the question how education should be organized in pluralistic and multicultural societies. The shift from an assimilationist view of culture to one of cultural pluralism marks one of the most profound social changes in contemporary Western societies, and educational governance structures have so far not kept pace. At a time when many other social sectors exhibit diverse mixtures of public, private, voluntary, and compulsory organizational structures, education is still largely a single-provider sphere with government as the main actor. Under these conditions we believe it important to broaden our views of legitimate forms of educational organization and to inquire into the roles of civil society, markets, governments, and the family in education. How can the idea of the civil society help to reorient education policy discussions that are sometimes stuck in either–or juxtapositions of "market versus government" or "individualism versus communitarianism"? What are some of the traditions of civil society–across countries and across history–that educators and policy-makers today can revive or build on?

These are some of the questions at the center of this book. Its goal is to further our understanding of how we can accommodate cultural, ethnic, and religious pluralism in a political and conceptual framework that is sufficiently flexible to combine choice with equity, and a commitment to a shared civil and political culture with openness to exploring and affirming the distinct ethnicity, race, creed, or culture of different groups.

To address these questions, the authors take up the notion of the *civil society*–an idea that has experienced a popular and scholarly revival in recent years as numerous citizens, action groups, political philosophers, and social scientists make the case that only a democratic civil society can sustain a democratic state. The implications of this development for education have to date been not sufficiently explored. This book is a step toward addressing this gap.

Going beyond simplistic juxtapositions of "market versus government" or "individual versus community," the book as a whole develops an integrative perspective informed by the idea of the civil society. It combines current policy issues with a look at their historical development, and evaluates U.S. educational policy in the context of a range of international cases. The authors–education scholars, sociologists, economists, historians, and philosophers–explore from diverse disciplinary, and philosophical points of view the potential of the civil society for education. At the same time, they share the hope that a thorough reconsideration of the role of the state, the market, and the civil society will help to energize ongoing experiments with a variety of plans to increase educational and school autonomy.

                                                   H.-D. M.
                                                   W.L.B

Chapter One

Civil Society, Pluralism, and Education— Introduction and Overview

HEINZ-DIETER MEYER

WILLIAM LOWE BOYD

The goal of this book is to explore comparatively and, where useful, historically, how the idea of the civil society (or any of its synonyms, such as *civic associations* or *third sector*), which has generated so much intellectual and political excitement during the post-1989 period (see, e.g., Berger & Neuhaus, 1996; Dahrendorf, 1990; Diamond, 1994; Dionne, 1998; Ehrenberg, 1999; Glendon, 1991; Hall, 1995; Keane, 1999; Walzer, 1995), can be used to reframe and reconceptualize some vexing problems of education governance and policy. As anyone familiar with education policy knows, the reform debate typically pits pro-government government advocates against pro-market advocates. For added complexity, another intellectual controversy is sometimes superimposed, that between communitarians and libertarians. The editors were curious whether the idea of the *civil society* could provide a conceptual and policy framework that would help to overcome these often sterile juxtapositions.

That the fall of the Berlin Wall and the implosion of communist collectivism in 1989 should have re-energized the civil society discussion, is, in retrospect, not surprising. For Eastern European dissidents, who had lived their adult lives under a regime that routinely and zealously squashed all social action independent of the state, the collapse of communism in one fell swoop shrank the totalitarian Leviathan and, for the first time, left the public square free for individual citizens to associate

1

voluntarily. In contrast, the causes for the rediscovery of civil society in Western Europe are more obscure, but among the likely suspects three factors stand out: a backlash against big government and the welfare state, a new sense of pluralism, and concern about civility and trust in the life of social communities.

At about the time that the Soviet Empire began its terminal decline, the Western capitalist economies were swept up in a trend toward deregulation and privatization prompted by a reaction against big government and a widespread reexamination of the proper responsibilities of government. As telecommunications, railways, postal services, air transportation, and other industries were deregulated, civil servants and government bureaucrats began to trade places with a myriad of unruly entrepreneurs. As a result, people who had been accustomed to think of airlines, telephones, or railways as extended arms of an ever-present government now viewed them as services offered by entrepreneurs competing for customers (Osborne & Gaebler, 1993).

Cultural Pluralism

A second impetus for the resurgence of the idea of civil society is the irreversible shift to ethnic and cultural *pluralism* that increasingly characterizes most Western societies. Pluralism, as many understand it today (e.g., Berlin, 1998; Glazer, 1997; Taylor, 1992, 1996; Walzer 1983), is a far richer and more encompassing notion than even twenty or thirty years ago. The earlier idea of a dominant culture organized around a core of shared values and surrounded by a few dissenting voices on the fringe (duly tolerated by the majority) has given way to the idea of a *thick* pluralism that sees divergent creeds, beliefs, and worldviews as matters of first importance in a group's self-understanding. Some observers view the emergence of a complex notion of pluralism, in which different and incompatible creeds and values are accepted as normal and even celebrated, as the result of an historic sea change. As the late Isaiah Berlin argued, the new pluralism is a long overdue correction of a rationalist view of humans as creatures of reason and reason only, a view in which shared feelings and beliefs—the stuff of culture—are relegated to a marginal corner in the life of communities. In the new pluralism, the cultural commitments of groups and communities are viewed not as obstacles to be overcome, or as residual remains of an obsolete past, but as durable attachments from which different groups weave their tapestry of collective understanding.

The expanded notion of pluralism differs from the earlier one in that its political accommodation does not yield easily to conventional institutional solutions centering on state neutrality and rigid separation of public and private spheres. Where pluralistic diversity reaches deeply into our understanding of our morality and beliefs, the neutrality stipulation acts, in fact, as a censoring device requiring citizens who want to participate in the public sphere (e.g., in the education provided there) to suspend all those beliefs and ideas that are informed by their ethnicity or race, religion or worldview. Increasingly, people find the cut-and-dried abstraction of a person that remains after such multiple cleansing operations hard to recognize.

Social Capital

Pluralism, a new sense of lean government, and the final erosion of the communist vision of an all-powerful government, are three key sources of the new interest in civil society. However, the renewed interest in the civil society is surely also a response to growing concerns with the moral fabric of society, what authors of an earlier age referred to as a people's virtue or mores. Ironically, as Eastern dissidents began to wrest an autonomous public sphere from the grip of authoritarian and totalitarian government, liberal democrats in Western societies became increasingly aware of the declining strength of the many informal bonds and 'social capital' that give cohesion to the life of communities (Coleman, 1990; Fukuyama, 1999; Putnam, 1995). In this period, Tocqueville's definition of individualism as a retreat "into the small world of family and friends" and a disposition to "leave the rest of the world to itself" (1969, p. 506) has for many taken on a new and urgent ring. To the extent that citizens of modern Western societies are less willing to contribute to the common good by joining forces voluntarily and spontaneously, the bonds of trust and the standards of civility that connect us as citizens are weakened, and a shared sense of community and obligation seems is eroded. Standards of civility are violated whether education of the young takes place in a sphere shot through with crime, violence, and graphic images of sex as an arena of power and exploitation, or whether a virtual government monopoly on education squashes the pluralism that is spreading through all other spheres of society.

Our main goal in this book is to explore the implications for education and education reform of these interrelated developments—the downsizing of governmental monopolies in many vital public services, a keener sense of cultural pluralism, and growing concern about the decline of morals and civility in liberal democracies. Naturally, any decline in morals and social capital must be especially pernicious where children, families, and our educational institutions are concerned. As alienation, cynicism, and readiness to challenge or disregard accepted standards of decency and civility increase, a rising chorus of voices claims that the public school—once a virtual center of community cohesion and civic pride—has often become a breeding ground for distrust and civic strife, held together not by shared beliefs and morals but by the force of metal detectors and police marshals. No less important is the concern that, as the social fabric of the country becomes more diverse and pluralistic, public education nevertheless remains a key bastion of a single-culture worldview.

The chapters assembled in this book represent a first step in the exploration of the implications of these developments and the potential of the civil society idea to reorient the education reform discourse. The common thread that runs through the chapters is the search for more complex and intelligent institutional frameworks that can accommodate pluralism while facilitating a conversation that strengthens the bonds uniting all citizens. Finding frameworks that can integrate diverse groups, without forcing them into the same mold, requires conceptual and historical research efforts. Our intellectual as well as our institutional history offers a rich inventory of ideas and institutional practices that can be fruitfully reconsidered under new social conditions. The arrangements that, historically and cross-culturally, are available to deliver education are extremely diverse. Even today they include home schooling, churches, philanthropy, and voluntary associations and partnerships of all kinds. One goal of this book is to explore this cross-national diversity. Another is to consider some of the intellectual antecedents of today's education-and-civil-society debate. A third goal is to scrutinize the institutions and reform strategies that are available to move education to the center of civil society today.

Throughout, our goal is integration and accommodation of diverse viewpoints, rather than polarization. Too often reform debates are merely a stage for the clash of diametrically opposed world views, which pit proponents of government intervention against advocates of greater reliance on the mechanisms of markets and private choice, and libertarian advocates of individual rights against communitarian champions of duty and obligation. Exacerbating the sense of polarization is the fact that these debates typically focus on the United States in isolation, ignoring the instructive similarities and differences experienced in other countries. As a result, particularly in the United States, many of the proposed solutions to the pressing problems of education and civic decline emerge from the fringes of the political and ideological spectrum, whereas the social and political middle ground that most Americans inhabit remains undeveloped. What is needed is a platform for debate and policy-making that can cut across those well-worn dichotomies and engage the diverse agents of education—government, markets, families, voluntary organizations, public-private partnerships, and churches—to produce an education that unites the citizenry without coercive uniformity, and that affirms their pluralistic commitments without engendering fragmentation.

This book is about how, under new conditions, the civil society tradition can be revived and strengthened and how education can benefit from being more firmly grounded in the civil society. The voluntary association of individuals to contribute to the public good is a hallmark of civil societies. Because education is a primary public concern, the extent to which it becomes a subject of the associative civic impulse is very much an indicator of the strength of civil society. Conversely, education that is organized by actors who enjoy some autonomy from both government and the market cannot fail to strengthen the civil society.

Civil Society as a Theoretical Framework in Education

How cultural pluralism can be accommodated in modern education is a problem that several of the chapters in this book address. At the beginning of the 21st century there are many indications that the legitimacy of the nation-state as the exclusive or main provider of mass education is waning, not least because government-organized education inevitably exhibits a high degree of uniformity of method, content, and, most important, mind set. Such uniformity bodes ill for thick pluralism, which requires room for diversity not only of ethnicity, religion, or culture but also of mental outlook. This harks back to Mill and Tocqueville who, more than 100 years ago, voiced concerns that the uniformity of thought that could easily result from a government monopoly in education was one of the easiest ways to establish a new kind of despotism, simply by attaching the stigma of deviance to non established ideas. Revisiting the writings of these authors is a useful point of departure for any contemporary debate about education and civil society (Meyer, chapter 2, this volume).

Government-organized education also creates uniformity on an institutional level because, in a pluralistic society, it becomes increasingly education of the lowest common denominator. What the members of a political and cultural community cannot agree upon, they must automatically exclude from the classroom. Under conditions of cultural pluralism, however, the area of moral and normative disagreement is, necessarily, large. As Strike argues, (chapter 3, this volume) included among our disagreements are often questions which individuals and groups care most deeply about: questions of belief and faith, morality, world view, or philosophy of education. By stripping education off its moral dimension, we promote, if only by default, an increasing indifference to the moral issues facing our communities—an indifference that many believe is partly responsible for the social ills and incivilities observable in today's schools and cities. As a result, the kind of moral conversation Strike calls for is severely curtailed. If public education is not to approach the moral vacuum of shopping malls, ways must be found to harness the moral energies of particular communities for the end of public education. The power of particular associations (such as religious or ethnic ones) to contribute to the moral fabric of society is unnecessarily and unwisely left unharnessed in a system of public education built on a rigid separation of universalistic and particularistic spheres. How the two spheres can be linked without shortchanging the rights of citizens or the commitments of members of particular communities is a key problem of institutions in a civil society. Richter (chapter

4, this volume) suggests that mixed-authority arrangements might be best suited to this end. He discusses the feasability of cutting back the government monopoly in education and opening the field up for a mix of public and private providers. Not surprisingly, the legal and constitutional problems are thorny, especially for countries such as Germany that have traditionally considered education as a privileged domain of government.

Historical Traditions of Civil Society

To favor diversity of educational institutions in the civil society is one thing, but to find arrangements that are legally and politically feasible may be quite another. The difficulty that any search for institutional arrangements encounters is reason enough to pay special attention to cases where this tradition has already been institutionalized in one way or another. Several chapters in this book show that many countries have developed distinct institutional arrangements in education that others may learn from. England has historically produced some of the most impressive examples for non-governmental mass education based on local initiatives and charitable giving (Stone, 1964; Whelan, 1996). In chapter 5, Walford discusses the English tradition of government as a 'fill-in-the-gap' provider of education, to which recent education reforms partially return. His survey of the results of these reforms provides a glimpse at what it takes to put good ideas into practice.

Perhaps the most interesting, and, from a civil society point of view, most far-ranging educational arrangements have developed in the Netherlands. As Djikstra and Dronkers show in chapter 6, the unique Dutch system of combining elements of private and public education emerged as a result of intense collective struggles between Catholics and Protestants, on one hand, and government (in turn under pressure from the artisan middle classes) on the other. To satisfy the demands of these conflicting constituencies, an intriguing arrangement was worked out which recognizes the right of parents to choose church-provided (but publically funded) schools as an alternative to government schools. Non-public schools are, of course, held publically accountable to satisfy certain minimum standards of quality, which are ensured through government inspection. Because many parents prefer the church-affiliated schools for their educational performance and moral orientation, religious schooling in the Netherlands has remained largely unaffected by the growing secularism in the surrounding society.

It is worthwhile to point out that these arrangements (as well as others, such as the German system of vocational education or the system of parochial schools in the United States) are the product of often long and intense struggles between conflicting collective interests, both class-interests and religious beliefs. Although the resulting arrangements were compromises, they nevertheless led to stable mixed-authority arrangements, in which government, parents, churches, private enterprise (in the case of the German vocational education system) and a host of other groups and institutions participate in a politically regulated legal and institutional framework.

Last but not least, comparing the different traditions of civil society-based education also shows that the educational practices of different nations are governed by different ideas and culturally shared beliefs and traditions, which law makers ignore at their peril. Herbst's comparison of German and Amerian traditions of civil society in education (chapter 7) contains a vivid demonstration that Americans have historically been far more averse to educational centralization and more explicitly concerned with civil society arrangements than Germans. His account also shows that German education reformers have scored some subtle victories in civic educational institution-building, as evidenced by the *Bürgerschulen*. More generally, Meyer (chapter 8) contrasts the different traditions of civil society in continental Europe and the United States. He identifies a stronger concern for solidarity and community in the European conception of civility, compared to a preoccupation with liberty and freedom from government interference in the American tradition. Civil society, he argues, requires both "faces," solidarity no less than liberty, and the greatest challenge might be to strike a balance between them.

Together, these chapters show another important aspect of the civil society: its ability to serve as a forum for the development of social movements and social advocacy. As Minkoff (1997) suggested, social movement organizations can play a vital role in the civil society and in building social capital. Similarly, many of the vital issues of education have been solved in the past through collective political struggle, compromise, and accommodation.

Policies to Strengthen Civil Society in Education

A third set of chapters in this book focuses on implementation and policy instruments. Naturally, this is the place for much debate over details, but —necessarily—also principled questioning of the difficulties and possible problems of deviating from a public school monopoly. Brown (chapter 8) shows how educational arrangements that make room for voluntary initiatives have the potential to strengthen the social capital of a school community. This chapter also shows that voluntarism and civic contributions in education can be increased in small, incremental steps, rather than awaiting all-out system reform. Cooper and Randall (chapter 9) provide an illuminating report on the pros and cons of vouchers, which many scholars, especially in the United States, consider a key policy instrument in any attempt to return control of education to families. They argue that, although vouchers have not yet been tested on a large scale, it would be premature to rule out a breakthrough for the voucher project. Under favorable and not altogether unrealistic political conditions, the viability of vouchers might still get a large-scale testing. In a dissenting vote, however, Weiss (chapter 10) points to potential problems and disadvantages of strengthening the third sector in education. Although he is arguing against the backdrop of the German educational situation, his reservations about private initiative in education will strike some as applicable to other countries as well.

The prospects for reform along the lines sketched in this book will depend to a good extent on whether the civil society concept will find its way into the discourse of education reformers and policymakers. In chapter 12, Boyd shows that the education policy discourse in both England and the United States has until recently focused mainly on market forces and individual choice, or their opposite, the state, while neglecting the importance of the civil society. He discusses these developments and reflects on the prospects for community, democracy, and civility in schools and society.

In the final chapter, Mundy and Murphy take the questions about education and civil society to the global and international level. They show that there is an emerging sense among the members of many international nongovernmental organizations that civility requires access to basic education in all parts of the world. Not unlike globally operating environmental and women's rights groups before them, these organizations have begun to build an agenda aimed at rallying diverse local and global civil society actors to the cause of education. Mundy and Murphy describe some of the relevant recent changes and assess the extent to which nongovernmental organizations and civil society-based groups can play a constructive role as global advocates of education for all.

Coda

This book is an attempt to reflect on the constitution of education at a time when diversity and pluralism are changing the way we think about education. Historically, the three big providers of large-scale education have been the family, the church, and the nation-state. The latter has been the organizer and provider of education in most Western democracies for more than a century. Given the widespread movement to redraw the boundaries around the proper sphere of government, we believe it important to think about more complex and more encompassing institutional frameworks in which private and public education are not necessarily polar opposites but different ways to carry out universal education in the civil society (see Loconte, 1999; Smith & Sikkink, 1999). In particular, we need to look for policy frameworks that can integrate diverse constituencies without forcing uniformity and sameness on everyone in their fold. Civil society might provide the basis for such a framework. Civil society generates public benefits by means of private, voluntary efforts. As such, civil society is coextensive with practiced pluralism and democracy. Civil society education is not a partisan project or a cause of exclusive interest groups of this or that stripe or persuasion. It is a democratic and a pluralistic project. It is part of the promise of liberal democracy, the idea that the power to shape and formulate the main tenets of one's childrens education ought to rest with the people.

One goal of the collaboration resulting in this book was to explore the diverse civil society traditions that have developed cross-nationally. Inevitably, different nations come to emphasize and stress different dimensions in the course of their political and social development. Inevitably, they become one-sided in their pursuit of justice and democracy. Europeans and Americans approach the strengthening of civil society in education from two different points of departure, the former (mostly) from a tradition of state-governed public education, the latter (mostly) from a tradition of local control. This provides great opportunities for learning and dialogue. Both Europeans and Americans have reason to look across the Atlantic for a more complete sense of how to strengthen civil society. For such learning and dialogue to be successful we must be prepared to scrutinize and reevaluate some of our most deeply held beliefs. On either side of the Atlantic people must ask themselves how good a balance their nation has struck between liberty and social justice, and what policy instruments are available to address whatever imbalance they have allowed to develop.

References

Berger, P. L., & Neuhaus, R. J. (1996). *To empower people. From state to civil society.* 2nd ed. (M. Novak, Ed.) Washington, DC: AEI Press.

Berlin, I. (1998). *The crooked timber of humanity.* Princeton, NJ: Princeton University Press.

Coleman, J. S. (1990). *Foundations of social theory.* Cambridge, MA: Harvard University Press.

Dahrendorf, R. (1990). *The modern social conflict: An essay on the politics of liberty.* Berkeley: University of California Press.

Diamond, L. (1994). Rethinking civil society. Toward democratic consolidation. *Journal of Democracy, 5*(3), pp. 4–17.

Dionne, E. J., Jr. (Ed.). (1998). *Community works: The revival of civil society in America.* Washington, DC: The Brookings Institution.

Ehrenberg, J. (1999). *Civil society: The critical history of an idea.* New York: New York University Press.

Fukuyama, F. (1999). *The great disruption: Human nature and the reconstitution of social order.* New York: The Free Press.

Glazer, N. (1997). *We are all multiculturalists now.* Cambridge, MA: Harvard University Press.

Glendon, M. (1991). *Rights talk. The impoverishment of political discourse.* New York: The Free Press.

Hall, J. A. (Ed.). (1995). *Civil society. Theory, history, comparison.* Cambridge, MA: Polity Press.

Keane, J. (1999). *Civil society: Old images, new visions.* Palo Alto, CA: Stanford University Press.

Loconte, J. (1999). Let's make religion public school's ally. *USA Today.* November 11, p. 17A.

Minkoff, D. C. (1997). Producing social capital. national social movements and civil society. *American Behavioral Scientist. 40*(5), 606–619.

Osborne, D., & Gaebler, T. (1993). *Reinventing government: How the entrepreneurial spirit is transforming the public sector.* New York: Plume.

Putnam, R. (1995). Bowling alone. *Journal of Democracy. 6*(1), 65–78.

Smith, C., & Sikkink, D. (1999). Is private schooling privatizing? *First Things,* 92, 16–20.

Stone, L. (1964). The educational revolution in England, 1560-1640. *Past and Present,* 28, July, 41–80.

Taylor, C. (1992). *Multiculturalism and the politics of recognition.* Princeton, NJ: Princeton University Press.

Taylor, C. (1996). Two theories of modernity. *The Reponsive Community, 6* (3), 16–25.

Tocqueville, A. (1969). *Democracy in America.* New York: Doubleday.

Walzer, M. (1983). *Spheres of justice.* New York: Basic Books.

Walzer, M. (1995). The concept of civil society. In M. Walzer (Ed.), *Towards a global civil society* (7–28). Providence, RI: Berghahn

Whelan, R. (1996). *The corrosion of charity. From moral renewal to contract culture.* London: IEA Health and Welfare Unit.

Chapter Two

Civil Society and Education:
The Return of an Idea

HEINZ-DIETER MEYER

An education established and controlled by the State should only exist, if it exists at all, as one among many competing experiments, carried on for the purpose of example and stimulus to keep the others up to a certain standard of excellence.
JOHN STUART MILL

Schools should be state-establishments and not establishments in the state. They depend on the state and have no resort but it; they exist by it and for it. They hold their right to exist and their very substance from it; they ought to receive from it their task and their rule.
NAPOLEON BONAPARTE

When it comes to education and how it is best organized and governed in modern democratic societies, there is an enduring schism among the pioneers of modern democracies. Although hardly anyone doubts that democracy and intellectual enlightenment of the citizenry go hand in hand, there is deep disunity over which organizational forms are best suited to the "diffusion of knowledge" (Jefferson) among the general population. Broadly speaking, we can distinguish a state-centered and a society-centered vision of education. Advocates of the state-centered vision, like Napoleon Bonaparte, want to harness education to the political ends of the state, whether these ends are military prowess, national unity, cultural assimilation, economic growth—or some combination of these. Advocates of the society-centered vision, like J.S. Mill, want to make society the guardian of education, and the state but one of its instruments.

A *State*-Centered Vision
of Education

The ancestry of the state-centered tradition can be traced all the way to classical antiquity. According to Plutarch, Lycurgus, the founder of Sparta, "was of a persuasion that children were not so much the property of their parents as of the whole commonwealth" (1992, p. 66). Aristotle too, believed that "education should be regulated by law and should be an affair of the state" and that "the citizen should be molded to suit the form of government under which he lives" (Aristotle, 1941, p. 1305). These ideas were revived in the education struggles surrounding the French revolution. La Chalotais, a French aristocrat jealous of the widespread educational influence of the Catholic Church, stressed "the right to demand for the Nation an education that will depend on the State alone . . . because the children of the State should be educated by members of the State" (in Glenn, 1987, p. 17). A member of the Jacobin wing of French revolutionaries warned that "you will lose the younger generation by abandoning it to parents with prejudices and ignorance who give it the defective tint which they have themselves. Therefore, let the Fatherland take hold of the children who are born for it alone" (p. 20). Likewise, the French aristocrat Richelieu did not think well of the widespread availability of education that was not provided or controlled by the state, condemning "the ease of access to this bewildering number of colleges that has enabled the meanest artisan to send their children to these schools, where they are taught free of charge—and that is what has ruined everything" (in McGinn, 1992, p. 165).

In the 19th and 20th centuries, the state-centered vision of education has received powerful support in both theory and practice. One of the most energetic architects of the idea of an education system as a creation of and by the state was Napoleon Bonaparte. According to him, schools should "depend on the state and have no resort but it" (see epigram at the head of this chapter). In Napoleon's hands the teaching corps of the French nation was reduced to a "means to direct political and moral opinion" (in Archer, 1986, p. 29). Given Napoleon's success in implementing his vision of a state-centered education system, it comes perhaps as no surprise that the most influential scholarly advocate of the state-centered vision also was from a French man, the sociologist Emile Durkheim. In Durkheim's view the vital function of education was to transform the young from asocial and unformed children into social beings, capable of functioning in society. To that end, they had to be inculcated with all the beliefs, morals, and ideas that were central to the particular society's mission (Durkheim, 1956):

> If, as we have tried to establish, education has a collective function above all, if its object is to adapt the child to the social milieu in which he is destined to live, it is impossible that society should be uninterested in such a procedure. How could society not have a part in it, since it is the reference point by which education must direct its action? It is, then, up to the State to remind the teacher constantly of the ideas, the sentiments that must be impressed upon the child to adjust him to the milieu in which he must live. If it were not always there to guarantee that pedagogical influence be exercised in a social way, the latter would necessarily be put to the service of private beliefs, and the whole nation would be divided and would break down into an incoherent multitude of little fragments in conflict with one another. (p. 79)

A *Society*-Centered Vision of Education

Another group of writers and political reformers articulated a very different view of education. No less committed to the ideal of democracy and public enlightenment, they were weary of the harm that could result from making government the national educator. In the eyes of these writers, liberty was endangered, not served, if government turned into a national schoolteacher. These authors were concerned with the coercive aspects of a wall-to-wall education state. The goal, as these authors saw it, was to enlighten the citizenry without undermining liberty in the process.

There can be little doubt that up until recently, the state-centered tradition has dominated thought and practice of most democratic nations. To keep the enemies of the revolution down and to instill the new, revolutionary and democratic ethos in the minds and hearts of the young, the state was believed to have to wrest education from the hands of parents and priests. Nor was the state's ability to boost political and military prowess a mere figment of the imagination. After Prussia's military victory over its longstanding rival France in 1871, French public opinion became convinced that France was "not beaten by the Prussian generals, but by the Prussian schoolmasters." For almost a century, the Prussian success in harnessing public education to the ends of national power found eager imitators all over the world, as nation-states strove to use education to advance economic competitiveness, nation-building, technological literacy, cultural assimilation, and the like.

Recently, however, this equation of education and state-organized schooling is increasingly called into question. For many, the state-centered vision of education constitutes something of an anachronism under conditions of cultural pluralism, which persists more because of institutional inertia than because of its intrinsic merits. Thus, a reevaluation of our heritage concerning democracy and education seems in order, and one that gives particular emphasis to the ideas that saw the constitution of education anchored in civil society (and the communities of which it is made up), not the state.

In this chapter I trace some of the intellectual roots of civil-society-thinking in education to counteract the underexposure of this line of thought. A second reason for reviewing the intellectual heritage of civil society thinking in education is that it contributes to the current civil society discussion more generally, for education was a key concern of the political and social theorists of the 18th and 19th centuries who advocated civil society.

Authors such as Locke and Montesquieu, Tocqueville and Mill, Jefferson and Madison, Hegel and Humboldt not only tried to map out a social sphere independent of the state and mediating between state and market. Most of these authors also cared deeply about education. For them, the advancement of civilization and the diffusion of knowledge among ordinary people were two sides of the same coin. In contrast to today's highly fragmented discourse on education, where the various sub disciplines often break down into so many non communicating specialties, these authors' educational ideas proceeded from broad conceptions of the nature of man and the nature of social institutions. At the same time, they articulated detailed ideas about the constitution of education in a civil society. That their views are well documented makes this attempt at a brief exposition possible. What makes it necessary is that

these ideas about education as a concern of society (of which government or the state may be one agent) have long been eclipsed by a conception of education as the prerogative of the nation-state, a conception
that has in many countries assumed the unquestioned and unquestionable
persistence of a widely shared prejudice.

Education and Civil Society:
Key Ideas

In most countries now education as well as charity has become a national concern.
The state receives, and often takes, the child from its mother's arms to hand it over to
its functionaries; it takes responsibility for forming the feelings and shaping the ideas
of each generation. Uniformity prevails in schoolwork as in everything else; diver-
sity, as well as freedom is daily vanishing.
ALEXIS DE TOCQUEVILLE (1969, pp. 680–681)

At the heart of the civil society tradition is the idea of an intermediate
social space lodged between state and market. In his writing about the
role of *corps intermédiaires* in maintaining liberty in the face of centralized power, Montesquieu (1989) was one of the first to advocate it. He
did so in response to the rise of centralized governments of proportions
unthinkable for the city-states of antiquity. Montesquieu was concerned
that a society squashed between central government on the one hand and
an unorganized mass of atomized individuals on the other would inevitably become despotic. As an antidote to that tendency he believed that
intermediate social bodies that were sufficiently independent of government could check the danger of despotism. The author of the *The Spirit
of the Laws* derived his remedy for government despotism from the experience of pre-monarchical France, where the power of the king's house
had once been limited and counterbalanced by the power of rivaling aristocratic families and municipalities. One of his most famous followers,
Alexis de Tocqueville, was later to reconceive this idea based on the
new realities of social life in modern democracies.

The distrust that Montesquieu expressed vis-à-vis the illiberal tendencies of centralized government was shared by many other French and
European writers of aristocratic heritage. One of the earliest writers to
apply the idea to education was Wilhelm von Humboldt. Two decades
before he became Prussia's minister of education, Humboldt rejected the

idea of "national education," which he believed to lie "wholly beyond the limits within which the State's activity should properly be confined" (1972, p. 54).

> *In fine*, if education is only to develop a man's faculties, without regard to giving human nature any special civic character, there is no need for the State's interference. Among men who are really free, every form of industry becomes more rapidly improved—all the arts flourish more gracefully—all the sciences extend their range. In such a community, too, family ties become closer; parents are more eagerly devoted to the care of their children, and, in a state of greater well-being, are better able to carry out their wishes with regard to them. Among such men emulation naturally arises; and tutors educate themselves better when their fortunes depend upon their own efforts, than when their chances of promotion rest on what they are led to expect from the State. (p. 53)

In 1806, after the defeat of Prussia at the hands of Napoleon, when he became head of the Prussian education ministry, Humboldt famously jettisoned his early views. In a situation when Prussia's very survival as a sovereign nation seemed to depend on the country's ability to educate all citizens in the spirit of German culture and language (as Fichte and others had argued), Humboldt revised his earlier views and placed patriotism over liberty. Yet, the genius of the reforms he inaugurated can be attributed to the fact that even when accepting the need for a government-organized national system of education, Humboldt successfully defended and implemented the autonomy of the education system against the political imperatives of the Prussian state. And if the older Humboldt compromised some of the key ideas advocated by the young Humboldt, the ideas themselves nevertheless survived and reemerged. The liberal Frankfurt constitution of 1848 implemented a key idea of civil society education when it held "every citizen entitled to open schools" (Kuper, 1977, p. 25). And as we shall see below, the spirit of Humboldt's reflections on the limits of government was later adopted by John Stuart Mill in his essay "On Liberty," in which he revived and elaborated Humboldt's idea and made it the starting point of his own reflections about government and liberty. Humboldt's educational ideals also found powerful advocates in Thomas Mann and in Karl Jaspers' (1959) educational thought.

The Frankfurt constitution's principle that democratic citizenship implies an entitlement to operate schools found more fertile ground in the United States where the notion of a lay-administered network of schools embedded in the civil society had powerful advocates. The framers of the American constitution refrained from charging government with a role in education, not because they were indifferent to the cause of widespread education but because they were concerned about the dangers inherent in making government the national schoolteacher. Thomas Jefferson, one of the first promoters of the idea of universal, nongovernmental education, supported his proposals by referring to the ease with which central governments could turn their power into tyrannies when dealing with an ignorant people. The first sentence in Jefferson's draft for a "Bill for the More General Diffusion of Knowledge" reads:

> Whereas it appeareth that however certain forms of government are better calculated than others to protect individuals in the free exercise of their natural rights, and are at the same time themselves better guarded against degeneracy, yet experience hath shewn, that even under the best forms, those entrusted with power have, in time, and by slow operations, perverted it into tyranny; and it is believed that the most effectual means of preventing this would be, to illuminate, as far as practicable, the minds of the people at large. (Jefferson, 1984, p. 365)

As Conant (1963) has shown in a sustained analysis of Jefferson's educational thought, Jefferson maintained his principled commitment to universal education carried out through institutions of civil society throughout his long literary and political career. For the administration of elementary schools he favored local school boards of the kind that had sprung up in New England townships. To expand higher education, and especially to support his brainchild, the University of Virginia at Charlottesville, he tried to tap the resources of private individuals as well as government.

Alexis de Tocqueville

Nor was Jefferson's campaign for civil society-based education exceptional in the early decades of the United States. According to Tocqueville, who visited the country two decades after Jefferson's death, education in America very much conformed to the civil society principle. Schools played a key role in the array of intermediate organizations:

> In America the force behind the state is much less well regulated, less enlightened, and less wise, but it is a hundred times more powerful than in Europe... I know of no other people who have founded so many schools or such efficient ones, or churches more in touch with the religious needs of the inhabitants, or municipal roads better maintained. So it is no good looking in the United States for uniformity and permanence of outlook, minute care of details, or perfection of administrative procedures; what one does find is a picture of power, somewhat wild perhaps, but robust, and a life liable to mishaps but full of striving and animation. (pp. 92—93)

The American civil society experience and especially the ubiquity of voluntary associations inspired Tocqueville to adapt Montesquieu's idea of intermediate organizations to the conditions of modern democracy. In Tocqueville's view, liberty was threatened not only by centralized monarchies but also by rule of the majority in democratic societies, which conceivably could produce a similarly unmediated juxtaposition of centralized power and unorganized masses. The mere fact that democratic government was elected by the majority did little to alleviate this problem. Tocqueville's lasting discovery was that, under democratic conditions, the role of intermediate bodies could be played by civic associations that could be at once independent of government and provide great numbers of people with an opportunity to learn and practice the art of self-government.

But Tocqueville did not limit himself to theoretical studies of modern democracy. The commentator on American democracy was also actively involved in French political and, notably, educational affairs. As a French political official, Tocqueville had ample opportunity to fine-tune his views on education and society. Given the highly centralized government monopoly on education in France, Tocqueville's main goal was to limit the educational role of the state. However, although he favored breaking the state's monopoly on general education, he did not intend to challenge the legitimacy of the state's educational involvement altogether.

As ably reconstructed by Sonia Chabot (1996), the older Tocqueville's view of the legitimate role of government in public education revolved around two main ideas: that the state had an obligation to guarantee basic instruction for all, but that it had no right to erect a monopoly on education and to suppress alternative forms of education chosen by the citizens themselves. For Tocqueville, the right to be instructed was an "inalienable right which nature gives and which society can but recognize; one of those rights which the French Revolution sought to assure for all citizens" (quoted in Chabot, 1996, p. 222). Although it was tempting to rely on centrally administered mass education to guarantee this right in practice, competition between governmental and non-governmental, public and private establishments of education was healthier for government and society. "Competition ought to be respected not only because it is necessary to preserve true freedom of parental choice in education, but also . . . because the exclusive influence of public power on instruction is dangerous for liberty and the progress of the social order. Any preference given to public education should be, to the extent possible, the result of trust" (p. 222).

To the extent that parents sent their children to state-administered schools as a result of free choice and trust, rather than for lack of alternatives, Tocqueville did not see a problem. But a state monopoly on education was dangerous for the diversity of thought and mental life because it would give undue power to a mandarin-type class, a tight-knit corps of state-employed intellectuals with a monopoly on the definition of received ideas and morals (Chabot, 1996, p. 225). For the same reason, Tocqueville was wary of certifications and degrees that would increasingly narrow the paths of individual growth and development. He was inclined to accept education certificates like the baccaulareate that were necessary to insure against favoritism in education. But he strongly recommended maintaining the option of alternative routes to prepare for school graduation and to take steps to insure that access to the exam would not be limited to the rich (p. 234). Last but not least, liberty of instruction implied for Tocqueville the liberty of association. "The families who wished to have Jewish, Catholic, or Protestant schools for their children should be able to found them or have access to them" (p. 223). This also applied to schools without a religious motif.

Just as Tocqueville opposed a church monopoly on education, so he opposed a monopolistic role of the state. In a letter to a friend he wrote: "You fear with reason a church monopoly. But does a monopoly of the state not make you afraid?" (p. 221) Here again Tocqueville's position was characteristically nuanced. The church was a legitimate competitor in the arena of public education as long as there was free choice. In his view, members of the clergy should even be allowed to teach in public schools, but their influence should be limited to primary schools. Tocqueville believed that education was a moral undertaking and that a strong influence of religion favored liberty. The best way for such an influence to blossom, however, was under conditions of institutional separation and free choice, rather than mandatory obligations.

In sum, Tocqueville's views as an educational reformer and politician were characterized by a belief in the healthy effects of choice and competition and the detrimental effects of educational monopolies, in elementary or higher education. At the same time, he did not advocate a tabula rasa. He realized the need to respect institutional traditions and to find solutions within the constraints of a concrete political situation. Above all, for all his skepticism vis-à-vis an expansive state role in education, he expected the state to remain the ultimate supervisor of education, public and private. He argued that government should retain "the right to inspect the schools which it does not direct" (p. 223), but he was quick to add that this right was based on its duty to fund them (p. 219).

John Stuart Mill

John Stuart Mill was a long-time correspondent and friend of Alexis de Tocqueville. The English political economist and scholar cared about many of the same problems that moved his French peer across the Channel to take up the pen. Like Tocqueville, Mill worried about the danger of a despotism peculiar to democratic societies: despotism of the mind. In his view, one of the most serious misunderstandings of democracy was the idea that "the people have no need to limit their power over themselves" (Mill, 1985/1859, p. 61). Not to do so would easily lead to new forms of tyranny, and Mill feared that such a state might in practice most easily come about through intellectual uniformity. Mill also shared many of the views the young Wilhelm von Humboldt had expressed in his *The Limits of State Action* essay and he even adopted Humboldt's phrase about the "absolute and essential importance of human development in its richest diversity" as the motto in his own essay "On Liberty" (p. 57). Not surprisingly, education figured prominently in Mill's thought (Harris, 1994), and opposition to state control in education was one of his leading principles:

> That the whole or any large part of the education of the people should be in State hands I go as far as anyone in deprecating. All that has been said of the importance of individuality of character, and diversity in opinions and modes of conduct, involves, as of the same unspeakable importance, diversity of education. A general State education is a mere contrivance for moulding people to be exactly like one another; and as the mold in which it casts them is that which pleases the predominant power in the government —whether this be a monarch, a priesthood, an aristocracy, or the majority of the existing generation—in proportion as it is efficient and successful, it establishes a despotism over the mind, leading by natural tendency to one over the body. (p. 177)

Mill opposed a uniform state education because it offered little "protection against the tyranny of the prevailing opinion and feeling" because "government operations tend to be everywhere alike. With individuals and voluntary associations, on the contrary, there are varied experiments and endless diversity of experience" (p. 180). On the same grounds Mill rejected the idea of making religion a compulsory school subject. Although he opposed the idea of supporting public schools only if they taught the Bible (p. 92), he argued that parents should have the right to add religion to their children's curriculum: "there would be nothing to hinder them [the children] from being taught religion, if their parents chose, at the same schools where they were taught other things" (p. 178).

There are many passages in "On Liberty" in which Mill's commitment to the liberty of the individual sounds dogmatic and indifferent to any competing demands social life might impose on individuals. At other points, however, Mill was sufficiently realist to know that principles have to pay their dues to the circumstances under which they are implemented. It is in the allowance to local variations and conditions where his argument remains of great interest.

State Education Versus State as an Enforcer of Education. Famously, Mill rejected all paternalistic justifications of state action. The only justification for government interference in an individual's action against his or her will is to prevent harm to others. "His own good, either physical or moral, is not a sufficient warrant" (p. 68). This classical anti welfare state stance also would exclude any governmental interference with education, as, indeed, Humboldt had argued. Parents, not the state, had to ensure that their offspring were educated. Parents had a strong moral obligation to provide their children with an education. In cases, however, where the parents failed to do so, Mill found a basis for state intervention: "If the parent does not fulfill this obligation, the State ought to see it fulfilled at the charge, as far as possible, of the parent" (p. 176). But even here the state merely was to use its policing power to make sure that somebody would provide the child with an education. The state did not and should not involve itself in the business of education: "the objections which are urged with reason against state education do not apply to the enforcement of education by the State, but to the State's taking upon itself to direct that education; which is a totally different thing" (p. 176).

Justified State Action in Education. Next to compensating for parental failure to provide their children with an education, the state was justified and even required to get involved in assuring a minimal level of educational quality. The pupils' retention of a minimum degree of knowledge and the certification of teachers were legitimate spheres of governmental action. Annual, state supervised examinations were an appropriate means to ensure the "universal acquisition and . . . retention of a certain minimum of general knowledge" (p. 178). By the same token, governments had a legitimate concern with teacher certification. "It is one thing to provide schools or colleges, and another to require that no person shall act as an instructor of youth without a government license" (quoted in Ryan, 1974, p. 174).

Significantly for Mill there was one condition under which governments were justified to go beyond these acts of quality and attendance control. This was the case when an entire society was in a backward state in which the state was the only social institution capable of ensuring a minimum level of education. A "ruler full of the spirit of improvement is warranted in the use of any expedients that will attain an end perhaps otherwise unattainable" (Mill 1985, p. 69). The best that could happen to a people under such circumstances was to be ruled by an absolute ruler who was also humane and civilized. On these grounds Mill justified the rule of the East India Company over India, and he may also have had Prussia's Frederick the Great in mind, whose friendship and correspondence with Voltaire spanned several decades. In the case of state action against alcohol abuse, Mill was of the opinion that while prohibition (of alcohol) was not justified in a civilized nation (because it treats free men as children), it may be justified as a last resort "after all efforts have been exhausted to govern them as free men" (p. 172). Mill applied this principle of the state as an actor of last resort also to education:

> [When] society is in so backward a state that it could not or would not provide for itself any proper institutions of education unless the government undertook the task, then, indeed, the government may, as the less of two great evils, take upon itself the business of schools and universities . . . But in general, if the country contains a sufficient number of persons qualified to provide education under government auspices, the same persons would be able and willing to give an equally good education on the voluntary principle, under the assurance of remuneration afforded by a law rendering education compulsory, combined with State aid to those unable to defray the expense. (p. 177)

Problems With State Action in Education. The minimal involvement of the state in education that Mill believed to be justified in a civilized society required a well-qualified Civil Service. For this reason Mill was a defender of the British Civil Service tradition, convinced that a governmental institution of well-qualified and impartial civil servants could do a lot of good (Ryan, 1974). But he was also concerned that such a class of civil servants might degenerate into a bureaucratic class, which—by endorsing the partial truths of scholarship with governmental authority—might ossify into mandarinism (Ryan, p. 177). Last but not least, Mill was concerned that in a mass democracy even the slightest involvement of government with the welfare of the people might set off a chain of expectation that imperceptibly would shift emphasis from staving off threats to individual liberty to positive assurances against unavoidable pain and suffering. "In many cases an individual, in pursuing a legitimate object, necessarily and therefore legitimately causes pain or loss to others, or intercepts a good which they had a reasonable hope of obtaining. . . . Whoever succeeds in an overcrowded profession or in a competitive examination . . . reaps benefit from the loss of others." But "society admits no right, either legal or moral, in the disappointed competitors to immunity from this kind of suffering" (p. 164).

On select occasions, the notion that education is a civil, not a governmental, affair has become a practical power in policy-making. In the well-known case *Pierce et. al. v. Society of Sisters* (1925), the state of Oregon tried to enforce a law requiring all children of school age to attend *public* school. The Supreme Court sided with a challenge of that law by the Society of Sisters, a Roman Catholic order offering "secular and religious education" to school-age children. The Supreme Court derived its rationale to strike down Oregon's law directly from J.S. Mill:

> The fundamental theory of liberty upon which all governments in this Union repose excludes any general power of the State to standardize its children by forcing them to accept instruction from public teachers only. The child is not a mere creature of the State; those who nurture him and direct his destiny have the right, coupled with the high duty, to recognize and prepare him for additional obligations. (Pierce v. Society of Sisters, p. 3052)

If Not Government, Who?

Reconsidering the society-based tradition of education as represented by writers such as Humboldt, Jefferson, Tocqueville, or Mill seems timely and appropriate under conditions of cultural pluralism and a new sense of limited and lean government. Taking this tradition seriously requires breaking with often deeply ingrained habits of thinking about education as a premier prerogative of government. The idea that the education of all children, not only of a small minority of religious dissenters or of the wealthy, might be carried out in the non state sector, represents, perhaps more than anything else, a challenge to our imagination. Are civic and private organizations and institutions really capable of carrying out the task of educating large numbers, perhaps even the majority of children in modern societies? To stretch our imagination and conceive of realistic alternatives to the state-centered mode of popular education, it is useful to look across time and space, to other countries as well as to other historic eras. Under which conditions does civic participation in education flourish most? Under which conditions do we find, cross-culturally, the greatest civic energies released in education? To understand what sorts of arrangements maximize civility and autonomy of education, careful comparative studies of the educational institutions of different countries are the most promising avenue. Some of the chapters in this volume make a start in this direction. In addition, a few general comments, gleaned from an informal survey of comparative arrangements, can be offered.

Private–Public Partnerships. Even a cursory look across educational arrangements employed by different nations shows a great variety of designs and configurations. We may still be at the beginning of evaluating their potential to facilitate civic associations. This would involve scrutinizing such different arrangements as the Dutch system of pillarization, the German Dual System, British grant-maintained schools, American charter schools, voucher systems, the Latin system in the United States, the selective public high schools in the United States (such as Stuyvesant High in New York), and other initiatives. The variety and diversity of these arrangements attests to the great inventiveness of the people in going about organizing education.

Many of the arrangements mentioned above rely on particular *private–public partnerships* to bring together a diversity of corporate actors in education: churches, parents, and government as in the Dutch case; manufacturers, craft guilds, chambers of commerce and government as in the case of the German dual system; parental associations and teachers' professional associations, as in the case of Waldorf schools; local educational authorities and parents and teacher associations as in the English grant maintained schools. Private–public partnerships offer good mechanisms for diverse constituents to make their contributions to education, at the same time checking each other's tendency to overreach (see Meyer, chapter 8, in this volume). To strengthen such arrangements, a more proactive, continuous, and predictable role of business organizations might be called for. Businesses are quite obviously a great beneficiary of education; they also create a lot of the expertise that is crucial to future generations of students and workers. Because of their dual role as consumers and producers of new knowledge, business employers depend on schools but they can also contribute a great deal to them. Examples such as the German dual system show that, integrated in a power-sharing arrangement, business enterprises can make great contributions to education. Corporate citizenship and corporate responsibility requires that companies absorb their share of the educational burden of society. They do so by engaging in well-structured partnerships with other private organizations as well as government.

Strong, professionally oriented teacher associations are also of great importance. In many countries teachers find themselves under siege from conflicting constituents (parents, administrators, policy-makers, students, and the courts). At times, they have responded to these pressures by imitating the tactics of blue-collar labor unions. Yet, as the experience of countries such as Japan and many European nations shows, the professionalization of teaching produces benefits for all constituents of education. Also, a more autonomous body of teaching associations, answering to their own professional rules rather than to local or central political authorities, is clearly more consistent with the principles of a self-governed civil society.

Social Capital. Although school teaching benefits from being organized as a profession, it should be pointed out that much of the complexity of schooling in contemporary societies arises not from the task of teaching youngsters how to read, write, and reckon (there are many examples of young people having accomplished this with only minimal aid from others) but from the very different task of maintaining a group of 20 or 30 youngsters in a state of attentiveness. Whatever makes this part of the job easy will make schools more effective. Experience everywhere shows that the most important ingredient to keeping a group of youngsters, seated in front of an (initially) unfamiliar adult, in a state of being ready to learn, are stable relations of trust and authority. As James Coleman (1990, pp. 300–324) and others have argued, the myriad social ties that connect actors in a community, in this case students, parents, teachers, and neighbors, form a social resource *sui generis,* which Coleman called "social capital."

When children can walk to their schools unattended by adults; when 8-year-olds can be entrusted to take their 6-year-old siblings to school; when parents know and trust each other to reciprocate supervisory responsibility regarding their children; when parents and teachers have an informal rapport, know each other by sight, and occasionally pause to chat—that is when we can assume that the social capital available to the participants in these situations will be of benefit for what goes on inside the classroom.

The informal ties that connect teachers, families, and neighbors are an eminently important, albeit highly intangible, part of civic associations. Therefore, one of the first orders of strengthening civic associations in education is a renewed commitment to harness the social capital inherent in neighborhoods and communities to the ends of education (see Driscoll & Kerchner, 1999; Smylie & Weaver Hart, 1999). This requires that we resist the temptation to disintegrate the neighborhood as locale of a child's primary schooling (Berger & Neuhaus, 1996), even if and especially if it is undertaken in the name of the noblest of goals (i.e., racial equality, equal access to quality schooling). It stands to reason that the net effect of taking 7-year-olds out of their neighborhood in order to bus them into racially more balanced but unfamiliar and often hostile neighborhoods 45 minutes away, can be negative. David Armor (1989) has provided a cogent argument showing that alternative methods of implementing desegration might have come with a better net balance of positive and destructive social capital effects. Having said that, we must hasten to add, however, that strengthening neighborhood schools will increase social capital only if the financial capital available is the same in all neighborhoods. If *neighborhood school* is just another name to justify the starkest discrepancies in educational funding, the gains for civil society will be nil. In the United States, where most states cling to the ancient institution of local control of education, this problem is particularly pronounced. In Europe, where school funding is based on centralized tax regimes, this incentive to leave a neighborhood is much weaker and often practically nonexistent (see also Dijkstra & Dronkers, chapter 5, in this volume).

Balance and Compromise. Perhaps most important about the educational views of the authors surveyed in this chapter is that they remind us of the need for compromise and trade-offs in education. They did not categorically reject government's involvement in education but tried to limit its role to its administrative as opposed to educational functions. They advocated mixed-authority arrangements, in which private, religious, and voluntary organizations along with state-sponsored schools all had their place. They thought that the involvement of non-state agents in public education (such as church members as teachers of religion) was unproblematic as long as parents had a choice in the matter.

They favored solutions of subsidiarity–the principle that whatever can be done by intermediate bodies ought to be done by them, rather than by the state. But they insisted on education as a universal right for all and on the need for government ensure that *all* young people receive the minimum education (however narrow or wide that minimum is defined by the majority of citizens).

Today, much public thinking about education is implicitly or explicitly dominated by concerns about efficiency (economic competitiveness, international comparability of achievements, administrative efficiency, etc.) and equality of access or opportunity–undoubtedly two very important concerns. But to advocates of civil society, liberty, pluralism, and morality in education were equally legitimate. And because in politics and society all good things do not always go together, because efficiency and liberty, equality and pluralism often conflict, it is important to understand the need for trade-offs and the art of compromise in education.

Rousseau taught that we must decide whether to educate men or citizens (1979, p. 40). He did not believe that it is possible to do both. In the opening chapter of the *Emile*, his famous essay on education, Rousseau declares the conflict between equally important goals an essential feature of all education. In contrast, we moderns believe all too often that our educational institutions can readily serve to make men *and* citizens. We believe that there is no conflict between political socialization and an education geared to raise men and women to their highest cultural potential. But in fact, such conflicts do exist and educational institutions will typically be institutionalized compromises. They will disappoint most purists.

Conclusion

I have begun this chapter saying that in the conflict between a state-centered and a society-centered constitution of education the former has, until now, typically maintained the upper hand. We might concede at this point that, up until recently, there may have been good reasons for this dominance. Many Western societies may have had to cope with some of those exceptional circumstances under which even a staunch liberal such as Mill found state control of education justified. Perhaps the need for cultural assimilation, national cohesiveness (in the face of fierce national hostilities), or economic development were so compelling that all other interests could legitimately be relegated to the back seat. Also, one of the first battles for civility in education has rightly been to make access to education independent of a person's wealth. Exclusive education for the rich would not be civil, and government was in many cases the only societal agent to effectively ensure that education was available for all.

If this has been so for the 19th century nation-state and even for much of the turbulent 20th century, the irreversible shift to more deeply pluralistic societies calls this institutional model into question. Under these conditions, civil society thinking in education provides a much needed alternative to more narrow efficiency-centered discourse in education. It highlights the fact that in today's pluralistic environment, a government monopoly on education can be maintained only by stripping education of its cultural and symbolic aspects, that is, only at the expense of *de-moralizing* education. But knowledge divorced from culture and identity affirming symbolism is a slim basis to maintain a sense of solidarity and community in the huge organizations into which schools, especially urban high schools, have evolved. Not only is it hard to imagine that the knowledge contained in our literature, history, politics, and even our science can be stripped of its cultural and symbolic connotations, which, in a pluralistic society will always find diverse interpreters and varied interpretations (cf. Meyer, 2000). Even to merely maintain a state of civil discourse and interaction among students in places that compel the attendance of large groups of adolescents is hard to imagine without some kind of binding community sentiment. This dependence of organized processes of knowledge diffusion on shared cultural belief and moral sentiments creates a conflict between accommodation and fragmentation. It is hard to see how that conflict can be resolved unless we decide that *society*, constrained, to be sure, by norms of civility, but otherwise infinitely more varied than the *state*, is the proper sphere of education.

References

Archer, M. S. (1986). Social origins of educational systems. In J. G. Richardson (Ed.), *Handbook of theory and research for the sociology of education* (pp. 3–34). Westport, CT: Greenwood Press.

Aristotle. (1941). Politics. In R. McKeon (Ed.), *The basic works of Aristotle* (pp. 1127–1324). New York: Random House.

Armor, D. (1989). After busing: Education and choice. *Public Interest*, 95, Spring, pp. 24–37.

Berger, P. L., & Neuhaus, R. J. (1996). *To empower people. From state to civil society.* Second edition (M. Novak, Ed.) Washington DC: AEI Press.

Chabot, S. (1996). Education civique, instruction publique, et liberte de l'enseignement dans l'oeuvre d'Alexis de Tocqueville [Civic education, public instruction, and liberty of teaching in the writings of Alexis de Tocqueville]. *La Revue Tocqueville.* Vol. XVII (1), 211–249.

Coleman, J. S. (1990). *Foundations of social theory.* Cambridge, MA: Harvard University Press.

Conant, J. B. (1963). *Thomas Jefferson and the development of American public education.* Berkeley: University of California Press.

Driscoll, M. E., & Kerchner, C. T. (1999). The implications of social capital for schools, communities, and cities: Educational administration as if a sense of place mattered. In J. Murphy & K. Seashore Louis (Eds.), *Handbook of research on educational administration* (2nd ed., pp. 385–404). San Francisco, CA: Jossey-Bass.

Durkheim, E. (1956). *Education and sociology.* Glencoe, IL: The Free Press:.

Glazer, N. (1997). *We are all multiculturalists now.* Cambridge, MA: Harvard University Press.

Glenn, C. L., Jr. (1987). *The myth of the common school.* Amherst, MA: The University of Massachussetts Press.

Harris, K. (1994). Mill, the state, and local management of schooling. *Journal of Philosophy of Education, 28*(1), pp. 55–63.

Humboldt, W. (1972). *The limits of state action.* Indianapolis, IN: Liberty Fund.

Jaspers, K. (1959). *The idea of the university.* Boston: Beacon Press.

Jefferson, T. (1984). *Writings.* New York: Library of America.

Kuper, E. (1977). *Demokratisierung von Schule und Verwaltung* [Democratization of School and Administration]. Munich: Ehrenwirth.

McGinn, N. F. (1992). Reforming educational governance. In R. F. Arnove, P. G. Altbach, & G. P. Kelly (Eds.), *Emergent issues in education* (pp. 163–172). Albany, NY: SUNY Press.

Meyer, H. D. (2000). Taste formation in pluralistic societies. The role of rhetorics and institutions. *International Sociology, 15*(1), pp. 33–56.

Mill, J. S. (1985). *On liberty*. London: Penguin. (original work published 1859)

Montesquieu (1989). *The spirit of the laws*. Cambridge, UK: Cambridge University Press.

Pierce et al. v. Society of Sisters, 268 U.S. 510 (1925).

Plutarch. (1992). *The lives of the noble Grecians and Romans*. New York: The Modern Library.

Rousseau, J. J. (1979). *Emile* (A. Bloom, Trans.). New York: Basic Books.

Ryan, A. (1974). *J. S. Mill*. London: Routledge & Kegan Paul.

Smylie, M. A., & Weaver Hart, A. (1999). School leadership for teacher learning and change: A human and social capital perspective. In J. Murphy & K. Seashore Louis (Eds.). *Handbook of research on educational administration* (2nd ed, pp 421–442) San Francisco: Jossey-Bass.

Tocqueville, A. (1969). *Democracy in America*. New York: Doubleday.

Chapter Three

Civil Society and Schooling: Particularistic Voices and Public Spaces

KENNETH A. STRIKE

Much of human life is and should be lived in local, particularistic communities. Such communities consist of people we know, who value us and whom we value. They are places where we belong. Without such communities human beings may be rootless and anomic. The values of such communities are particularistic in that they may not be widely shared. Nor, in liberal societies, and insofar as the values are those of religion or culture rather than those of justice, is it the business of government to see to it that they are widely shared. It is such particularistic values and their associated communities that make most modern societies irreducibly pluralistic.

The values that form and inform particularistic groups are neither those of the state nor of the market. For example, the state and the market distort the values that bind families together by viewing the family either as based on an arm's length exchange of goods or by seeing it as a miniature polity. Such characterizations do not give enough weight to love, belonging, solidarity, or commitment. Much the same can be said about the values that form most religious congregations or cultural subgroups.

Groups informed by particularistic values are essential to human development. They are the source of views about human flourishing as well as of love, belonging, and solidarity. They are essential to the nurturance and education of children. Inculcating and sustaining the commitments and values associated with particularistic groups is a task that is beyond the province of the state and that will be done badly by the market. Yet liberal democratic and capitalist societies must permit and encourage such groups if they are not to degenerate into societies whose members are motivated largely by self-interest and untutored desire. Hence a dilemma of liberal capitalist societies: Particularistic groups should be encouraged because they perform tasks that neither the state nor the market can do well. However, liberal societies must also be decently impartial between such groups if they are not to become oppressive, and capitalist societies must find ways to prevent particularistic groups from being dissolved by the solvent of the market.

My concern for the health of particularistic groups is broader than that exhibited by much of the civil society literature. That literature is largely concerned for the health of democracy (Putnam, 1993). Although it seeks a place between state and market, it rarely extends to a concern that particularistic groups are able to successfully maintain their distinctive convictions. Moreover, most accounts of how the associations of civil society work are "structuralist" in that they attend more to how social structures and organizational characteristics affect social capital and less to the role of substantive convictions. In these ways the civil society literature may be shortsighted. The substantive values of particularistic groups may be cognitive and motivational sources of social capital.

Framing the Argument

One function of civil society is to provide discursive forums outside of the sphere of government. Such forums help build consensus and advise government of the will of the people (Taylor, 1995). Civil society also develops participatory competence and establishes social bonds (Putnam, 1993; Rosenblum, 1998). One place where these functions should intersect is the school. Thus, although schools are generally agencies of government, it may nevertheless be important to think of them as though they were potentially among the institutions of civil society.

Currently the United States is having a state versus market debate about education. On one side are advocates of systemic reform (Fuhrman, 1993; Smith, Scoll, & Link, 1996; and, for discussion, Strike, 1997). This view emphasizes educational standards formulated at the state or national level, accountability mechanisms to enforce these standards, and devolution of responsibility for realizing these standards to local school districts. The other side claims that so long as schools continue to be public monopolies no reforms can succeed. The keys to school reform are school autonomy and the discipline of the market (Chubb & Moe, 1990; Friedman, 1962).

These antagonists share some assumptions. They believe that schools exist to build human capital. Also, they emphasize raising academic achievement, believing that academic achievement is the key to economic competitiveness. And they agree that the state versus market issue should be decided by looking at the effects of school governance on achievement scores. Thus governance arguments are assimilated to productivity debates and are fought by economists armed with regression equations (Hanushek, 1997). This debate largely ignores the role of schooling in developing social capital or in helping form views of human flourishing. That schools should help young people to form a reasonable conception of a good life has become almost an alien thought. That the "get an education to get a job to get money to get stuff" ethos that pervades public schools in the United States may be part of the solvent that dissolves the bonds and erodes the beliefs and cultures of particularistic groups and undermines the sense of citizenship crucial to democracy is an idea barely entertained.

In contrast, Bryk, Lee, and Holland (1993) in their book *Catholic Schools and the Common Good* argued that the modern Catholic school is more successful when measured against the civic aspirations of common schools than most public schools. Catholic schools emphasize success for everyone, they create communities, informed by a humanistic tradition emphasizing the life of the mind, that are just and caring, and they teach the values of this tradition to their students. In contrast, many public schools

> convey a vision of a society in which individuals strive for personal success while pursuing their self-interest. . . . Institutional norms are competitive, individualistic, and materialistic . . . affluence and poverty in adult life are . . . seen as appropriate consequences, with questions about broader societal responsibility for inequality less likely to arise. (p. 319)

This passage suggests that the civil society perspective on the democratic, capacity-building features of associations needs to inform discussion of the question of whether schools should be public or private institutions. Bryk et al. seem to suggest that the common good is likely to be best served in private schools. Their argument also highlights tension over the role of particularistic groups, for it traces much of the success of Catholic schools to the substantive values of Catholic humanism. Although Catholic humanism has its roots in Aristotle as much as in Catholicism, its values are still the particularistic values of a particularistic group.

The civil society perspective often seems of two minds about particularistic groups. On the one hand, some claim that associations formed on the basis of religion or ethnicity are an essential part of civil society. They help build democratic capacity, and they bring important perspectives to debates conducted in public space. Thus Hollenbach (1995) argued that the privatization of religious views demanded by some liberals "may ironically have the effect of threatening democracy through alienation and anomie rather than conflict and violence" (p. 145).

Others view particularistic groups more as sources of ethnic or sectarian strife than of social capital. They may frustrate the formation of thick democratic communities, or they may bring sectarian premises into public arguments raising the stakes and making issues less resolvable. Gutmann (1987), for example, argues that students should be taught a public language that avoids religious conceptions:

> The case for teaching secular but not religious standards of reasoning . . . rests . . . on the claim that secular standards constitute a better basis upon which to build a common education for citizenship than any set of sectarian religious beliefs—better because secular standards are both a fairer and a firmer basis for peacefully reconciling our differences. (p. 103)

Others argue that public discourse needs to be characterized by "dialogical restraint" (Ackerman, 1980). In public space we should give reasons that can be shared by citizens independently of their ethnicity, religion, or fundamental convictions.

These views generate different paradigm cases about the associations we should encourage as we seek to build civil society. On one view the paradigm case of a desirable association might be a congregation. For the second it might be a volunteer fire company. The essential difference is this. Congregations are associations whose members share a thick, particularistic, moral or cultural tradition. Volunteer fire companies, in contrast, are associations constituted of purposes and values that can generate a membership consisting of people who are rooted in different moral traditions and cultures. I will refer to such associations as *democratic/cross-cutting*.

Importing this tension in the civil society literature into the context of schooling poses some hard choices. Those who emphasize the virtues of particularistic communities have non-market reasons to argue for increased privatization of schooling. They may argue that having a coherent and rich view of human flourishing depends on being initiated into some tradition. They may also argue, as Bryk et al. (1993) do, that sectarian schools with a strong and humane tradition do a better job than public schools in developing democratic citizens. However, those who emphasize democratic/cross-cutting associations have reasons to wish schools remain firmly in the public sector. They may emphasize the importance of dialogue among those from different traditions in promoting an autonomous choice of a good life. They may find public schools essential to promoting tolerance. My argument admits the force of the claims of both sides and suggests that what is needed are institutions that seek a balance between these tensions. However, it also emphasizes the importance of the substantive convictions of particularistic groups in creating social capital.

Rawls and the Civic Role of Particularistic Traditions

First I consider the role of particularistic associations in forming political and social capital through a discussion of Rawls's distinction between what he refers to as the two moral powers. Second, I consider the issue of dialogical restraint.

Rawls, the Two Moral Powers, and the Independence Thesis. In both major works, *Theory of Justice* (1971) and *Political Liberalism* (1993), which have dominated debate among political philosophers for the last quarter of the 20th century, Rawls claims that human beings need to develop two moral powers: a capacity for a sense of justice and a capacity for a conception of the good. In *Political Liberalism*, he links having a conception of the good with having a comprehensive doctrine. A comprehensive doctrine is rooted in an intellectual tradition that "covers the major religious, philosophical, and moral aspects of human life" (p. 58), and is the basis of decision-making about values.

Rawls sees the development of a sense or conception of justice as independent of comprehensive doctrines or a conception of the good. I call this the *independence thesis*. He claims that his conception of justice is warranted by arguments that do not presuppose any particular comprehensive doctrine. He also provides an account of the development of a sense of justice, which depends significantly on the bonds formed through human associations, but he attaches little weight to the substantive content of the values and beliefs of these groups. Thus, the two moral powers are independent in two ways. They are independent argumentatively, and they are independent psychologically and motivationally.

The following comments from *Political Liberalism* illustrate:

> Many if not most citizens come to affirm the principles of justice incorporated into their constitution and political practice without seeing any particular connection, one way or another, between those principles and their other views. It is possible for citizens first to appreciate the good those principles accomplish both for those they care for, as well as for society at large, and then to confirm them on this basis. Should an incompatibility later be recognized between the principles of justice and their wider doctrines, then they might very well adjust or revise these doctrines, rather than reject those principles. (p. 160)

I suspect that in the minds of many people the commitment to justice is more strongly associated with their comprehensive doctrine than Rawls supposes.

Religion illustrates this point. Religions often make claims about justice. The believer is not someone whose conception of the good includes, say, personal salvation or the glorification of God and who must decide if these commitments are consistent with an independent conception of justice. Instead, the believer already has elements of a view of justice. When faced with the need to cooperate with those outside the faith, the believer's task is to find a way to understand a religious view of justice that permits cooperation with these others. If there is to be an overlapping consensus, antecedently held and religiously based views of justice are what must overlap. When the believer encounters liberal justice, the question is whether the faith can be understood so as to allow liberal justice to be seen as a variant of the views of justice internal to the faith. To be sure, this is, as Rawls claims, a question of consistency, but for the believer it may be one in which the believer's fundamental convictions stand in judgment of and shape any conception of liberal justice.

Some examples: The three major monotheistic faiths hold that human beings are created in the image of God and are thus objects of worth. The Christian scriptures teach that "in Christ there is no Jew nor Greek, no rich nor poor, no male nor female." They also suggest that we should "render unto Caesar that which is Caesar's." Many religious groups, believing that God values only uncoerced faith, teach doctrines of free faith. Arguably ideas such as these contain the germs and antecedents of such liberal conceptions as the centrality of personhood, the equal protection of the laws, the separation of church and state, and religious tolerance.

If so, the problem for the religious person in liberal society is not to see if justice, independently justified and acquired, is consistent with the picture of the good life taught by the faith. It is rather to see whether liberal ideals such as respect for persons, the equal protection of the laws, and the separation of church and state provide suitable interpretations of views already held. Sometimes the issue may be one of translatability. Can the believer who holds that human beings are created in the image of God treat the emphasis on respect for persons as more or less the same thing? For the believer, the justification for an overlapping consensus is not freestanding.

Although the attempt to reconcile one's comprehensive doctrine with an overlapping consensus may involve modification of the comprehensive doctrine, I see this process as more dialogical and dialectical than does Rawls. I see the pursuit of an overlapping consensus as a kind of conversation between people from different traditions who wish to find mutually acceptable ways to live together while holding to their comprehensive doctrines conscientiously. The interaction may lead religious people to seek new meaning for such notions as "In Christ there is no Jew nor Greek" or that human beings are created in the image of God. But in such conversations the comprehensive doctrines people hold are unlikely to disappear as argumentative resources either in their own minds or in their interactions with others.

It is also unlikely that justice will be motivationally independent of comprehensive doctrines. The sense of justice, Rawls claims, develops out of bonds forged first in the family and then in larger communities. Consider then how congregations forge common bonds. Congregations share stories, songs, and suppers, something of a shared life together. They care for the sick and visit widows and orphans. It is, perhaps, these communal practices more than ideas and arguments that forge bonds. However, these practices are intertwined with a creed, which in turn is often sustained by a tradition of argument. Songs, suppers, and sharing are warranted by doctrine and creed. Love of brothers and sisters is practiced because it is commanded. In congregations the activities that form and sustain bonds are intertwined with a religious tradition that gives them meaning and apart from which they are unlikely to endure.

What motivates one to comply with abstract principles of justice? Justice has no songs and symbols. It inspires few congregational suppers, visitations of the sick, or prayers for the bereaved. Its congregations (if philosophers could be thought of as such) argue more than celebrate. They split hairs rather than break bread. Associations that forge strong bonds do so with songs, symbols, and suppers, not arguments. If there is to be a strong commitment to justice in a society, as Rawls suggests, social bonds must be formed in more local and particularistic groups and then transferred to the members of the larger society. But moralities of association are infused with the assumptions of culture and creed. No expansion of the bonds forged in a morality of association to the larger society that does not expand particularistic conceptions of culture and creed to include the other and which does not take advantage of their motivational force is likely to succeed.

Thus Rawls's independence thesis is doubtful. It is doubtful because people live their lives locally. Their identities, views, and character are formed first and foremost by their face-to-face associations and by the commitments their families and communities transmit to them. People are unlikely to treat their fellow citizens with justice or decency, they are unlikely to forge common bonds with them, unless their local culture forms and sustains such bonds cognitively and affectively. The support that such civic virtues as justice, trust, decency, and charity receive from local culture and particularistic doctrines is a far more significant matter than is suggested by Rawls's independence thesis.

Public Discourse and Dialogical Restraint. Charles Taylor (1995) said that the public sphere is a space outside of government where public opinion is formed through rational discussion. Government, Taylor suggested, should pay attention to what is said in the public sphere both because discursively formed public opinion may be enlightened and because responding to enlightened public opinion gives meaning to the idea that the government rests on the consent of the governed.

The picture of democracy that forms the background of Taylor's view of a public sphere is deliberative democracy. Deliberative democracy views democratic processes as a search for the common good through reasoned argument. In a deliberative democracy citizens must give one another reasons that in principle all could accept. Deliberative democracy is not likely to work well unless its citizens possess a set of virtues. Chief among these should be a virtue that Gutmann and Thompson (1996) called reciprocity or Hollenbach (1995) called solidarity. Hollenbach writes:

> What I propose to call intellectual solidarity is a spirit of willingness to take other persons and groups seriously enough to engage them in conversation and debate about how the interdependent world we share should be shaped and structured. Thus, it calls for discussion about public discourse about diverse visions of the good life. Such discourse is quite different from the tolerance recommended by Rawls as the best we can do in responding to pluralism. Tolerance is a strategy of disengagement and avoidance of fundamental questions of value in public life. (p.150)

Hollenbach's picture of deliberative democracy seeks for deliberation about the nature of the common good in a way that involves discourse about "diverse visions of the good life." He opposes this notion to Rawls's concept of tolerance and public reason. Rawls's notion of public reason is one instance of what I earlier called dialogical restraint. The passage quoted above from Gutmann (see p. 37) is another one. The general idea of dialogical restraint is this: In the public sphere, citizens should try to give one another reasons that all can accept. They should attempt to avoid giving reasons that appeal to premises that are distinct to their comprehensive doctrines because such reasons are unlikely to be shared. Instead, they should attempt to provide public reasons. Citizens are asked to recognize that not every reason they consider to be a good reason is a public reason. For example, reasons that appeal to religious doctrines may be good reasons, but because they are rooted in comprehensive doctrines, they cannot be public reasons.

Hollenbach rejects the notion of dialogical restraint because it takes discourse about diverse visions of the good life off the table and out of public space. Does it? Should it?

Consider three different kinds of conversations:

1. *In-group conversations about collective concerns*: Such conversations are discussions among members of particularistic moral traditions about carrying out their shared outlook. The purposes of such conversations include instruction of new members in the group's view, the resolution of issues against the background of shared assumptions, and the development of positions on matters of public concern.

2. *Between-group conversations about matters of mutual concern*: An example might be a discussion between Protestants and Catholics about their respective views of religious authority, the meaning of these views for their lives, and what different views of religious authority imply for democratic citizenship. The purposes of such conversations include mutual understanding, inquiry into the truth of the matter, and the pursuit of an overlapping consensus. Insofar as such conversations provide opportunity for discussants to modify their own views, they also promote individual autonomy and the examined life.

3. *Public discussion about some matter potentially before the legislature*: An example might be a debate about welfare policy. The purposes are to build an informed public consensus about a matter of public policy and to inform and advise the legislature.

I make two assumptions about these conversational types. First, I assume that participation in these conversational types not only forms opinion but also helps develop the capacities and virtues on which having such conversations depend. Second, I assume that a good education requires space for each of the three conversational types. Two questions need to be asked. To which of these conversational types might the notion of dialogical restraint apply? Which of these conversations are public conversations that might take place in public space?

In choosing between the dialogue that Hollenbach advocates and the avoidant tolerance Rawls recommends, it makes a great deal of difference whether the results of the dialogue are likely to be written into law. Dialogical restraint becomes a suitable norm to the degree that discussion anticipates the coercive use of public power. Here the search for sharable reasons is an attempt to avoid oppression, not to avoid a more robust dialogue about the nature of a good life.

Dialogical restraint is not, however, a plausible view for the other forms of conversation. Indeed, it would make them impossible, and, because these conversations serve important educational and public purposes, this is surely undesirable. Moreover, to apply dialogical restraint to these conversations would be inconsistent with freedom of religion and free speech.

In-group and between-group discussions can be seen as public conversations that appropriately take place in public space. Taylor, for example, thinks of the public sphere as a place apart from government control where citizens deliberate about public matters in a way so as to advise the legislature. A newspaper or the Internet are examples. But the purposes of such forums exceed the need to advise the legislature. They are places where people may explore their differences over wide-ranging areas to their mutual benefit. It would be odd and objectionable to exclude between-group conversations or expression of particularistic views from such forums. Because between-group conversations can occur in these public spaces, they are in some sense public conversations. Moreover, they may serve public purposes such as building tolerance and mutual understanding even if their purpose is not to advise the legislature. So long as they do not envision some use of public authority as resulting from the discussion, there is no violation of dialogical restraint.

If we think of public spaces as places in which public purposes are appropriately discussed, all three types of conversations are public conversations and the places in which they occur are public spaces. A church may be a public place because the public good is appropriately discussed among members of religious congregations whose members may feel the need of a view suitably informed by their faith. It also may be a public place because it is a place where ideas and values that either sustain or thwart liberal democratic societies are forged. Finally, public purposes are at stake in congregations because the conversations that take place in congregations include those that concern the nature of an overlapping consensus. The dialogue that molds the nature of a society's political values cannot take place without discussions that are internal to communities formed by comprehensive doctrines.

In short, the notion of dialogical restraint must be applied with sensitivity to context and intent. It needs to consider whether the forum is a church, the Internet, or a legislative floor and whether the intent is to coerce or to teach, inform, or persuade. At the end of the day, public policy should be rooted in public and sharable reasons. As the context comes to envision legislation, the search for sharable reasons, and hence dialogical restraint, becomes important. However, if dialogical restraint is understood to preclude people from deliberating among themselves in their particularistic languages about public matters, or if it is viewed as a broad prohibition against people sharing their particularistic reasons with others, it is a repressive and miseducative notion. A society that wishes to promote a robust discussion among citizens about the common good needs to construct any notion of dialogical restraint narrowly.

The implication of these arguments is that the search for spaces between state and market should not seek a civil society that consists largely of democratic/cross-cutting groups. In such a society, in-group conversations will be thwarted, and eventually because in-group conversations are a resource for between-group conversations, between-group conversations will become degraded. Discussions about the nature of the good life are unlikely to be very sophisticated if individuals are unable to debate and refine their distinctive views and avail themselves of their distinctive traditions through discussions with the like-minded. Hence any society that believes in the examined life and in meaningful dialogue about the good life will need robust particularistic groups organized by coherent moral or cultural traditions. Moreover, as I have argued earlier, the conversations of particularistic groups are a significant resource for producing the beliefs and the virtues on which the practices of liberal democracy depend. I do not mean to ignore the fact that such groups are also a source of sectarian and cultural strife. The trick is to discover how to enhance their capacity to produce social capital while diminishing their potential for conflict.

Islands of Particularity in the Public Sector

One educational strategy is to encourage and institutionalize between-group conversations. It is these conversations that are most likely to promote mutual understanding and tolerance and to create the virtue of reciprocity that is required for conversations about the use of public power to be conducted in good faith. So far as education is concerned, it is particularly important to have children participate in all three types of conversations. It would certainly be desirable if all three types of conversation were to occur in the same school. However, under current conditions (particularly in the United States), between-group conversations are unlikely in both public and private schools. Let's consider why.

School communities may be formed either through free association or by geography. In the United States, although there are exceptions such ·as charter schools or magnet schools, most public school communities are formed through geography and most schools that are formed through freedom of association are private. Religious schools in the United States must be private by law.

Hence, the educational conversations of particularistic associations are privatized and occur in forums where others are not present. This means that religious schools as well as schools rooted in some distinctive culture (e.g., Afrocentric schools) are likely to be dominated by in-group conversations. Between-group conversations may be unlikely, or, if they do occur, perhaps through the agency of reading material or the questioning of skeptical students, nonorthodox perspectives are unlikely to be forcefully and persuasively defended. Even discussions about public policy are likely to be in-group discussions because there is little need to respect the norm of dialogical restraint in a particularistic school.

In-group conversations and between-group conversations are unlikely in public schools. That in-group conversations are unlikely is obvious. Public schools are democratic/cross-cutting organizations where conversations presupposing the views of some particular comprehensive doctrine are inappropriate. But why might between-group conversations be unlikely? One reason is that in liberal societies schools are supposed to be neutral among different conceptions of the good. Hence, liberalism inhibits a curriculum that is rooted in any particular vision of a good life. However, a neutral curriculum is likely to lack the coherence a moral tradition can provide. It may be instrumental because the purposes that inform it are likely to belong to individual students (or their parents), not to the school as a whole. The liberal school may be more like a shopping mall than a deliberative forum. It will provide a diversity of curricular goods to be employed by students for their own purposes, but which will not be shared or discussed.

Also, the sensitivities that many parents have about how schools deal with matters that impinge on their sundry religions and cultures exert a significant chilling effect on between-group conversations. In public schools, discussions about good lives will be conducted by teachers who will be expected to be nonpartisan. Teachers may be poorly trained to mediate such conversations or to be sensitive to the range of deeply held views that students may bring to them. Moreover, many parents will resist any attempt at a neutral presentation of their views. What counts as neutral will be a matter of considerable contention. And some parents will view any presentation not committed to the truth of their views either as a kind of sacrilege or as the encouragement of their children to defect. In the United States religious sensitivity usually produces avoidance. In less touchy cultures (England may be an example), an attempt to teach such matters in schools may tend toward vacuity. Neither avoidance nor vacuity is a virtue.

What follows is that substantive between-group conversations, conversations that are important both to the examined life and to the development of civic virtue, are unlikely to be common in any of the forms of schooling potentially available in the near future.

Full privatization of schooling is not a solution to this dilemma. Even if one supposes that the U.S. Supreme Court would countenance public funds flowing to religious schools, under the current arrangements the only result would be the substitution of schools with one kind of inadequacy for schools with another.

The general form of a solution is this: We need to find ways to have a higher level of free association in the public sector. That is, we should look for ways that members of particularistic groups can associate together for educational purposes within public institutions. Such associations need to perform the delicate balancing act of promoting all three of the conversational types I have just described while carefully avoiding the imposition of any particular group's views on others. They would be islands of particularity, but because they also occupy the space of a public school and are subject to public regulation, they can be islands in communication with one another in a public sea that mitigates their potential for strife. Some examples follow, which are intended more as illustrations than as recommendations.

1. *An expanded role for the conversations of particularistic associations in the extracurricular activities of public schools:* Currently U.S. law permits students to form religious clubs under the same conditions that regulate other student-sponsored activities. Such clubs must be student-led and initiated (*Board of Education v. Mergans,* 1990). Another

example is the black gospel choir (open to members of all races). Such choirs have met legal opposition in some places because of their emphasis on religious music. One can imagine an expansion of the educational significance of such groups by permitting more adult participation and by encouraging interaction between them.

2. *Reauthorization of shared time:* Schools in the United States were once open to religious instruction provided by clergy who taught religion on a voluntary basis during school time and on school property. In *School District of Grand Rapids v. Ball* (1985), the Supreme Court declared shared time to be unconstitutional; however, it has recently shown signs of relenting (*Agostini v. Felton*, 1997). Something like shared time (one might refer to it as *particularity time)*, available to all particularistic groups, might be reintroduced in public schools. A nonreligious example would be elective studies in African American history (again, available on a nondiscriminatory basis). Here too it would be important for schools to promote some form of interaction between groups so constituted.

3. *Charter schools as house plans:* Charter schools are schools that have relief from some state and local regulations, that are operated by license by people who have a distinctive vision of a school they wish to create, and that are attended by those who are willing to salute this vision. House plans involve breaking the local comprehensive high school into separate "houses" in which smaller numbers of students go to class together and work with the same teachers over a longer period of time than is common. Their point is to make schools more intimate and communal places. These two ideas could be combined by creating a number of charter schools within the space of a single comprehensive high school. Here charters would be available to particularistic groups, and the larger school could work to encourage the sharing both of resources and perspectives.

4. *Associations of mutual exploration:* One can imagine schools deliberately constituted to share different traditions. There is in Cambridge, U.K. a school run as a cooperative venture between Anglicans and Catholics where students are encouraged to respect and understand one another's religious traditions while also being led to see them as

"non-malignantly suboptimal." (I owe the example and phrase to Terence McLaughlin of Cambridge University who is a governor of this school.)

The purpose of these examples is to illustrate institutional arrangements that make possible all three of the conversational types sketched above in order to find a way to allow students to be initiated into a praiseworthy conception of a good life while also creating patterns of association and interaction with those with different visions. Their point is to permit schools to have aspects of both particularistic and democratic/cross-cutting associations. These aspirations seem equally necessary, but are in tension. Their institutionalization is not easy. Indeed, I am painfully aware of the difficulties of proceeding with such ideas. Open discussion of deeply held views can be contentious and painful. Institutions that promote between-group discussions would create strong demands for both tolerance and reciprocity without which they would certainly fail. No enterprise would be likely to succeed apart from much planning and pedagogical sensitivity on the part of the school staff. However, the ability to have such conversations is also a learned skill important to liberal democracies.

In conclusion, I want to note that these proposals are in service of a view that might be called *local cosmopolitanism*. Local cosmopolitanism tries to balance two ideas. The first is that life is lived locally. Human beings thrive in thick particularistic communities where they are nurtured by people they know and trust and where their lives are formed and informed by a praiseworthy view of the good life (Strike, 1997). However, the public ethic of a liberal democratic society must be something like an overlapping consensus. It must be thin enough to be acceptable to all reasonable people. Consequently it cannot be thick enough to provide a coherent picture of human flourishing. Yet people need to be initiated into a praiseworthy view of a good life, one that, in a pluralistic society, cannot be shared. Initiation into such a view of the good life is part of localism. But localism need not and should not be parochialism or partisanship. Any worthy localism must grant others the right to their own local education, and should seek to understand, appreciate, and learn from others. This is what I mean by cosmopolitanism. A good education is both local and cosmopolitan. An education that builds the social capital for liberal democratic societies must be both as well.

Current visions of educational reform, both the statist systemic reform and the market-oriented emphasis on competition and choice, are neither of these. They provide no space between the state and the market. Both offer schools in which students are seen as competing with one another for advantage in the marketplace. Whether such schools will raise test scores I do not know, but it seems evident to me that they are unlikely to help students achieve a praiseworthy conception of a good life or to develop the social capital for a liberal democratic society. If we bring the civil society perspective to schooling, we will ask a wider range of questions, but if the civil society perspective is to fulfill its potential, it must view particularistic groups as resources for the development of social capital, not just as sources of sectarian strife.

References

Ackerman, B. (1980). *Social justice in the liberal state.* New Haven, CT: Yale University Press.

Agostini v. Felton, 118 S. Ct. 40 (1997).

Board of Education v Mergans, 496 U.S. 226 (1990).

Bryk, A. S., Lee, V. E., & Holland, P. B. (1993). *Catholic schools and the common good.* Cambridge, MA: Harvard University Press.

Chubb, J. E., & Moe, T. M. (1990). *Politics, markets, and the American school.* Washington DC: The Brookings Institution.

Friedman, M. (1962). *Capitalism and freedom.* Chicago: University of Chicago Press.

Fuhrman, S. H. (1993). The Politics of coherence. In S. H. Fuhrman (Ed.), *Designing coherent educational policy* (pp. 1–34). San Francisco: Jossey-Bass.

Gutmann, A. (1987). *Democratic education.* Princeton, NJ: Princeton University Press.

Gutmann, A., & Thompson, D. (1996). *Democracy and disagreement.* Cambridge, MA: Harvard University Press.

Hanushek, E. A. (1997). Outcomes, incentives, and beliefs: Reflections on analysis of the economics of schools. *Educational evaluation and policy analysis, 19*(4), 301–308.

Hollenbach, D. (1995). Virtue, the common good, and democracy. In A. Etzioni (Ed.), *New communitarian thinking* (pp. 143–153). Charlottesville, VA: University Press of Virginia.

Putnam, R. (1993). *Making democracy work: Civic traditions in modern Italy.* Princeton, NJ: Princeton University Press.

Rawls, J. (1971). *A theory of justice.* Cambridge, MA: Harvard University Press.

Rawls, J. (1993). *Political liberalism.* New York: Columbia University Press.

Rosenblum, N. (1998). The moral effects of associational life. *Philosophy and public policy, 18*(3), 8–13.

School district of Grand Rapids v. Ball, 473 U.S. 373 (1985).

Smith, M. S., Scoll, B. W., & Link, J. (1996). Research-based reform: The Clinton administration's agenda. In N. R. Council (Ed.), *Improving the performance of America's schools* (pp. 9–27). Washington, DC: National Academy Press.

Strike, K. A. (1997). Centralized goal formation and systemic reform: Reflections on liberty, localism and pluralism. *Educational policy analysis, 15*(11), 1–24.

Taylor, C. (1995). Liberal politics and the public sphere. In A. Etzioni (Ed.), *New communitarian thinking* (pp. 183–217). Charlottesville, VA: University Press of Virginia.

Chapter Four

The Idea of an Education Mix:
A Proposal to Strengthen Civil Society and Education in Germany

INGO RICHTER

T he public school system in the Federal Republic of Germany is based on the so-called *social state* clause (e.g., on the constitutional statement contained in Article 20, § 1 of the Basic Constitutional Law that the Federal Republic is a "social" state). This constitutional social state clause does not, however, guarantee any specific organizational form of society; it is merely a declaration of the type of society that is to be aimed at, and although it is not merely a political program but objective law, it is left to the legislature to decide on the precise shape of this society (Jarras & Pieroth, 1992).

The social state uses the schools as an instrument for the production of necessary skills and social planning; it wants to compensate for individual and family deficits and to use the schools to guarantee social justice. In this process, people sometimes overlook the fact that school is also a place where children and juveniles live and learn, by themselves, with each other, and with one or more teachers, and that in this way they grow up to be young adults.

The Crisis of the Social State and the Schools

The social state in the Federal Republic, having tried to fulfill all these tasks and having to a large extent fulfilled them, is now in a crisis that is being widely debated. People are talking of a restructuring of the social state. They claim that the social state cannot or can no longer achieve its aims of social security (see, e.g., Heinze, Olk, & Hilbert, 1988, p. 13), that the social state is too expensive and the whole system is inefficient, that the social state cannot give an answer to the new social question that arose with the development of a segment of society labled *new poverty* (families with many children, single-parent families, foreigners and homeless, old women, chronically sick, long-term unemployed; see Geissler, 1976).

The public school system, which is a public enterprise of the social state, seems to be fixed in the social landscape like an immutable monolithic structure that has survived the centuries. But this impression is erroneous. The criticisms of the social state certainly apply equally to the functions of school within the social state. The school system has been accused of failing to achieve such aims as protecting against the risks of life (Tillmann, 1994), teaching the knowledge and skills society needs (e.g., Klemm, Rolff, & Tillmann, 1986), supporting the children's upbringing in the family (Fünfter Familienbericht ([5th Family Report], 1995, p. 232), guaranteeing equal opportunities in education (Rodax, 1989, p. 311) as well as democratic thinking (on the basis of the Youth Survey of the Deutsches Jugendinstitut). This criticism may well be unjustified and too much of a generalization; but it cannot be denied that it is a point of view that is shared by many people and therefore raises doubts about the aims of the social state in schools.

The second point of criticism, the high cost of the social state, is also widely accepted in the debate about the school system. Education expenditures, both from the public coffers and from the private sector, have more than tripled in 20 years. If, as appears to be the case, the crisis in the social state also affects the functions of the social state in school, the question then arises whether the suggestions for restructuring the social state can and should also be applied to school.

The Restructuring of the Social State and the Schools

The restructuring of the social state is taking place in various ways, two of which I discuss here: privatization and expanding the so-called third sector and the welfare mix.

Privatization. The social security system has always known benefits provided by the private sector. Health care is traditionally available from private doctors and pharmacists, and private hospitals co-exist with public and church-owned ones. In the field of health insurance, pensions, disablement insurance, and accident insurance, numerous private insurance companies offer alternative or additional insurance policies. The monopoly of the Bundesanstalt für Arbeit (the Federal Employment Agency) on job placement has only recently been abolished. The privatization of further services provided by the social state is under discussion.

Privatizing schools run by the state or by local authorities by transferring them to the private sector has so far not been seriously discussed in the Federal Republic, at least not the financial aspect. Such a discussion would in fact be pointless because private schools are bound by Article 7, paragraph 4 of the Basic Constitutional Law to observe certain standards and because the state has to safeguard financially the existence of an economically viable private school system. Furthermore, whether private schools can operate more economically than public schools is highly debatable (Haug, 1998; Weiß, 1988a, 1998b). The privatization of individual school functions is only being considered in a half-hearted and not very serious way as well. It would for example be conceivable that schools might leave sports and music lessons to local authorities, to clubs or associations, or to commercial providers, who could—after bids have been made—ask a certain fee for this. Entrusting language instruction to commercial providers is probably out of the question in principle due to the high costs of the long courses. Experiments along these lines in the United States in the 1970s were unsuccessful (Richter, 1975, p. 84). Privatization therefore does not seem to be a suitable method of restructuring the social state in the field of education.

Welfare Mix and Education Mix. What remains—if we accept the limited possibilities of restructuring the social state in the field of education—is the formation of the third sector, or the welfare mix. In organizational theory, the *third sector* is defined as the area between and beyond the state and the market, in which public welfare organizations and private and public organizations, in particular trusts and corporate bodies, carry out public tasks that can be effectively performed by the state, but which it is not considered politic to leave to commercial providers. In social policy, the *welfare mix* is defined as forms of activity in which both the state and the market and organizations of the third sector together provide social services, paying particular attention to the policy of self-help. The principle behind this is that the combination of these different organizations will increase the overall efficacy of the system. Whereas the theory of the third sector is aimed rather at the organizational forms, the theory of the welfare mix is more concerned with the forms of activity (e.g., Backhaus-Maul & Olk, 1992, p. 94, 101).

German social policies can be seen as a classic area for both approaches as the German social security system has always been organized by public institutions and bodies and social security benefits are provided by public agencies and private providers cooperating together. Aid systems are dominated by organizational structures run by the state or the community; but the principle of subsidiarity guarantees that charitable bodies occupy a special place in the system of benefits, and the self-help principle—including voluntary activities—is firmly anchored in it (for applications in social policies, Kaufmann, 1987; Heinze, Olk & Hilbert, 1988).

In the school system, by way of contrast, these approaches have so far been ignored. The third sector does not exist and cannot exist under the current laws because a school run by the state or by local authorities is a public school, and if it is not a public school, then it is a private school (Heckel & Seipp, 1976, p. 142). For the same reason, an education mix is quite impossible; school law does not envisage a school run both by the state and by private bodies. It may be possible for private providers to offer specific services at a public school, for example computer training, and the state can prescribe the courses offered at private schools and demand specific examinations, but there can certainly be no question of the state, local authorities, associations, and private providers together offering services at schools.

What would the situation be if it were precisely the third sector and the welfare mix approaches that could best achieve the restructuring of the social state by resolving the crisis of the social state without occasioning any additional costs? Might this offer possible solutions for the school system, too? How could the school system be organized as a third sector and how could an education mix be created?

A Public School System. It is easy to justify a third sector in the school system; the state would invite bids for a specific sector of the school system and grant licences for services that cost less per capita than in the public school system. Applications would be invited from organizations run by local authorities, by associations, and by private providers, as long as these organizations fulfilled the published conditions and had been granted charitable status. The result of this would presumably be that between the poles of the public school sector and the commercial one a wide variety of mixed public–private organizations would spring up, all competing to be awarded the contract. The school system in the Netherlands has often been cited as a model, although there are no calls for bids (Liket, 1993). These organizations would, however, not only be competing with each other within the context of the call for bids, but they would also be vying with state schools, with commercial ones, and with each other for pupils, so that pupils and parents would have genuine choices.

It can be assumed that within such a system it would come to forms of limited cooperation between the various organizations, specifically when such cooperation would provide advantages for all concerned. Organizations from the third sector in particular would try and involve voluntary helpers in order to reduce personnel costs; the result would be a broad self-help area in connection with the third sector. Such cooperation is, however, conceivable not only within the third sector; commercial schools could also make use of specific services that are available in the third sector in order to increase their chances in the marketplace. The state could invite bids under certain conditions for specific courses of education and in this way develop special forms of cooperation with the third sector, with the British system of opting out serving as a model. In this manner, something could be created between the three sectors, which—taking its cue from the phrase welfare mix—could be called *education mix*. An education mix would create a very varied school system, whose ability to function could only be guaranteed by a unified system of examinations and entrance standards.

However, before imaginations roam wild as this picture gets fleshed out, the question "Can we even consider such a picture?" must be answered. Article 7, Paragraph 1 of the Basic Constitutional Law says that the entire school system is under the supervision of the state—nothing more and nothing less. This does not necessarily mean that schools are to be run by the state or the community. The guarantee for private schools in any case rules out a monopoly for schools run by the state or the community. But if the freedom of private schools is

guaranteed as a basic right, then the Basic Constitutional Law ought not
to prevent the creation of a third sector.

But what about the guarantee of a public school system, which—in
contrast to the Constitutions of Frankfurt and Weimar—is not
specifically mentioned in the Basic Constitutional Law, although the
social state clause distinctly implies it? According to the Constitutions
of Frankfurt and Weimar—notwithstanding the guarantee for private
schools—public schools were to be provided in sufficient quantity for
the education of young people. But again according to the Weimar
Constitution the Reich, the states, and local authorities were to cooperate
to establish such public schools, and the teachers at these public schools
were to have the rights of civil servants. Leaving aside the fact that this
constitution in no longer in force, the text can be interpreted in such a
way that an education mix is permissible. The Reich, the states, and
local authorities would work together to establish the schools, but would
not necessarily have to run them; and the teachers would have both the
rights and the duties of civil servants, but would not necessarily have to
be civil servants.

Far more important than such pettifogging attempts to interpret the
text of a former constitution is the question of the function of the supply
of public schooling contained in the constitution. Why should public
schools be provided in sufficient quantity for the education of young
people? In part the constitution wanted to limit the freedom of private
schools (consider the prohibition of nursery schools and the near
monopoly of the state in the primary school sector contained in Article
7, Paragraphs 2 and 3 in the Weimar Constitution); but the Constitution
of Weimar was primarily concerned with three educational policy aims
that were to be served by a public school system:

1. Schools, especially secondary schools, were to be opened to all
social classes (Article 145—the ban on school fees and charges for
books etc.; Article 146, Paragraph 1—the organizational structure of the
school system according to the requirements of the employment system
and the ban on social selection; Article 146, Paragraph 3—scholarships;
and Article 149, Paragraph 1—the ban on social segregation in private
schools).

2. Schools were to be opened up to pupils of all religious
denominations by the introduction of the communal school with

voluntary religious instruction as the standard school, and by the stipulation that special permission was needed for denominational schools (Articles 146 and 149).

3. Schools were to be opened up to the contents of educational theories that were not classical–humanistic (Article 148—"ethical education, patriotic attitudes, personal and professional hard work in accordance with German traditions and international understanding," "civics and work education").

Because these educational demands contained in the Weimar Constitution have been almost completely fulfilled in the states in the Federal Republic of Germany, it is important to ensure that they remain fulfilled even if a third sector and an education mix are created. Leaving the distinctions between state-run and privately-run schools aside, public schools would then be those schools that fulfilled these criteria of openness and accessibility.

Would "public schools"—understood in this sense—be better able to meet the current criticism that the present educational system does not properly fulfill its tasks in the social state?

1. Even in such a system, ensuring that the socially disadvantaged are protected would rather be the task of the state, unless special incentives were provided for fulfilling the task of protection. The answer would therefore be: No.

2. The knowledge and skills acquired in such a system would presumably be more functional than in the present system, as an education mix could permit more flexible contents and forms of learning more closely geared to specific needs. To this extent the answer would then be: Yes.

3. The task of upholding the family would remain the state's, unless special incentives were provided for fulfilling these. Again the answer would be: No.

4. Social inequality would, however, increase in such a system unless the government intervened in order to guarantee that schools remained accessible to all. So here, too, the answer would be: No.

5. The wide variety of such an educational system would per se rule out the possibility that the educational system would favor the creation

of a specific form of society. This is in accordance with the picture of free pluralism in society, and so to this extent the answer would be: Yes.

Assuming that in such a system the costs of the educational system would be lower, it can be assumed that the effectiveness of the educational system would be higher because the demands of society would be better fulfilled. Creating a third sector or introducing an education mix would lead to the fulfilment of the first two aims of the Constitution of Weimar, namely the opening up of schools to children of all social classes and all religious denominations. This would contribute towards solving the crisis of the social state. It cannot, however, be expected that such a system would contribute towards solving the new social question.

In the final analysis it can be said that creating a system of public schools along the lines of a third sector and an education mix would tend to increase the effectiveness of the educational system, but would probably reduce the social equality. It would therefore be a question of weighing up these two factors if the problem of restructuring the social state in the educational system is to be tackled.

References

Backhaus-Maul, H., & Olk, T. (1992). Intermediaere Organisationen als Gegenstand sozialwissenschaftlicher Forschung. In Schmaehl, W. (Ed.), *Sozialpolitik im Prozess der deutschen Wiedervereinigung*, pp. 90–103. Frankfurt: Campus.

Fünfter Familienbericht. (1995), *Familien und Familienpolitik im geeinten Deutschland—Zukunft des Humanvermögens,* edited by Bundesministerium für Familie, Senioren, Frauen und Jugend. Bonn, BT-Drs. 12/7560

Geissler, H. (1976). *Die Neue Soziale Frage. Analysen und Dokumente.* Freiburg, Basel, Wien: Herder.

Haug, R. (1988). Ausgabenkennwerte staatlicher Schulen. *Recht der Jugend und des Bildungswesens, 4,* 450–455.

Heckel, H., & Seipp, P. (1976). *Schulrechtskunde* (5th ed.). Darmstadt: Luchterhand

Heinze, R. G., Olk, T., & Hilbert, J. (1988). *Der neue Sozialstaat. Analyse und Reformperspektiven.* Freiburg im Breisgau: Lambertus.

Hoffmann-Lange, U. (1994). Zur Politikverdrossenheit Jugendlicher in Deutschland—Erscheinungsformen und Ursachen. *Politische Studien, 336,* 92–106.

Hüfner, K. (1992). Organisationsuntersuchung im Schulbereich. *Recht der Jugend und des Bildungswesens, 2,* 197–205.

Jarras, H. D., & Pieroth, B. (1992). *Grundgesetz* (2nd ed.). München: Beck

Kaufmann, F.-X. (1987). *Staat, intermediaere Instanzen und Selbsthilfe. Bedingungsanalysen sozialpolitischer Intervention.* München: Oldenbourg.

Klemm, K., Rolff, H.-G., & Tillmann, K.-J. (1986). *Bildung für das Jahr 2000. Bilanz der Reform. Zukunft der Schule.* Reinbek b. Hamburg: Rowohlt.

Liket, T. M. (1993). *Freiheit und Verantwortung. Das niederländische Modell des Bildungswesens.* Guethersloh: Bertelsmann.

Richter, I. (1975). *Die unorganisierbare Bildungsreform. Innovations-, Legitimations- und Relevanzprobleme im amerikanischen Bildungswesen.* München: Piper & Co.

Rodax, K. (1989). *Strukturwandel der Bildungsbeteiligung,* 1950–1985. Darmstadt: Wissenschaftliche Buchgesellschaft.

Strasser, J. (1983). *Grenzen des Sozialstaats?* (2nd ed.). Köln: Bund-Verlag.

Tillmann, K.-J. (1994). Gewalt in der Schule: Was sagt die erziehungswissenschaftliche Forschung dazu? *Recht der Jugend und des Bildungswesens, 2,* 163–173

Weiss, M. (1988a). Erwiderung. *Recht der Jugend und des Bildungswesens, 4,* 455–459.

Weiss, M. (1988b). Kostenkennwerte staatlicher Schulen. *Recht der Jugend und des Bildungswesens, 3,* 341–348.

Weiss, M. (1992). Zur 'inneren Ökonomie' des Schulwesens. *Recht der Jugend und des Bildungswesens, 2,* 206–216.

Chapter Five

Church, State, and Civil Society: The Netherlands' System of Schooling

ANNEBERT DIJKSTRA
JAAP DRONKERS

In the international discussion about enlargement of parental choice and private deliverance of education, the Dutch arrangement is quite often regarded as a unique system. Central to this arrangement is the constitutional principle of freedom of education. This principle has resulted in approximately 70% of parents sending their children to schools established by private associations and managed by private school boards, yet fully funded and highly regulated by the central government. In the opinion of national interest groups as well as educational experts (e.g., Hermans, 1993; van Kemenade, Jungbluth, & Ritzen, 1981), this freedom of education and equal financing of public and private education from public funds makes the Dutch system exceptional. Foreign observers are also of this opinion, as illustrated by the last Organisation for Economic Co-operation and Development (OECD) review of Dutch education, in which the constitutional provision for freedom of education and the underlying compartmentalized organization of society has been designated as unique (OECD, 1991). The Dutch system developed over the course of the 19th century from a relatively secular school system, dominated by the national government at the beginning of the last century, to a plural system, with private school sectors dominated by religious groups. According to international observers—"the evolution of the Dutch system of . . . education is unique in the Western World" (James, 1989, p. 179)—this history is also regarded as remarkable.

The Dutch arrangement (and a few others, such as the Danish system) is of particular interest to those involved in the debate about parental choice and public financing of private education. For several societies, the analysis of the effects that are to be expected from enlargement of parental choice and privatization in education is often based on analytical evaluations or small-scale experiments (e.g., the Milwaukee Parental Choice Program in the United States; cf. Witte, 1993). Yet, the Netherlands offers an experiment in private production of education on a national scale, which includes the entire education system and is a century old. As Brown (1992, p. 177) so concisely puts it: "The Netherlands is the only country with a nationwide school choice program." In the choice debate, the Dutch experiment is often advanced as an argument in favor of providing more private deliverance of education in other countries (e.g., Dennison, 1984) although sometimes it is also considered as a warning not to go down that road (e.g., Walford, 1995). The unique features of the Dutch system evidently offer points of departure for arguments in favor of as well as against enlargement of freedom of education and private production of education. A number of years ago, Glenn (1989) already warned that references to the Dutch situation are "often with little factual basis," underscoring the necessity for proper insight into the Dutch system, before any general lessons can be learned. In this chapter, we discuss some characteristics of the system of schooling in the Netherlands, as well as recent developments in this long-standing, nationwide experiment of private deliverance of education.

The Dutch System of Choice

Parental choice of school was one of the most important topics in the Netherlands in the 19th century. The political struggle between the liberal, dominant class and the Catholic and orthodox Protestant lower classes gave rise to Christian-Democratic parties, which have held central political power since the start of the 20th century until the mid-1990s.

The liberal party, representing the higher social classes and moderate Protestants and Catholics, had reorganized primary and secondary education profoundly since its rise to power. It also started the improvement of schools by a higher level of funding, either by the state or by the municipalities. From the liberal point of view, schools had to teach general Christian values in order to avoid religious conflicts in school and society. This resulted in a conflict with the orthodox Protestants, who insisted that their Protestant values be taught in the public schools. When it became clear that the orthodox Protestants, with their base in the lower socioeconomic strata in society, could not win this conflict, they established their own religious schools outside the state system, demanding financial support for these schools from the government. The refused requests for public funding were the start of the so-called School Conflict. Later in the 19th century (because of their minority position in the Netherlands), the Catholics started founding their own schools also. Because they shared the opposition to the general character of the (Christian) public school, the Catholics joined the orthodox Protestants in the School Conflict, despite their century-long rivalry. During the School Conflict (which spanned the last quarter of the 19th century and the first decades of the 20th century), the orthodox Protestants split away from the conservatives and established their own political parties. The Catholics did the same and, despite earlier support by the liberals for restoring the Catholic Church in the Netherlands, formed their own political party as well. The socialist party supported the demands for state funding of religious schools in order not to alienate the religious groups in the labor class and to get support from the religious parties for universal franchise.

This political struggle was not unique to the Netherlands; it was the unintended result of three interacting processes: the struggle between the state and the established churches in continental Europe; the fight between the 18th century ancien régime (representing one state-church and suppressed religious minorities) and the 19th century liberal state (which claimed to be neutral to all churches); and the emergence of new social classes in the 19th century (skilled workers, craftspeople, laborers) who rejected the dominant classes, either liberal or conservative. In several continental European societies (Austria, Belgium, France, German *Länder*), these processes had more or less comparable results, with public and religious-subsidized school sectors offering parents a choice between schools with the same curriculum and usually under comparable financial costs. For good reasons, these processes had a quite different effect in the United Kingdom (Archer, 1984); other societies, such as the United States, have never experienced these long conflicts over the schools between the state and the church, or between the ancien régime and the liberal state.

In the Netherlands, choice between religious and public schools was not only an educational choice, it was closely connected to other choices in life—voting, church activities, membership of clubs, unions, newspapers, and the like. The choice between public and religious schools was linked to the choice between the Catholic, orthodox Protestant and public subcultures, or pillars, as they were called in the Netherlands (for a description of this pillarization in Dutch society, see Post, 1989). A consequence of these religious grounds for the rise of subsidized schools was that parental choice on educational grounds (quality of schooling in public and religious schools) did not exist during the first half of the 20th century. Religious considerations and the belonging to a specific subculture were dominant, with perhaps only some elite groups making an exception to this rule. Free parental choice of schools was primarily a religious choice. Because religious socialization was seen as being closely connected to education, this freedom to choose a public or religious school under equal financial conditions was known as freedom of education, a concept that originally referred to one of the basic human rights formulated during the French Revolution—the freedom to teach without church approval, contrary to the situation of the ancien régime. Later, it came to mean freedom of persons and juridical bodies to establish and maintain schools of different denominations under the same conditions as public schools maintained by the state (cf. Box, Dronkers, Molenaar, & de Mulder, 1977).

The religious, political, and social contrasts at the time of the School Conflict have greatly affected the structure of the pillarized education system. As already mentioned, the 19th-century supporters of Christian education strove for their own schools, convinced of the dilution, as they saw it, of the Christian character of the public school. After the attainment of this freedom of education in the 1848 constitutional amendment, the conflict then moved to government financing of private schools. The School Conflict was finally put an end to with the Pacification of 1917, which provided for the complete subsidizidation of private schools from general funds, laid down in the constitution. The freedom of education amendment and the provision of public funding represent the basic historical background of the contemporary framework within which private religious schools in the Netherlands operate, and continue to be a delicate political issue today. As a result, the constitutional amendment on education has not undergone any change, despite its old-fashioned wording and inapplicability to current issues (e.g., recent tendencies toward ethnic segregation since the arrival of new minority groups in Dutch society; cf. Karsten, 1994) and despite later revisions of the Dutch constitution. The old-fashioned wording of the education article is simply too sensitive to change without reviving the School Conflict of the 19th century.

The constitution prescribes the equal subsidizing by the state of all school sectors; they are subjected to strong control of equal examinations, salary, capital investment, and so forth by the state (see also James, 1989). Although the constitution addresses the funding of only primary education, later legislation expands this public funding to all types of education, including schools for higher vocational training, until the Protestant and Catholic universities were also subsidized by the state to the same extent as public universities in 1972, all without any change to the constitution.

The Dutch educational system is considered unique in several aspects when compared with other European countries with similar state - subsidized religious and public school sectors. First, in most such countries the religious schools are of one denomination, mostly Catholic or the former Protestant state church. This is not the case in the Netherlands, whose creation in the religious wars of the 16th century resulted in a large Catholic minority within a moderate Protestant state. Since the 1920s, as a result of the 19th century political struggle, there exist three main private school sectors, a Catholic, a Protestant, and a secular private school sector, all with independent private school boards. In addition, there are several small private religious sectors, and the public sector, the

latter governed by local municipalities. Within the Catholic and Protestant school sectors, there are national umbrella organizations that also
function as lobbies, but they do not replace the autonomous board, nor do
they coordinate all Protestant or Catholic schools. These boards generally
have the juridical form of a foundation, with a high degree of self-
selection of new board members.

Second, the principle of freedom of education or parental choice under conditions of equal funding was enshrined in the constitution of
1917. From the Dutch point of view, certain debates in other societies on
parental choice or vouchers closely resemble debates on this topic in the
Netherlands in the second half of the 19th century. Those debates focused, among other things, on the lower quality of religious schools or
the alleged elite characteristics of such schools, the unfairness of paying
taxes for public schools and extra money for the preferred religious
school, and the appropriateness of public funding of religious schools.

Third, the equal subsidizing of all religious and public schools has
promoted a diminution of prestigious elite schools outside the state-
subsidized sector. As a consequence of equal subsidizing and prohibiting
the use of extra funds for teacher grants, smaller classes, and the like,
there does not exist an institutionalized hierarchy of schools within each
school type, as in most Anglo-Saxon societies (e.g., the English public
schools or independent grammar schools; the Ivy League, or the large
difference in quality between schools in the poor inner cities and those in
the wealthy suburbs in the United States).

Religious Schools in a Secular Society

From the middle of the 20th century onward, the religious substructures
or pillars in Dutch society broke down rapidly. In 1947 only 17% of the
population did not officially belong to any church; halfway through the
1990s the proportion had increased to around 50%. The same trend can
be seen in the votes in favor of Christian-democratic parties in national

elections: in 1948, 55%; in 1998, less than 20% of the vote. Secularization in the Netherlands is considered to be among the most widespread in Western societies (Greeley, 1993). One might have expected this secularization to result in a decline in the popularity of institutions such as religious schools that depend on religious affiliation for their recruitment. However, although such a decline has occurred in a number of other institutions (such as unions, journals, clubs, and hospitals), it has not reached the educational system. In 1950, 73% of all pupils in primary education were attending a nonpublic school; in 1996 the figure was 68%.

How then can one explain the persistence of religious schools or the failure of public schools to attract the growing number of children of nonreligious parents (cf. Dronkers, 1992)? This issue of legitimacy is also of interest to modern societies characterized by an increasing number of religious schools and increasing pressure for public funding, and perhaps even more so in societies with a not very active religious population. The Dutch case might offer some insights into the mechanisms of stability or increase in religious schooling in relatively secular societies. Several explanations and theories explaining this paradox are suggested in the literature (cf. Dronkers, 1995) and we address some mechanisms that might add to the explanation of the continuing existence of religious schools in Dutch society (for a detailed account, see Dijkstra, Dronkers, & Hofman, 1997).

One of the explanations suggested is the strong position of religious schools through political protection by the Christian-Democratic party, by laws protecting freedom of education, and by the dense (administrative) network of the organizations of religious schools. This hypothesis has some validity. The central position of the Christian-Democratic party on the Dutch political map untill halfway through the 1990s made it possible to maintain the pillarized school system and the religious schools within that system, despite the society's decreasing secularization, and even to establish new religious schools in areas with low numbers of active church members. Nevertheless, these mechanisms can't fully explain the flourishing private religious-school sectors, because the Dutch system enables parents to vote with their feet. Despite all regulations and the strong formal position of religious schools, parents can favor other school sectors without facing serious geographical or financial barriers because of the free choice of schools (the Dutch system does not contain catchment areas) and the equal government funding of public and private schools.

Schools are financed according to the number of pupils enrolled, and the way to establish a new school is to find enough parents who will send their children to that school of a given denomination. Several groups of parents (orthodox Protestant, Evangelical, Islamic, Hindu) have recently used this tactic of voting with their feet with success against the powerful, already-established organizations of private religious schools, to found schools of their own religious preference. The essential question here is why nonreligious parents did not use the same tactic to increase the number of nonreligious schools or the number of pupils attending them. It is hard to argue that these parents are less powerful or less numerous than the orthodox Protestant, Evangelical, Islamic, or Hindu parents and their organizations—actually, the opposite might be true. Nonreligious parents are on average better educated and have more links with the established political parties than the other groups. What we conclude from this is that nonreligious parents no longer feel deterred by the religious socialization of religious schools—that is, to the extent religious schools still offer such socialization (cf. Vreeburg, 1993)—and thus do not see the need to change to nonreligious schools. If this is true, the mechanism of protection is not sufficient to account for the continuing existence of religious schools.

Another explanation offered for the attractiveness of religious schools is their (on average) mild educational conservatism, compared with the (on average) more progressive tendency of public schools. Among the reasons for this mild educational conservatism is the different exposure of public and private schools to social policy initiatives around the school. The board at public schools is the council of the municipality. These councils might favor educational experiments in order to accomplish political goals, because education is one of the major instruments of policymakers to promote desirable social developments. Although the boards of private religious schools are often in indirect ways connected with the more moderate political parties, boards of private schools have less direct connections with policymakers, and represent (mostly indirectly) more parents. Therefore they will feel less need for educational experiments for political reasons. Another difference between public and private schools is that the former experience more pressure from the national government because they cannot use the principle of freedom of education as a shield to protect themselves. Religious schools can only be obliged to conform to educational experiments by national law that declares the educational experiment a matter of quality, necessary to qualify for public funding. In all other cases, religious schools are free to participate in educational experiments, but are not required to.

Dutch educational research also contains evidence of positive effects of Catholic and Protestant schooling on academic achievement (for a review, see Dijkstra, 1992). These effects, all adjusted for differences in the student intake of public and private schools, are reported in terms of educational outcomes such as the dropout rate, test scores, degrees, attainment, and so forth. Although, as in other societies, there is debate as to whether these differences are of any substance, private religious schools do distinguish themselves by a reputation for offering educational quality, which research indicates is an important motive in the process of parental choice favoring religious schools in the Netherlands.

One possible explanation for the educational advantage of religious schools has to do with the effect of making a deliberate choice. A deliberate choice for an unconventional school (compared with a traditional choice for a common school) might increase the possibility of this unconventional school becoming a community in which students perform better. Through the mechanism of these deliberate educational choices, and the self-selection following from such a choice, both religious and public schools can become communities with shared values and dense social ties affecting student achievement, as suggested by Coleman and Hoffer (1987). Roeleveld and Dronkers (1994) found evidence that the effectiveness of schools was the highest in districts where neither public,

Protestant, nor Catholic schools attracted a majority of the students, after taking student composition into account. In districts without schools of a dominant position on the educational market, there is no such thing as a conventional school choice, and thus the parental choice is more deliberate. In districts in which public, Protestant, or Catholic schools had either a very small share of the market (under 20%) or a very large one (over 60% of all students), the effectiveness of these schools was lower. In these district's the conventional school choice is most common and the parental choice more traditional.

Especially after the secularization of Dutch society peaked in the 1960s, religious schools were forced to compete for student, and could no longer rely on their recruitment along the religious, pillarized lines in society. For these schools, profiling themselves along lines of educational and pedagogical quality became more important than appealing to their religious constituency, relying on a deliberate educational and pedagogical choice of parents. Religious schools were on average better equipped for this competition, because of their history (during the 19th century, religious schools had to compete for students and won this struggle on the pupil market), because of their private governance and administration (more flexibility compared with public schools under authority of the local government, cf. Hofman, 1993; Hofman et al. 1996), and because of their reputation for educational quality (Dijkstra, Dronkers, & Hofman, 1997). Perhaps public schools also lost this battle because their leading advocates expected the religious-school sector to break down automatically, as a consequence of the growing secularization and irreligiousness of Dutch society.

Recent Developments

As already indicated, the equal funding of private and public schools has promoted the diminution of prestigious elite schools outside the state-subsidized sector. The equality of financial resources between religious and public schools has prevented a creaming-off of the most able students by either the public or the religious schools. Before the 1970s, the choice of a religious or public school was made not on educational but on religious grounds. As a consequence, the long existence of parental choice did not increase educational inequality in Dutch society.

The educational differences between religious and public schools are recent and could be the beginning of a new form of inequality, despite efforts of the Dutch administration to diminish unequal educational opportunities. Differences between parents in their knowledge of school effectiveness, which correlates with their own educational level, can perhaps be seen as the basis of this new form of inequality (Dijkstra & Jungbluth, 1997). In the Netherlands, as well in other European societies, the importance of deliberate choice of parents to promote the educational opportunities of their children seems to be an important element in understanding the persistence of educational systems with religious school sectors as substantial components, despite secularization. But also, in a school system without private religious sectors of some size, varying degrees of knowledge of school effectiveness by parents can result in educational inequality between schools.

The system of equal funding has led to a high degree of central regulation, and a relatively uniform curriculum and structure. Whereas the private sector is considered responsible for determining the philosophical or religious direction of education, the government is given responsibility of overseeing and guaranteeing the general quality of schooling. Although the central government is not allowed to determine the exact content of the curriculum, nor the specific texts and pedagogy, the government does have significant control regarding standards of quality, such as teacher qualifications, working conditions and salaries, curriculum subjects and the time allotted for each, the use of finances, and the examinations given to all students at key transition points (cf. OECD, 1991, p. 16). Because of these centralized standards and the equalization of resources available to both private-and public-schools, there is a relatively high degree of uniformity as well as equality between private and public school sectors. The standardized exams given at key transition points and the diplomas granted by schools (which indicate a similar level of achievement) mean that students are able to move in and out 65 different sectors with relative ease. Thus, although the Dutch system is designed to give parents significant choice regarding the philosophical or religious orientation of schools, there is considerably less choice as to the level of resources a school has and the academic quality that is often associated with such funding (cf. Naylor & Dijkstra, 1997).

A dual educational system is not less expensive. Koelman (1987) estimated the extra costs of the Dutch system of both public and religious schools at about 631 million guilder per year for primary education only. The extra costs come from the many small schools of different sectors existing in one community, given the small minimum number of pupils necessary to maintain a school. Efforts by the government to reduce these costs are promoting larger schools by increasing the minimum number of pupils in a school. In secondary education this has led to a fusion of schools into larger units, but the mergers have been mostly within the given boundaries of the public and religious sectors (with some tendencies to merge Protestant and Catholic schools into a united Christian school). However, in primary education this fusion movement partly collapsed because the government could not raise the minimum number of pupils to a sufficient level. The main cause of the failure has been pressure from smaller communities, which have feared losing their only school. Although maintaining small schools (public or religious) is more expensive, most religious schools have lower overhead costs because they are not obliged to use the more expensive services of their municipalities but can shop around to obtain the cheapest and most effective assistance for administration, repairs, building, cleaning, and the like. Religious schools also use more voluntary help (owing to their more direct link with parents), which also lowers overhead costs. A total balance sheet of the lower overheads costs of religious schools and the higher costs of maintaining a multisector school system has never been agreed upon; the figures are disputed by all sides.

A new form of religious schooling was introduced to the Netherlands with the establishment of Islamic schools, although their number is not yet very large. The motives for establishing Islamic schools are comparable to those given by Protestant and Catholic parents during the School Conflict in the 19th century. Because the constitution and educational laws were developed to accommodate these religious-based educational preferences, the Dutch system essentially allows for the establishment of schools organized around new denominations, despite objections raised in the current political debate. Besides problems regarding the actual establishment of Islamic schools (the mobilization of parents, religious and cultural differences among the Islamic communities the schools want to serve, and the lack of qualified Islamic teachers), there are concerns that segregation will hamper the integration of Islamic children into Dutch society. The strongest opposition comes from advocates of public rather than Catholic and Protestant schools, because the integration of all religious groups into one school has always been the ideal of public schools. However, so far there is no indication that pupils in Islamic schools achieve less, nor that they achieve more compared to pupils in other schools (Driessen, 1996).

On the whole, the Dutch case does not indicate that private religious schools result in more educational inequality then comparable public schools, as long as these religious schools are treated in the same way by the state as the public schools, and as long as the religious schools are not allowed to collect extra resources for their schools.

The Pacification of 1917 assumed that only a few different religious groups in Dutch society would use the opportunity to establish state-subsidized religious schools (basically Catholic and Protestant) and thus formulated rules for how to require a state-recognized religious school charter. However, since 1917 the religious and philosophical diversity of society and thus of schools has increased greatly, forcing the Dutch government more and more into the unattractive position of having to decide whether the charter of a new school reflects legitimate religious or philosophical diversity. This development suggests that the disparity between the supply of schooling (organized around religious diversity) and demand of schooling in a predominantly secular society might need some adjustments in the regulations regarding the establishment of private religious schools in the near future. Especially noteworthy was a report published by the Dutch Educational Council (the so-called *Onder-wijsraad*, an influential advisory council to the national government) which might become the marker of an important change in the current system of choice. The Educational Council, commonly seen as powerful watchdog regarding the arrangement of freedom of education, is propos-ing to adjust the educational system to the new social realities of Dutch society. In effect, the report radically reinterprets the design of the sys-tem of choice in education (Leune, 1996; Onderwijsraad, 1996). The Council suggests no longer taking into account the religious charter of the school in the granting of subsidies, but basing this solely on a nu-merical criterion (i.e., the number of students), thus removing from legis-lation all criteria regarding the need for a religious or philosophical foundation for schools. Although the Educational Council (Onder-wijsraad, 1996, p. 95) puts the existence of discrepancies between the supply of schools and educational preferences of parents into perspective and is of the opinion that the current situation offers a sufficient balance between supply and actual demand, the Council recognizes the need for drastic adaptation of school planning, and suggests founding and main-taining schools only on the basis of number of pupils. The main reason for the proposed adaptation is to attune the teaching activities more to parental wishes, although arguments in the field of retrenchment should not be left out, even though they are seldomly mentioned. However, these not-yet-implemented recommendations do not affect in any way the existing combination of nongovernmental control of private schools and government funding. In practice, this will make it easier for existing schools to change or adapt their religious charter to better reflect parental preferences, if parents really want to change that charter. In the current system, the denomination of the school as an important factor in the regulation regarding funding is a hindrance for schools who wish to change (or merge) their religious charter, when, for example, the student population has changed its identity. In a system in which a religious or philosophical charter is no longer a criterion for state funding, it might become easier to realize parental preferences through adaptation of the school's religious charter (Netelenbos, 1997, pp. 11–14). So, by providing for diversity along lines other than religious or philosophical, the government hopes that the system would allow for more of a linkage between changing parental preferences and the teaching activities. Furthermore, the system would be more consistent, no longer having as its rationale the religious diversity that Dutch society no longer exhibits. However, given the earlier discussed stability of the Dutch system, it is questionable whether a majority of the parents really want to change the religious charters of their schools, despite the clear discrepancy with their own religious beliefs. And even if these parents do not change these charters, the larger formal adaptivity legitimizes the disparity between the supply and demand of religious schools in a secular society.

Conclusion

The Dutch case shows that promoting more parental choice in education and more competition between schools can be a good way to improve the quality of schooling, and to reduce the costs within schools. The Dutch case also shows that it is possible to strike a fair balance between the parental freedom of school choice and the aims of a national educational policy. It assumes, however, the equal funding and treatment of public and private religious schools by the state. Advocates of a strong market orientation and the absence of the state in education tend to forget these important conditions of equal treatment and subsidizing. Without these conditions, the introduction of religious schools might produce a lower quality of teaching for the average student, more educational inequality, and a less-balanced provision of education relevant to the needs of society. A balanced combination of the forces of the market and the state produces a better education for the larger part of the population than a reliance on either the state or the market. The missing counterbalances against the inevitable negative aspects of either a powerful state or an almighty market will produce a suboptimal result.

Acknowledgments

An earlier version of this chapter was presented at the 18th Conference of the Comparative Education Society in Europe/CESE: *State-Market-Civil Society. Models of Social Order and the Future of European Education*, July 1998, Groningen, The Netherlands. We wish to thank Wendy Naylor for her helpful comments on an earlier draft.

References

Archer, M. S. (1984). *Social origins of educational systems*. London/Beverly Hills: Sage.

Box, L., Dronkers, J., Molenaar, M., & Mulder, J. de. (1977). *Vrijheid van onderwijs* [Freedom of education]. Nijmegen: Link.

Brown, F. (1992). The Dutch experience with school choice: Implications for American education. In P. W. Cookson, Jr. (Ed.), *The choice controversy* (pp.171–189). Newbury Park, CA: Corwin Press.

Coleman, J. S., & Hoffer, T. (1987). *Public and religious high schools. The impact of communities*. New York: Basic Books.

Dennison, S. R. (1984). *Choice in education*. London: Institute of Economic Affairs.

Dijkstra, A. B. (1992). *De religieuze factor. Onderwijskansen en godsdienst* [The religious factor. Educational opportunities and religion]. Nijmegen: ITS.

Dijkstra, A. B., Dronkers, J., & Hofman, R. H. (Eds.). (1997). *Verzuiling in het onderwijs. Actuele verklaringen en analyse* [Pillarization in education. Current explanations and analysis]. Groningen: Wolters-Noordhoff.

Dijkstra, A. B., & Jungbluth, P. (1997, July). *The institutionalization of social segmentation? Segregation of schooling in the Netherlands*. Paper presented at the 33th World Congress of the International Institute of Sociology, Cologne.

Driessen, G. (1996). Prestaties, gedrag en houdingen van leerlingen op islamitische basisscholen [Achievement, behavior and attitude of pupils at Islamic elementary schools]. *Migrantenstudies, 12*, 136–151.

Dronkers, J. (1992). Blijvende organisatorische onderwijsverzuiling ondanks secularisering [Persistent organizational pillarisation in education]. *Beleid en Maatschappij, 19*, 227–237.

Dronkers, J. (1995). The Existence of Parental Choice in the Netherlands. *Educational Policy, 9*, 227–243.

Glenn, C. L. (1989). *Choice of schools in six nations*.Washington, DC: U.S. Government Printing Office.

Greeley, A. M. (1993). Religion around the world is not dying out. *Origins, 23*, 49–58.

Hermans, C. (1993). *Vorming in perspectief. Grondslagenstudie over identiteit van katholiek onderwijs* [Education in perspective. Study of the foundation of the identity of Catholic schooling]. Den Haag: ABKO.

Hofman, R. H. (1993). *Effectief schoolbestuur. Een studie naar de bijdrage van school-besturen aan de effectiviteit van basisscholen* [Effective school administration. A study on the impact of school boards on the effectiveness of primary schools]. Groningen: RION.

Hofman, R. H., Hofman, W. H. A., Guldemond, H., & Dijkstra, A. B. (1996). Variation in effectiveness between private and public schools. The impact of school and family networks. *Educational Research and Evaluation, 2,* 366–394.

James, E. (1989). The Netherlands: Benefits and costs of privatized public services. In G. Walford (Ed.), *Private schools in ten countries: Policy and practice* (pp. 179–199). London: Routledge.

Karsten, S. (1994). Policy on ethnic segregation in a system of choice: The case of the Netherlands. *Educational Policy, 9,* 211–225.

Kemenade, J. A. van, Jungbluth, P. L. M., & Ritzen, J. M. M. (1981). Onderwijs en samenleving [Education and society]. In J. A. van Kemenade (Ed.), *Onderwijs: bestel en beleid* [Education: System and policy] (pp. 95–242). Groningen: Wolters-Noordhoff.

Koelman, J. B. J. (1987). *Kosten van verzuiling; een studie over het lager onderwijs* [The costs of pillarisation; A study for primary education]. Den Haag: VUGA.

Leune, J. M. G. (1996, November). *The meaning of government legislation and funding for primary and secondary schools with a religious character in the Netherlands.* Paper presented at a colloquium on "The ambigious embrace of government." Erasmus University, Rotterdam.

Naylor, W., & Dijkstra, A. B. (1997, March). *Private schooling in the Netherlands: The institutionalization of directional diversity.* Paper prepared for the annual meeting of the AERA, Chicago.

Netelenbos, T. (1997). *De identiteit van de school in een pluriforme samenleving* [The identity of the school in a plural society]. Den Haag: OCW.

Onderwijsraad. (1996). *Advies Richtingvrij en richtingbepalend* [Direction-free and de-termination of direction]. Den Haag: Onderwijsraad.

Organisation for Economic Co-Operation and Development. (1991). *Reviews of national policies for education.* Paris: OECD.

Post, H. (1989). *Pillarization: An analysis of Dutch and Belgian society.* Aldershot, UK: Avebury.

Roeleveld, J., & Dronkers, J. (1994). Bijzondere of buitengewone scholen? [Special or typical schools?] *Mens en Maatschappij, 69,* 85–108.

Vreeburg, B. A. N. M. (1993). *Identiteit en het verschil. Levensbeschouwelijke vorming en het Nederlands voortgezet onderwijs* [Identity and the difference. Religious educa-tion in Dutch secondary schools]. Zoetermeer: De Horstink.

Walford, G. (1995). Faith-based grant-maintained schools: Selective international policy
    borrowing from the Netherlands. *Educational Policy, 10,* 245–257
Witte, J. F. (1993). The Milwaukee parental choice program. In E. Rasell & R. Rothstein
    (Eds.), *School choice. Examining the evidence* (pp. 69–109). Washington, DC: Eco-
    nomic Policy Institute.

Chapter Six

The State and Civil Society in Education in England: Past Developments and Current Problems

GEOFFREY WALFORD

The concept of the third sector is relatively new and relies on an implied dichotomy between private and public provision of goods and services. Within education this dichotomy has also been seen as one between market and state control of schools and colleges. But the concept of third sector has grown within a particular sociohistorical and geographical context—largely late 20th-century United States. It is not a concept that has been widely used in English schooling provision. Indeed, to do so directly would make little sense, for the English system (if it can be seen as a system at all) is far more complex than in most other countries and has many more than three sectors. In particular, there has never been a strict private-public distinction that would imply the existence or need for third sector involvement. Further, just as the precise meaning of the private sector varies in different countries and historical periods (Walford, 1989), there is a diversity of somewhat contradictory views about what is meant by the third sector. It would be particularly inappropriate and anachronistic to apply uncritically the concept of the third sector in any discussion of the historical development of the English system.

This does not mean, however, that the concept has no utility in an examination of English schools. Thinking about what might be considered to be the third sector can sensitize critics and advocates to the fact that schools have been, and still are, provided by a diversity of different groups. It can help illuminate this diversity and force a recognition that

"things do not have to be as they are now," both in England and elsewhere.

Pre-Victorian Third Sector Involvement

In England, before the 19th century, the education of children was considered to be the private affair of parents. All schools were private
schools--but, whereas most were fee-paying schools, they were not
necessarily run for a profit. It is not only instructive to examine some of
this early provision but essential to a full understanding of modern
provision, for the current diversity of schools in England can be traced
back several hundred years. Indeed, there are still many schools that can
trace their own histories back to the 15th and 16th centuries. One central
feature to note is that, as most of these early schools were fee-paying,
the nature of provision varied greatly according to the social class of the
family. The education of children was not only considered to be the
private affair of parents but of the particular social-classed parents of
each specifically gendered child.

It is worth examining the Victorian and pre-Victorian periods in some
detail, for it was during the Victorian era that the framework for the current English schooling system was laid down. It was also a period when
many new schools were established through the work of individuals or
groups. In pre-Victorian England, the majority of children from what
was to become the workingclass received little or no formal schooling,
as most parents could ill afford to pay school fees or to refuse the additional income that a child at work would bring to the family. If they had
any schooling at all, it was in dame schools or charity schools. Over the
centuries, and even at one particular time, the quality of the schooling
given in dame schools varied considerably but, at their best, children
would be taught the rudiments of reading and writing. A few of these
dame schools developed into present-day preparatory schools for the
major private schools (Leinster-Mackay, 1984). These schools are reasonably thought of as private, market-led, provision for the poor but, in
contrast, charity schools for the poor might be seen as the start of third
sector involvement. The event usually used to date the start of the char-

ity schools movement is the founding of the Society for Promotion of Christian Knowledge (SPCK) in 1698, whose schools were intended to restore morals and religious belief to the poor children of what was then seen as an increasingly degenerate country. The schools were supported by the churches, both through direct charitable donations and through the local clergy often teaching in the schools for no fee. As urbanization and industrialization progressed, the somewhat contradictory drives of philanthropy, religious conviction, and the practical need for a better-educated and disciplined workforce led to the gradual expansion of a network of schools for the poor. By the end of the 18th century, elementary schools, which provided a few years of schooling for children from age 5 upward, were operated by the Church of England, the Roman Catholic Church, various Protestant denominations, and some other charitable foundations. But there was great geographical unevenness. In the newly developing cities, in particular, there were far too few schools for all children.

In broad terms, the government was unwilling to become involved in the provision of schooling, preferring to leave it to the various churches and other third sector organizations if at all possible. Intervention during the 19th and early 20th centuries was reluctantly made, and done so because it was evident that children in some poor families were not being schooled in the way that the state required. Intervention was as much for the good of the state as for the good of the children themselves. Thus, it is indicative that the first formal involvement of the state in education was the Health and Morals of Apprentices Act of 1802, which forced employers to provide for the teaching of apprentices during the working day and for at least an hour on Sundays. Such teaching was supposed to counteract the "moral degeneracy" of such apprentices (Walford, 1990).

In 1833, the first grant of £20,000 was made by government to aid "private subscription for the erection of school houses." This grant was given to the two main religious providers of schooling at the time—the National Society for Promoting the Education of the Poor and the British and Foreign School Society. Grants to build schools gradually increased over the century and an Education Department was established in 1856 to control this funding. The government of the day recognized the need to ensure that education was provided, but was still happy to leave this to the charitable and religious organizations wherever possible, and would only help financially where other sources were insufficient.

It was only following the 1870 Education Act that the state became involved in the provision, maintenance, and organization of its own elementary schools. Again, the state's involvement was restricted to areas where other providers were unable or unprepared to meet the perceived needs of all children. A national system was established, but it was one where responsibility for provision was still shared by a multitude of providers.

Strangely enough, the pre-Victorian and Victorian schooling for children from the middle and upper classes was also provided by a mixture of fee-paying for-profit and charitable organizations. In contrast to working-class boys and girls who received a fairly similar basic schooling, girls from the upper class and from the expanding middle class of the 19th century usually received a very different form of schooling from their brothers. Schools for these social classes were single sex and provided very different learning environments for boys and girls. At the center of discussion of the schools for upper-class boys was a small group of so-called Great Schools, which were investigated by the Clarendon Commission in 1864. The seven boarding schools of Eton, Winchester, Westminster, Charterhouse, Harrow, Rugby, and Shrewsbury were often linked together as a loose group, and were investigated by the Clarendon Commission alongside the two ancient day schools of St Paul's and Merchant Taylors, with Marlborough, Cheltenham and Wellington as examples of recently founded schools. All nine Great Schools were nonprofit, charitable foundations. Thus, King Henry VI founded the College of Our Lady of Eton by Windsor in 1440, not only to provide free education for 70 boys but also as a college of priests, an almshouse, and a pilgrimage church. Although, in this case, the endowment was sufficient for the 70 scholars to remain to this day, several hundred fee-paying students were also being educated by the time of the Clarendon Commission. In a similar way, Bishop William of Wykeham had started his school for poor scholars to the number of sixty and ten, studying in grammar in 1394. Westminster was founded in 1560 by Queen

Elizabeth I; Charterhouse in 1611 by the will of Thomas Sutton; Harrow in 1571 by John Lyon; Rugby in 1567 by Lawrence Sheriff; Shrewsbury in 1552 by King Edward VI; St Paul's by Dean John Colet in 1509; and Merchant Taylors in 1561 by the Master, Wardens, and Court of Assistants of the Worshipful Company of Merchant Taylors (McConnell, 1985). All of these foundations were charitable, and might be considered to be prime candidates for third sector status if they were modern foundations. There is some considerable debate about exactly how poor the poor scholars were originally intended to be, but by the 19th century these schools were patronized almost exclusively by the aristocracy and landed gentry (Bamford, 1967). There was considerable variation among these schools but, by the time of the Clarendon Commission, all seven of the boarding schools drew their pupils from all over Britain. However, although they were Great Schools, few would have designated them good schools. In the first 50 years of the 19th century they led a precarious existence. The number of pupils in the schools fluctuated dramatically from year to year, and the schools made little attempt to provide a relevant or up-to-date education. The content of the curriculum had become of no practical importance, and focused on Latin and the classics, maintained through tradition and unchanged statutes. By and large, the schools preferred to retain their elite clientele rather than modernize and draw from a wider social mix. Further, by the early Victorian era, the Warden and Fellows of Winchester and Eton Colleges, for example, had exploited the endowments for their own use, leaving the boys badly taught, poorly fed, and meanly accommodated. The special position of Eton as the training ground for statesmen outweighed these inconveniences, and in 1868, it still had 850 pupils, but the number of boys at Winchester had slumped. Westminster, Charterhouse, and Harrow were also doing badly, in contrast to the reinvigorated Rugby and Shrewsbury. In any discussion of the third sector it is worth remembering that one of the main purposes of the Clarendon Commission was to pave the way for legislation that would remove the corruption, inefficiency, and ineffectiveness that the Great Schools had fallen into by the mid-19th century.

During the Victorian period there were several different ways in which new schools were developed for the sons of the growing middle-class. First, in some of the major cities, groups of citizens came together to form joint-stock companies to start new proprietary day schools. The Liverpool Institute was one of the first of these in 1825, and between 1830 and 1840 these proprietary day schools met the needs of most of the middle class. However, with the coming of the railways, the expansion of the middle class, and the social changes of the mid-19th century, boarding schools came to be seen as appropriate. There were many new foundations, based on the joint-stock company route, such as Cheltenham College, as well as others that resulted from religious zeal. For example, the Reverend William Sewell, Professor of Moral Philosophy at Oxford and a moderate follower of the Oxford Movement, founded Radley College in 1847. His belief was that there was a need for schools that would teach "Christian gentlemen and Christian scholars" (Boyd, 1948). Although Radley was designed for the middle class, Sewell's original plan was that the profits from the schools for the rich should finance schools for the poor—a plan that did not come to fruition as Radley had continual financial problems for much of its early history. Nathaniel Woodard had more success with his overall plan of a system of three grades of school to suit the three social classes, although his schools were also in perpetual financial crisis. Woodard's passion was to spread High Anglicanism, and Hurstpierpoint was founded in 1853, followed by Lancing in 1857 and Ardingly in 1870 (Kirk, 1937). The group eventually grew to 19 schools.

A further way of developing schools for the middle class was to build on existing grammar schools. Throughout the 16th and 17th centuries, the establishment of free grammar schools for local children was seen as a particularly appropriate way for wealthy merchants or nobility to be remembered. The usual pattern was for the foundation to provide a fixed sum for a schoolmaster from property rents, and for the schoolmaster to be required to provide free teaching in Latin and Greek in return. Although this arrangement had originally worked reasonably well, as the importance of the classics declined, the growing, vocal middleclass of the late 18th and 19th centuries began to try to divert the endowed schools from their original purpose to provide schools for their own children—predominantly their sons. In many cases, foundation income that was originally intended for poor children was used for middle-class boys instead. In a few cases, an Act of Parliament was passed to change the statutes of the particular grammar school, and in other cases they were simply ignored. Further wholesale changes occurred as a result of the Taunton Commission of 1864 and the resulting Endowed Schools Act of 1868.

The Taunton Commission is an interesting case of government re-structuring of third sector schooling provision. The Commission reported on over 800 endowed grammar schools, and roundly condemned practically all of them. Officially most of them were still tied to ancient ideas of an appropriate curriculum, but many had also fallen into decline. The office of Schoolmaster was either a sinecure or one not taken very seriously. The Taunton Commission proposed that the schools and their endowments should be restructured such that three separate sections of the middle class should have appropriate schools for their children. These were to be fee-paying schools, but reduced by virtue of any endowment income. The Commission was clear that "indiscriminate gratuitous instruction" was a waste of endowments, which meant that the working-class children for whom many of the endowments had been intended were to be removed from their free schools. A limited number of competitive scholarships were established instead.

Up to this time, there had been little consideration given to the schooling of upper-and middle-class girls. This is mainly a reflection of pre-Victorian and early Victorian society. It is true that there were some fee-paying boarding schools for girls as early as the 17th century, and many girls were taught by governesses, or through attendance at fee-paying day schools. But by the first half of the 19th century, women from the upper and middle classes were expected not to work. Girls were thus required to learn what was thought necessary to be ladies of leisure--the accomplishments of reading, writing and religion, but also a great deal of needlework, dancing, music, household management, and French. Academic schooling for girls began to flourish only at the middle of the century. The schools that will forever be identified with the names of Miss Beale and Miss Buss, Cheltenham Ladies College and

North London Collegiate, opened in 1854 and 1850, respectively (Walford, 1993).

The establishment of the Taunton Commission in 1864 acted as an important spur to girls' education for the middle classes. It was originally intended that the Commission would only examine the private and endowed grammar schools for boys, but, as the girls' schools were not explicitly excluded, pressure from such activists as Frances Buss and Emily Davies led the commissioners to include them. The final report officially recognized the general deficiency in girls' education and pointed to the problem of misuse of school endowments. It would have been difficult to do otherwise, for they found 820 endowed schools for boys and only about 20 comparable schools for girls (Avery, 1991). In some cases, the original benefactions had been specifically for boys, but in many the sex of the children who were to benefit was left unstated in the original will or statutes. Where the governors had interpreted this as being for boys only, the commissioners made it clear that this was inappropriate, and ordered the governors to redirect some of the income toward girls. In some case, even where the original endowment was specifically for boys only, the Taunton Commission directed that it should be extended to support girls as well. The governors did not always welcome this change, and many took several years to begin to comply, but middle-class girls were certainly the beneficiaries of the Commission, at the expense of both working class girls and boys.

The Period after 1944

It is not possible to follow all the twists and turns of policy since the 1870 Education Act. That Act divided the country into school districts and made provision for school boards to fill the gaps in existing provision established by the churches, private benefactors, and guilds. In brief, third sector provision was insufficient, and public elementary schools were to be provided through money raised by local rates. The 1902 Education Act established a system of secondary schools in the same way as the 1870 Act had for elementary schools. Again, the state was only concerned with establishing its own secondary schools where there were insufficient places provided by the churches and other charitable bodies. However, fees were payable at these state secondary schools until after 1944.

Prior to 1944, all children not in private schools attended elementary schools from 5 until 14, or until they were selected out from the elementary schools at 11 or later to enter grammar or other secondary schools. The 1944 Education Act dramatically changed this. Coming into law while the war was still in progress, it promised a brighter and fairer future to all children irrespective of social class. The slogan secondary education for all meant that all children would leave their elementary or primary schools at age 11 and move on to secondary schools that were supposedly appropriate for their differing abilities and aptitudes. In most places, the Local Education Authorities (LEAs), which were given responsibility for implementing the new system, developed two or three different types of school to which children were directed according to the results of an 11-plus selection examination. But another cross-cutting factor was the religious orientation of the students and the schools. Many of the pre-existing secondary schools were run by the Church of England or the Roman Catholic Church. To make it possible to provide free secondary schooling for all children it was seen as necessary to include as many of these schools as possible into the system. Although some religious schools remained as fee-paying private schools, the majority entered into funding agreements with the state in one of three categories—voluntary controlled, voluntary aided, or special agreement. The main distinction between the three was the degree of control that the governors maintained over the school and the size of the financial contribution expected from the churches in return for this remaining power. Although these schools retained their religious denominational character and the churches had a degree of control over teacher appointments and the curriculum, they became an integral part of the state-maintained local authority system and charged no fees. There also remained a group of mainly religious-based direct-grant grammar schools that received a grant from central government in exchange for offering a set proportion of places to children who passed the 11-plus. These grammar schools were positioned between the full fee-paying private schools and the fully state-maintained schools, as they were officially private schools that accepted fee-payers yet also gave free places to academically able children (Walford, 1990).

During the 1960s and 1970s, the selective system of secondary schooling was gradually replaced by comprehensive schools, still provided by the churches together with the LEAs. By 1979, about 90% of secondary-age children in the state-maintained sector were in comprehensive schools. There were about 28% of primary-aged pupils in voluntary schools and 17% of secondary pupils. Over all ages, 22% of pupils were in voluntary schools, which were made up of 11% Church of England, 9% Roman Catholic, and less than 1% each of Jewish and Methodist (O'Keeffe, 1986). Additionally, nearly 2% of pupils were in nonreligious voluntary schools, which had been originally established by the type of guilds and charities discussed earlier. A further 8% of school-age children were in fee-paying private schools, most of which were originally established by church-related groups or individuals.

Since 1944, two interlinked trends have affected the voluntary schools, both directly related to the declining importance of organized religion in English life. First, the proportion of funding that the government requires the schools to contribute to the capital and maintenance costs of the school buildings has gradually decreased. The churches have simply been unable or unwilling to devote the substantial funding to schooling that they once did. The proportion of funding required by government has shrunk such that it now stands at 15% for voluntary-aided schools. In addition, all recurrent expenditure for these schools is paid by the state through the LEAs. Second, the schools have become increasingly secularized. Whilst being more true of the Church of England schools, which are often hardly distinguishable from LEA schools, it is also true for Catholic schools (Arthur, 1995; McLaughlin, O'Keefe, & O'Keeffe, 1996). Many of the teachers in these religious schools no longer adhere to the beliefs of the founding church, and religious practice within the schools is often restricted to a brief assembly and the compulsory study of religious education by the students. Indeed, the degree of secularization of the existing religious voluntary schools was one of the main reasons for some evangelical Christian groups wishing to establish their own private schools and, subsequently, campaigning for state support for these schools.

Quasi-Markets and the Third Sector

Within England, the 1988 Education Reform Act has come to be seen as the crucial legislation that introduced market mechanisms into state-maintained schooling. The quasi-market that resulted from that Act gave families the right to express a preference for any state-maintained school they wish to use, and gave funding to schools largely according to student numbers.

Such developments have been common within the educational systems of industrialised countries around the world (Walford, 1996). During the 1980s and 1990s, many countries introduced schemes that are supposedly designed to increase choice of school and to enhance the efficiency and effectiveness of state-maintained schooling. However, again in common with most of these schemes, Although the 1988 Education Reform Act was central to establishing a quasi-market, it did little to encourage the supplyside of that market. It provided no new ways by which interested charitable or religious bodies could establish new state-maintained schools. That this is true is not immediately obvious, for the Act included legislation on grant-maintained schools and City Technology Colleges. Both of these would appear to be supply-side developments, but the reality is different. Although the concept of grant-maintained schools was certainly new, the reality was that existing LEA schools were simply removed from LEA control and became self-managing schools under the overall direction of central government through the Funding Agency for Schools. Early research has shown that grant-maintained schools generally offer little that is distinctive beyond cosmetic changes such as smarter uniforms for students (Halpin, Power, & Fitz, 1997; Power, Halpin, & Fitz, 1994). Local management of schools (LMS) within the LEA sector has meant that the grant-maintained schools differ only slightly from the LEA schools in their degree of autonomy and hardly at all in the day-to-day experiences of staff or students.

In a similar way, the 1988 Act's legislation on City Technology Colleges was not introducing new routes to establishing schools. In this case, the Act was merely making minor adjustments to a program that was already under way—and which was already under pressure and liable to fail. The City Technology College program had been launched in 1986 and the first CTC was announced in February 1987. The intention was that industry and commerce would provide the major capital funding for their own technological schools. In essence, the government was attempting to stimulate new third sector involvement. The resulting schools would be officially private schools but would charge no fees to students, as the bulk of the recurrent costs were to be met by central government. Even after the 1987 reelection of a Conservative government, fears that a future Labour government might withdraw funding led to clauses in the 1988 Act that began to protect the investment of sponsors. In practice, even with this safeguard, sponsors were highly reluctant to provide substantial funding to build new schools. The conditions that had to be met were gradually adjusted such that sponsors had to find only 20% of the capital costs, and the government paid the rest. However, the scheme stalled with a total of just 15 CTCs and, as with grant-maintained schools, the evidence suggests that CTCs offer little that is radically different from other schools (even in technology) and have yet to move away from traditional modes of teaching and learning (Walford & Miller, 1991; Whitty, Edwards, & Gewirtz, 1993).

It was not until the 1993 Education Act that significant changes were made to encourage new third sector sponsors to increase the supplyside of the quasi-market. As a result of that Act, since April 1994 it has been possible for groups of parents, and charitable, religious, or independent sponsors to apply to the Secretary of State for Education and Employment to establish their own grant-maintained schools. According to the Government White Paper that preceded the Act, the explicit intentions behind such developments were to widen choice and diversity of schools and to allow new grant-maintained schools to be created "in response to parental demand and on the basis of local proposals" (Department for Education, 1992, p. 26). If the Secretary of State approves individual proposals, it is possible for England and Wales to have state-funded schools that have the aim of fostering, for example, Muslim, Buddhist, or Evangelical Christian beliefs, or that wish to promote particular educational philosophies. Groups of sponsors can propose either an entirely new school or that an existing faith-based or other private school for which they are responsible should be reestablished as a grant-maintained school.

These new sponsored grant-maintained schools differ from existing grant-maintained schools in that sponsors have to pay for at least 15% of costs relating to the provision of school buildings and some other capital expenditure. Their financial position is thus very similar to voluntary-aided schools run by the churches—except that the voluntary-aided schools are to receive their recurrent expenditure funding through their LEAs whereas these new grant-maintained schools are funded by central government through the Funding Agency for Schools (FAS). In return for this financial contribution, through the school's Trust Deed and Instrument of Governance, the sponsors obtain some guarantees that the school retains the purpose for which it was established. The composition of the governing body allows the sponsors to ensure that the religious objectives of the school are maintained. Although the schools do have to teach the national curriculum, special arrangements for the teaching of religious education can be detailed in the trust deed, and arrangements can be made with regard to the character of collective religious worship that differ from those demanded in most state-maintained schools. The admissions process can give preference to children from families with particular beliefs in the same way as existing Roman Catholic or Church of England voluntary schools.

Sponsored Grant-Maintained Schools

The details of the process that sponsors have to follow was gradually developed over a period of several years by the FAS and the Department for Education (DFE). The FAS was established through the same 1993 Education Act and came into existence in April 1994. Its main functions are to provide capital and recurrent and special grants to grant-maintained schools. In respect of new sponsored schools, the FAS provides advice and must be officially consulted by the sponsors. The FAS is one of several bodies (in fact, the most important body) that gives its opinion about the proposal to the DFE before the Secretary of State makes a decision.

Various schools or sponsor groups have made some initial contact with the FAS since April 1994. By the time of the General Election in May 1997, only 20 full proposals had been published. Only eight of these proposals had been successful—all but one were from existing private Roman Catholic secondary schools, the exception being an existing private Jewish primary school. Four of the successful secondary schools were part of a group formerly owned and run by the Order of Christian Brothers.

At the time of the election, only two applications had been rejected by the Secretary of State for Education, but one had been withdrawn and there were still nine applications outstanding. Some of these had been with the Secretary of State for more than a year. At the same time, a further 15 or so promoters were in serious discussion with the FAS.

Since the General Election the Labour government has produced its own White Paper, *Excellence in Schools* (DFE, 1997), and has proposed a new organizational structure for schools. Grant-maintained schools are to be brought back into a revised local education authority system, and the FAS is to be abolished. However, somewhat incongruously, the new Labour Secretary of State for Education and Employment has made decisions on several proposals that had been with the past Secretary of State for many months. Six schools have been allowed to proceed, including two Jewish primary schools (one entirely new), and a rather exceptional small school for disaffected students. Crucially, two existing private Muslim primary schools and one existing secondary Seventh Day Adventist school have also been accepted as grant-maintained schools. Of the remaining three schools, one withdrew its application and two have been rejected (one Jewish primary school and one Transcendental Meditation primary school).

The result is that the overall policy has thus not been as successful as the original supporters of the 1993 legislation had hoped. Very few schools or sponsors have managed to meet the demands made on them during the application process. Many have fallen by the wayside before their applications were passed to the Secretary of State for consideration, and only 14 schools have successfully become grant-maintained under these new regulations. All but one of the sponsored grant-maintained schools so far have involved the transfer of an existing private school into the state-maintained sector. The one entirely new school is scheduled to open in September 1999, after grant-maintained status is due to have been abolished.

What happened since 1994 was that procedures and criteria were developed that became an impediment to new proposals. In essence, any potential sponsors of a new school had to document in advance a vast range of information about the demand for the school, the appropriateness of the site and buildings, the way in which the school would be managed and the curriculum delivered, and the long-term financial viability of the proposed school (DFE, 1994). To establish demand for the school they had to show not only that there would be sufficient pupils for the foreseeable future but also what the effect of this would be on existing schools. It became clear that no new schools would be established if there were sufficient places in existing schools unless the sponsors could claim that their proposed school would add to choice and diversity within the local system. Sponsors of religious schools also needed to prove denominational need which means that they had to show there would be sufficient students with their given religious background to fill the school, and that similar provision was not easily available elsewhere. Sponsors then needed to show that an appropriate site and building was available and that they had (or could obtain) the necessary funding for at least 15% of the capital costs of this building and any necessary modifications. Most significantly, since 1995 the FAS has emphasized the need for "value for money" and stated that where sponsors "are able to contribute a higher proportion of the capital costs of a project . . . we will therefore be better placed to give overall support for the proposal" (FAS, 1995, p. 15). In short, potential sponsors of new schools faced substantial difficulties in proving demands for the school, finding a site and buildings, and in ensuring sufficient capital funding was available.

As a result of these difficulties, in 1995 a new organization was formed taking the title of the "Third Sector Alliance" (Hodgetts, 1996). This has the aims of pressuring government to broaden the range of schools that can obtain funding from the state and of easing the application procedures for schools wishing to apply for sponsored grant-maintained status. It has had little impact so far.

Conclusion and Speculation

The historical section of this chapter has shown that the state in England has always acted in cooperation with other providers to ensure that sufficient school places are available. The Church of England, the Roman Catholic Church, and the Jewish communities have long had a significant role in schooling with a more minor role being played by the Methodist Church and various charitable foundations. But as England has become more secularized and schooling more expensive, the amount of funding that churches have been able or prepared to give to schools has greatly decreased. Correspondingly, the degree of control that they retain over their schools has reduced. All state-maintained schools now follow a full National Curriculum and have to abide by a series of regulations concerning funding, admissions, governorships, and management. Many Church of England schools, in particular, now have a majority of teachers who are not believers, and it is difficult to discern any particular religious emphasis. Although this is less evident in Roman Catholic schools, and not evident in most Jewish schools, this slide towards secularisation is of considerable concern to the religious authorities.

Civic society, or the third sector, was of great importance in the Victorian era in the establishment of new schools for the middleclasses, and in the continuance of support of charitable schools for the poor. There were two main driving forces behind such activity—self-interest and religious zeal. The joint-stock company schools, such as Cheltenham or Clifton, were formed by groups of individuals from the growing middle class because the local grammar schools did not meet their requirements. Shareholders' self-interests were served as they received the right to nominate pupils for the school. In contrast, schools such as Radley or the Woodard schools developed through the religious conviction (or even fanaticism) of individuals or small groups who wished to spread their own particular religious beliefs. Both such forces are also likely to be central to any present-day support of new schools.

It is also worth noting that the Victorian middleclass was not beyond diverting funds from previous charitable donations towards their own priorities. As has been shown, sometimes this was done simply by ignoring statutes, but the Taunton Commission's restructuring can be seen as a legal way of diverting foundation income toward particular social-class self-interests. It might serve as a warning for any present-day donors who believe that legal documentation will ensure that their interests and intentions are preserved in perpetuity.

Within the last two decades there have been two attempts to encourage greater involvement in the provision of schools by a wider variety of organizations. The City Technology College initiative of 1986 was based on the idea that industry and commerce would wish to run and partly fund their own schools for technology. This belief was rapidly proved incorrect. Many major British companies stated clearly that they did not wish to support individual schools (Walford & Miller, 1991). If they wished to be involved in schooling, their aim was to influence as many different schools as possible. But, even where companies were supporting schools in this way, they were not prepared to fund the building of new schools on the scale envisaged by the Conservative government. The amount of funding required of sponsors was rapidly scaled down, and various companies that supported the Conservative cause were persuaded to provide funding (Whitty et al., 1993). Even here, there was little interest in actually running the CTCs. Further, even to reach the limited final total of 15 CTCs, the scheme had to be extended to include the revamping of some existing schools. There has been more success in the later revised developments of Colleges for the Arts, Sport,

Modern Languages, and Technology—but, here, the total contribution required from what can be a multitude of sponsors is just £100,000.

The 1993 Education Act appeared to offer a real chance for groups and individuals to establish their own third sector schools. In particular, it seemed to offer a chance for minority religious groups to obtain statesupport for their own schools on a par with Church of England and Roman Catholic believers. The reality has been that a very few existing private schools have been able to obtain state support and, so far, only one entirely new school is to be established. In this case, the procedures that were developed to deal with the new legislation came into being during a period of great change. At the time of the 1993 Education Act, John Patten was Secretary of State for Education and was strongly enthusiastic about increasing diversity. But in July 1994 he was replaced by Gillian Shephard who was perhaps more able to see potential problems. In particular, the extra costs of increasing diversity at a time when education budgets were being cut made the idea of value for money a prominent concern. The FAS and DFE became more interested in saving money by encouraging capital expenditure to be contributed by sponsors than in offering diversity as such (Walford, 1997).

The entry of the two Muslim schools and one Seventh Day Adventist school into the state-funded sector is of considerable interest. They have had to meet stringent criteria to ensure equal opportunities and adherence to the national curriculum. It will be several years before it is possible to assess the extent to which these schools divert from their original purpose and become secularized due to their move from the private sector to the third sector.

References

Arthur, J. (1995). *The ebbing tide. Policy and principles of Catholic education.* Leominster: Gracewing.

Avery, G. (1991). *The best type of girl. A history of girls' independent schools.* London: André Deutsch.

Bamford, T. W. (1967). *The rise of the public school: A study of boys' public boarding schools in England and Wales from 1837 to the present day.* London: Nelson.

Boyd, A. K. (1948). *Radley College 1847–1947.* Oxford: Blackwell.

Department for Education (1992). *Choice and diversity.* London: HMSO.

Department for Education (1994). *Guidance to promoters on establishing new grant-maintained schools.* London: DFE.

Department for Education and Employment (1997, July). *Excellence in schools.* London: The Stationary Office.

Funding Agency for Schools (1995). *Guidance for promoters.* York: FAS.

Halpin, D., Power, S., & Fitz, J. (1997). Opting into the past? Grant-maintained schools and the reinvention of tradition. In R. Glatter, P. A. Woods, & C. Bagley (Eds.), *Choice and diversity in schooling.* (pp. 23–52) London and New York: Routledge.

Hodgetts, C. (1996). Third sector alliance: Schools that want to join the state system. In F. Carnie, M. Large, & M. Tasker (Eds.), *Freeing education.* (pp. 57–83). Stroud, Gloucestershire: Hawthorn Press.

Kirk, K. E. (1937). *The story of the Woodard schools.* Abingdon: Abbey Press.

Leinster-Mackay, D. (1984). *The rise of the English prep school.* London: Falmer.

McConnell, J. (1985). *English public schools.* New York and London: W.W. Norton.

McLaughlin, T., O'Keefe, J., & O'Keeffe, B. (Eds.). (1996). *The contemporary Catholic school.* London and Washington DC: Falmer.

O'Keeffe, B. (1986). *Faith, culture and the dual system.* London and Washington DC: Falmer.

Power, S., Halpin, D., & Fitz, J. (1994). Underpinning choice and diversity? The grant-maintained schools policy in context. In S. Tomlinson (Ed.), *Educational reform and its consequences.* (pp. 97–112). London: IPPR/Rivers Oram.

Walford, G. (Ed.). (1989). *Private schools in ten counties: Policy and practice.* London and New York: Routledge.

Walford, G. (1990). *Privatization and privilege in education.* London and New York: Routledge.

Walford, G. (Ed.). (1993). *The private schooling of girls: Past and present.* London: Woburn Press.

Walford, G. (Ed.). (1996). *School choice and the quasi-market.* Wallingford, Oxfordshire: Triangle Books.

Walford, G. (1997). Sponsored grant-maintained schools: Extending the franchise? *Oxford Review of Education, 23*(1), 31–44.

Walford, G., & Miller, H. (1991). *City Technology College.* Buckingham, UK, and Phila-

Philadelphia: Open University Press.

Whitty, G., Edwards, T., & Gewirtz, S. (1993). *Specialisation and choice in urban education. The City Technology College experiment.* London and New York: Routledge.

Chapter Seven

Schools Between State and Civil Society in Germany and the United States: A Historical Perspective

JURGEN HERBST

A t the end of the 20th century, school choice has become a hotly debated subject in both Germany and the United States. The term refers to the efforts of public officials, educators, intellectuals, parents, and other laypersons and laywomen to create for children freely available alternatives to the education provided in public or officially sanctioned private schools. Spurred on by parental dissatisfaction with government- sponsored public schools, the school choice movement today is part of the present rediscovery of civil society as a driving force of public policy. As an educational initiative it is linked to German *Reformpädagogik* and American progressive education of the 1920s. Like them, it is the dialectical counterpart to monopolistic school practices and acts like the yin to the yang of our public common schools. One would not exist without the other.Fearing that the individuality of children was threatened by the impersonality and overpowering force of the public school system and greatly dissatisfied with the results of public schooling, parents, educators, and others created school communities of their own removed from the direct and complete supervision of government. As constituent parts of civil society, many of these communities flourished. Others were and are threatened by politically and ideologically motivated groups and individuals. When a political party writes school choice upon its banner and the term becomes a fashionable cause of rational-choice philosophers or free market economists, school choice proponents find themselves hard pressed to maintain their concern for educational reform. They are caught between the pressures of public school advocates and radical libertarians, between the demands of government on the one hand and the siren song of markets on the other.

A promising educational movement thus becomes endangered by partisan bickering, arcane academic contretemps, and ideological rancor.

The specific reasons that move parents to demand school choice are varied. Some parents are dissatisfied with the academic or instructional standards of the school their child has been assigned to; some object to the skin color, social class, or gender of their child's schoolmates; others disagree with specific subjects taught in school, usually subjects that carry moral overtones; others again object to the absence of religious instruction, or, in reverse, to the specific kind of religious instruction offered; yet others want a different teaching style for their children. Finally, there are those parents who resent the administrative or bureaucratic atmosphere that characterizes the public schools.

Although many current school choice plans are offered as additions to or modifications of public school systems, parents in both Germany and the United States have always included tuition- or fee-charging secular and religious private schools among the available alternatives for schooling. In both countries the existence of such private schools has been legally guaranteed. Any parents who are financially able to send their children to such a school are free to do so. The situation differs between the two countries with respect to the availability of fee- or tuition-free religious instruction. In Germany, denominational religious instruction is a recognized subject in the public schools. Parents exercise their right to school choice when they enroll their children in either a Protestant or Catholic public school. Jewish, Muslim, or agnostic children may be excused from attendance and instead enroll for instruction in ethics. There are no special fees for these classes; they are part of the regular curriculum. In the United States, the separation of state and church forbids the teaching of religion in public schools and public funding of religious schools. Schools in which religion is taught are by definition private schools and ask parents to finance the education of their children through the payment of tuition. Financial considerations thus restrict the parental ability, if not the parental right, to choose a religious school.

Some school choice advocates in the United States today demand that through vouchers students (or their parents) be funded publicly to attend religious schools. Because of objections raised to this proposal, John Chubb and Terry Moe (1990) seek to avoid this dilemma by asking in their *Politics, Markets, and America's Schools* that religious schools participating in their choice plan keep sectarian functions separate from educational ones and be chartered as public schools. They would then receive public funding directly from federal, state, or district sources rather than indirectly through parents or students. It is, however, not clear whether religious schools would or could comply with this demand and, if they could, whether their compliance would meet constitutional objections and survive a test in the courts.

Before Modernization

Before schools and school providers appeared on the scene to educate the children of their communities, that task fell to parents, especially mothers. The parental claim to and responsibility for the education of their children thus precedes that of any other individual, group, or institution. Civil society in the form of local churches and synagogues, manorial landlords and patrons, villages, towns, school societies, and districts often prodded or aided parents in that educational assignment. Not before the late 18th and early 19th century did state or federal governments join the existing school sponsors. In Germany, society, church, and state shared the educational burden in roughly equal proportions (Schmale & Dodde, 1991, pp. 13–31). In the English-speaking colonies in North America, and subsequently in the United States, both civil and religious communities carried the responsibility for schooling until, here too, in the 19th century the state made its appearance as co-director. Everywhere public schooling as a state-inspired and executed function appeared as a second step, building on preexisting activities and institutions of civil society.

In its early stages, the extension of influence over schools from communities to the state or nation changed little or nothing in local arrangements. In Prussia children were expected as before to follow in the footsteps of their parents. All schools were class-specific: Country schools prepared peasant children with a minimum of elementary drill and a maximum of religious and disciplinary instruction for their roles as field and homemakers. Schools in cities, usually as common *Bürger-* or higher *Gelehrtenschulen,* offered religious and moral instruction together with academic learning for future artisans, merchants, and professionals. Few parents would have asked for different arrangements.

In Massachusetts, schooling remained a matter for family, church, master artisans, and community. Together they represented the colony's ethnic-religious traditions. The provincial government, called the General Court, was primarily concerned with Latin education for the colony's future secular and religious leaders. In 1642, it delegated the responsibility for elementary education to parents and to masters of indentured servants. By 1647, it ordered towns of 50 or more families to appoint teachers for reading and writing schools. Towns of 100 or more families were to open a grammar school to prepare boys for Harvard College. Boston, Charlestown, Dorchester, and a handful of other towns, prodded by their ministers and concerned community leaders, had begun hiring Latin schoolmasters even before the Court had acted. In addition, private neighborhood and dame schools existed to offer elementary instruction. The initiatives for schooling thus had been taken locally, though the colony's government lent its support to the agencies of civil society. Within the bounds of social and religious tradition parents had a limited amount of choice in selecting schools for their children (Herbst, 1996, pp. 11–12, 17–19).

In other colonies—especially in Pennsylvania, New York, and New Jersey—ethnic and religious diversity made centrally directed colony-wide efforts less feasible. Pennsylvania with its "Noble Experiment" as a haven of toleration for Quakers, Mennonites, Pietists, Moravians, Lutherans, Baptists, and others favored community and church sponsorship of schools. New York and New Jersey with their mixture of Dutch, Swedish, Finnish, German, and English immigrants did the same. In New York City, as Carl Kaestle (1973, p. 27) put it, "the tolerance of the coexisting minorities . . . born of social necessity" led to a mixture of parental efforts, private schoolmasters, apprenticeship contracts, and church-sponsored instruction. All these were unregulated by central authority and prevailed into the early 19th century. Parents thus enjoyed some choice among the educational opportunities of civil society.

In the premodern era, in summary, many agencies of civil society undertook to school children and youths. When governments concerned themselves with schooling they were motivated by economic requirements and demands for social discipline. Wherever possible, government asked churches and employers of youth to take on these educational responsibilities. Parents were free to avail themselves of or to ignore these opportunities offered to their children. Given the force of tradition and the limited opportunities available, the diversity of educational means available did not translate itself into school choice as we know it today. School choice was not a relevant issue.

Prussian Efforts to Nationalize Education

When, toward the end of the 18th century governments moved toward direction and supervision of education, statesmen and educators on both sides of the Atlantic raised the issue of school choice publicly for the first time. They developed rationalist, enlightened, and progress-conscious ideologies with which they attacked inefficiency and waste of resources. Warm-hearted humanists pointed to misery and poverty which, they felt, could be eradicated by bringing schooling to all in a fair and equitable manner. They agreed that this could be done best by centralized administration of public schooling.

In Prussia, teachers of the cameral and police sciences had already discovered the connection between schools and a country's welfare in the first third of the 18th century. One of them, Johann Heinrich Bergius, wrote in 1774 that the state could no longer rely on parents to educate their children in love of country, industriousness, and productive competence. But it was Karl Abraham Freiherr von Zedlitz, Prussia's Minister of Justice responsible for the country's religious and educational affairs, who took the decisive step. In 1787 he published *Suggestions for Improving Education in Kingdoms*. Arguing that the purpose of schooling was to prepare everyone for life in society, Zedlitz subordinated concern for the student as an individual to the interests of the nation. His most enduring contribution, however, was the creation of the *Ober-Schulkollegium*, a National Higher School Board, consisting of five appointed educators, directly responsible to the Crown. The board was charged with supervising and inspecting all of Prussia's schools, including the existing private ones, and with examining teacher candidates (Heinemann, 1974, p. 168).

Opponents spoke up from the beginning. They argued that state interference in education would provide a privileged education to some and it would condemn others to continued poverty. It would ignore parental responsibilities and deprive the country's schools of the expertise of educators. Proponents, however, countered that parental responsibilities had to yield before the rights of children which the state had to protect. Class distinctions being inevitable, the state should educate everyone according to his or her estate. Thus the state would assuage the unhappiness of individuals who could not live within their social conditions. And as for the expertise of educators, the state would safeguard it through examinations and supervision.

Opposition to the idea of state supervision received a boost in 1792 when Ernst Christian Trapp and Wilhelm von Humboldt, two of Prussia's leading intellectuals, separately penned essays on limiting the state's power to regulate schools. Trapp, in 1779 in Halle the first professor of education at a German university, rejected state as well as church supervision of schools, their curricula, and their teachers. But he asked that the state support public schools, that they be open to everyone, and that private schools and instruction be permitted to exist without state interference (Berg, 1980, pp. 22–36). Humboldt's (1792/1972) famed essay, "The Limits of State Action," rejected the argument that republican antiquity could serve as model for monarchical Prussia. In a monarchy, subjects lived under the thumb of royal authority and needed to be protected against arbitrary power. State schools could neither provide a raised level of civic awareness nor guarantee against abuse of governmental power. The state, Humboldt wrote, thought of subjects, not, as did private educators, of human beings. It produced a uniform character type and thus showed itself ill-suited to assume the oversight of education (Humboldt, 1809/1964a, pp. 56–233).

The Königsberg pedagogue Johann Friedrich Herbart and the Berlin Protestant theologian, philosopher, and university reformer Friedrich Schleiermacher agreed with Humboldt. Herbart wrote in 1810 that state schools of necessity dealt with masses of children and thus resembled factories. As education was to be concerned with individuals and their development, tutors in homes and small community institutes were the best educators. There, parents could be in close touch with the education of their children. Such instruction constituted Herbart's preferred, though never realized, version of private and public education in civil society (Berg, 1980, pp. 37–45). Schleiermacher, equally critical of state supervised and of private schooling, allowed for a program in which civil society cooperated with the state in creating a community-conscious national school system. However, if national schooling failed to arouse in its students a high degree of community consciousness, it should be handed back to civil society, provided that, for boys—the country's future civil servants—private education remain out of the question (Schleiermacher, 1814, pp. 28–29).

Prussia's educational policy did not follow the paths outlined by either Humboldt, Herbart, or Schleiermacher. After the creation of Zedlitz's National Higher School Board in 1787, the Prussian state gradually gained increased control over its schools. When in 1809 Humboldt was placed in charge of the reconstruction of Prussia's schools and universities, he regarded his earlier ideas on the limits of the state as an "ideal" that, under the circumstances in defeated Prussia, had to be viewed as an "unattainable model." He was, however, not willing to give it up entirely (Humboldt, 1809/1964a, pp. 181–184; Scurla, 1970, p. 81). On it rested his 1809 plans for the rebuilding of schools in Königsberg and Lithuania and his 1810 report on financing Prussia's schools. That report called for a national school fund separate from the state treasury and administered by local authorities (Humboldt, 1810/1964b, pp. 278–285). The realities of Prussia's reconstruction, however, forced Humboldt to abandon his locally administered national school fund.

The opposition to Humboldt's views was most forcefully expressed in 1807 by the philosopher Johann Gottlieb Fichte. In a series of public lectures called *Addresses to the German Nation,* Fichte sketched out a vision for a unified state educational system to bring the German-speaking peoples to national consciousness, liberation, and service (Lilge, 1948, p. 52). A common philosophy, rationally conceived and uniformly embraced and adopted by all, would lead them to reject their private and parochial interests. A uniform national education in state-directed schools was to shape the German nation in the 19th century (Fichte, 1846, pp. 271–427). Obviously, in such a system there would be no room for the agencies of civil society or for parental choice.

By 1810, a basis for the country-wide future development of Prussia's schools had been laid. The conflict of opinions had produced a vigorous interplay between state and civil society that resulted, as Karl-Ernst Jeismann (1988) expressed it, in education and schooling becoming "a political factor of relative autonomy and an instrument dominated equally by the state and social groups in the pursuit of the common or particular interests" (pp. 11–13). Prussia's General Land Law of 1794 required that children were educated for their roles as citizens. In most cases, this meant, they were expected to attend public schools. But the law also recognized the claims of varied school sponsors, whether secular or religious, and the rights of parents to direct the education of their children (Heinemann, 1974, pp. 320–327). The continued presence of the agencies of civil society insured that school choice remained an option for parents who wanted to avail themselves of state-approved private schools and, in subsequent decades, of the *Bürgerschulen,* community-sponsored secondary schools. Local school authorities were left to navigate between the claims of all parties—state, parents, school sponsors and children—on a case by case basis.

States and National Plans in the United States

Across the Atlantic, in Virginia, Thomas Jefferson was attempting to introduce public schooling under statewide legislation. He did so against the background of a tradition of parental responsibility, private schoolmasters, apprenticeship arrangements, church and community efforts, and a widely dispersed plantation society. For Jefferson, public schooling was a necessity in a democracy with a republican form of government. All citizens were potential legislators responsible for the commonweal and had to be prepared for their task. Jefferson, however, never succeeded in persuading the Virginia House of Burgesses to adopt his proposals. People preferred to stay with their accustomed ways.

The same fate awaited several proposals for public and national education submitted by American intellectuals after the end of the Revolutionary War. Benjamin Rush of Pennsylvania called for "one general and uniform system of education" in which pupils were to be taught that they were "public property." Rush agreed with Noah Webster that "education should . . . be the first care of a legislature" and that in the American republic "knowledge should be universally diffused by means of public schools." In Delaware Robert Coram demanded that government secure education to every child and that parents and guardians "be compelled to bind them [children] out to certain trades or professions." Samuel Smith, who with Samuel Knox had won the prize offered in 1797 by the American Philosophical Society for the best essay on a national system of education, declared it to be "the duty of a nation" to place the education of children "under a control, independent of and superior to parental authority." Knox seconded Smith in calling for a uniform national system of education with publicly supported common schools in each county, academies for secondary education, state colleges, a national university, and a national board of education whose members were to be appointed by the states (Rudolph, 1965).

These reformers placed little confidence in the educational efforts of local communities. But nothing came of their proposals. In Massachusetts, a rural population, jealous of republican self-government and determined to preserve their right to resist outside taxation, insisted on local control over their schools (Kaestle, 1983, pp. 77–78). In New York, a State Board of Regents, in existence since 1784, was of limited effectiveness and restricted chiefly to financial support of local schools (Herbst, 1996, pp. 21–25).

Nonetheless, the ideas set into circulation in the 1780s and 1790s did not die, and in the new century led to regulation of education in several states. In Boston, Massachusetts, primary schools came under public local control in 1818. Three years later the city opened the country's first public high school. Compulsory local taxation for common schools followed in 1827. In New York, state supervision of private academies and colleges began with the establishment of the State Board. It was followed in 1795 with a state school fund that was to support public schools in towns and cities and, in the City of New York, denominational and charity schools as well. In 1812, the state inaugurated a system of common schools (Cremin, 1951, pp. 94–98). Georgia, like New York, created a state board to supervise the state's private academies and common schools. Twenty years before it became a state, Michigan in 1817 created a system of common schools, academies, colleges, and a university. At admission into the Union, nine academies received state funding for their classical, English, and teacher-training departments.

In both New York and Georgia, however, the state boards encountered the hostility of local interests, which asserted themselves through their respective state legislatures. In Georgia the legislature abolished state funding of the academies in 1837. In Michigan, as in New York and in Georgia, financial distress and popular dissatisfaction led the legislature in 1846 to abolish state appropriations for the academies and prepared the way for these schools eventually to be replaced by public high schools (Herbst, 1996, pp. 58–60). Nearly everywhere governmental efforts to direct and control education were checked by traditions of local, community, and church establishment of schools. A more widespread series of state efforts to support and supervise public education would come only during the late 1830s and 1840s when reformers set under way what has come to be known as the public school revival. Until then civil society as represented by local interests largely prevailed in the direction of public education.

Prussia's Schools Between Reform and Reaction

The interplay between state and civil society that had characterized Prussia's educational arrangements up to the Wars of Liberation was disturbed in 1819 when the Karlsbad Decrees placed new emphasis on class- and estate-specific schools and on reliance on the church as an ally of the state. Baron von Altenstein, the minister responsible from 1817 to 1840 for the country's educational, religious, and cultural affairs, tried to keep alive as much as possible the reforms of the Humboldt era while yet he had to conform to the letter, if not the spirit, of the reaction that followed the Karlsbad decrees (LaVopa, 1980, p. 123). In a royal edict of June 15, 1822, one of his conservative colleagues, Ludolf von Beckedorff, censored the efforts of progressive directors in the teacher-training seminars who proposed to introduce the principles of Pestalozzianism. Elementary school teachers were sufficiently trained, the edict stated, if they were able to teach reading, writing, arithmetic, and religion. Subjects such as grammar, geography—at least in so far as it concerned foreign countries—political and natural history, science, and drawing were unnecessary, wrote Friedrich Wilhelm III (Herbst, 1989, p. 44). The opposition of German teachers to these policies continued, but remained ineffective. It also did little to promote the concerns of parents whose opportunity for choice in their children's schooling was limited to deciding between Protestant and Catholic public schools. Apart from that, social class and locality determined which school children attended.

Parental concerns received a better hearing in the cities than in the country. Parents of the lower bourgeoisie successfully opposed state directives that favored a Latin academic education for future civil servants and professionals. Just as in colonial Massachusetts localities had protested the General Court's insistence on founding Latin grammar schools and had preferred academies (Herbst, 1996, p. 19), so German civil society asserted its interests in a less classically oriented and more vocation directed schooling for their children, primarily boys. Parents demanded *Bürgerschulen* and *Realschulen* in which the natural sciences and modern languages received greater attention than Latin and Greek. Eventually they succeeded in obtaining them and in having many *Gymnasia* incorporate classes of the *Realschul* type (Herrlitz, Hopf, & Titze, 1993, pp. 65-66).

After the Public School Revival in the United States

In the United States, the common-school revival that had gathered momentum in the late 1830s began to threaten local control and the influence of laymen over common school education. The proponents of the revival, led by Horace Mann in Massachusetts and Henry Barnard in Connecticut, battled against what they considered the excessive decentralization of the district system. The supporters of that system, in turn, condemned the reformers' penchant for centralization as "associated . . . with King George, Prussian autocracy, and monopolies"(Tyack, 1974, pp. 33–34). In Massachusetts, victory came to the reformers in 1840 when they defeated a bill for the abolition of the State Board of Education and the normal schools (Kaestle & Vinovskis, 1980, pp. 213–232). In other states they also succeeded with their crusade. Local determination of school policy through school boards responding primarily to parents and taxpayers slowly gave way to the ascendancy of the schoolmen's professional bureaucracy.

Throughout the century's second half battles were fought on many fronts and the outcomes varied. In Illinois and Wisconsin, rural residents vigorously opposed the introduction of the township high school. They feared that such schools would seduce their children into leaving home and the farm. In Wisconsin, too, farmers resisted the efforts of the professionals to abolish their locally elected county superintendents. As Wayne Fuller (1982) explained it, the schoolmen "threatened to deprive the farmers of their right to supervise the education of their children, and [the farmers] would not have it" (p. 155). After the turn of the century, Midwestern farmers fought against school consolidation because they opposed the closing of their district school houses, the loss of control over the schooling of their children, and the costs involved. They disliked "wagoning" their children and the new "friends" the children would encounter. By the time of World War II, however, the decline in the country's farm population gave added impetus to the demands of the schoolmen, and consolidation ultimately won the day (Fuller, 1982, pp. 226–245). As David Tyack (1974) put it so well: American schoolmen were on their way to devise the "one best system" for educating the country's children.

German Schools After 1850

In Prussia, and subsequently Germany, the failed revolution of 1848 had prompted the government to assert its full force in bringing the country's educational efforts under its complete control. The government held that Prussia's elementary schools were to be seen as instruments of state policy. Because schools were to shore up the social and economic stability of the country, the government insisted that elementary education was to be limited to information and indoctrination. For the same reason, parents were to fulfill their duties as subjects by keeping their children in their family's place in the existing social class system. They were not to encourage their children to seek social or economic advancement because that would endanger the existing order. Teachers were to acknowledge the ministers of the church as their spiritual guides and professional supervisors, and they and their students were to remain loyal to fatherland and church.

Again, these efforts succeeded better in the country than in the cities, where civil society remained in constant tension with the state. As Karl-Ernst Jeismann (1988, pp. 29–30) observed, the struggle between society and the administrative state continued throughout the 19th century.

After the mid-19th century and throughout the 20th century, the Prussian and later the German state maintained and still maintains its supervisory powers over civil society. Although it recognizes parental rights and responsibilities for the education of children and acknowledges the right of private schools to exist, it claims that it exercises its supervisory powers over parents and both public and private schools to assure the protection of the rights of children for the benefit of the nation.

As a result, state officials authorize curricula and teaching materials for both public and private schools, inspect classrooms, administer teachers' examinations, supervise the moral conduct and political loyalty of teachers, and, in the public schools, require the teaching of confessional religion. Religion, they argue, is a pillar of social stability (Heckel, 1967, pp. 50–51). As for private schools, they have in effect, as one author wrote, become quasi-public institutions (Deutscher, 1976, pp. 154–155).

It was only in the 1960s that as part of the worldwide social upheaval a loosening of the governmental direction of schools occurred. The traditional German school structure of primary and continuation schooling on the one hand and secondary education on the other as well as the largely class-based tripartite separation of *Hauptschulen, Realschulen,* and *Gymnasia* came under attack. Parents and citizens had complained all along that although the state school system provided a variety of school types for its children, this diversity did not imply opportunities for school choice. Attendance at a given school was largely determined by parental residence, social class, and religion. Nor could parents who opted to send their child to a private school thereby exempt their children from the influence of state policy.

The protests and demonstrations found their echo in proposals developed by the *Deutsche Bildungsrat,* appointed by the federal government in 1965. The result of these endeavors was the creation of the integrated *Gesamtschule*—a type of comprehensive high school—that was to bring to fruition the goal of equal opportunity for all. Girls, children from rural areas, and the sons and daughters of Catholic and working-class parents were no longer to be shortchanged by being assigned to gender-, class-, or religion-specific schools. The initiatives that had arisen first in civil society and were in time supported and directed by governmental action also aroused vigorous opposition by parents who resented social integration and feared the decline of academic standards. The result has been that much of the original impulse has been lost, and the future success of the integrated *Gesamtschule* remains hard to predict.

American Schools From the 19th to the 20th Century

Localism had been the initial driving force in the United States to stave off the inroads of centralizing governmental into the common-school system. But it was not the only banner under which Americans fought the growing tide of uniform state regulation. In the 19th century, American Catholics, native born and immigrant, first objected to the Protestant religiosity that pervaded the public schools. They particularly resented the use of the King James Bible in the classroom. They protested having to pay taxes for what they considered Protestant public schools when they received no tax revenues for Catholic parochial schools. They asked that, like in Prussia, public schools be either Protestant or Catholic or, if that was not possible, that their children be allowed to receive Catholic religious instruction from teachers of their faith in public school classrooms. As Catholics failed to gain these concessions, they began to build a parochial school system of their own. By 1890 that system enrolled 626,496 students and was, as Tyack and Hansot (1982) wrote, "the largest 'alternative school system' in the United States" (p.78).

When in 1925 in *Pierce v. Society of Sisters* the United States Supreme Court unequivocally upheld every American parent's right to send their children to private schools, double taxation for the public and their own parochial schools became the crucial issue for American Catholics. They argued that, as a matter of fairness and to avoid a violation of religious liberty, tax credits be given to parents who sent their children to parochial schools (Blum, 1958, p. 958). Their claim found support in the child benefit theory that the Supreme Court endorsed in 1930 in the *Cochran v. Louisiana State Board of Education* decision and reaffirmed in several later cases (Ravitch, 1983, pp. 30–31). Still, the original Catholic claim for full public support of all private schooling foundered on the shoals of the doctrine of the separation of state and church.With the *Brown v. Board of Education* decision of 1954, which declared unconstitutional the practice of racial segregation in public schools, new forms of community opposition to state regulation of schools appeared. Many of these resulted in school-choice programs. As integration proceeded, White opponents sought tuition grants to obtain their own form of segregated school choice. Federal courts, however, declared such legislation unconstitutional (Ravitch, 1983, p. 133). In the North, racial minorities demanded improved academic and vocational education for their children in inner-city schools. Activists pushed urban public school systems to loosen their bureaucracies and confronted them with alternative educational institutions. In New York City in 1966 and 1967 they brought to the fore the issue of community control, that is, parental influence over local schools (Ravitch, 1974, pp. 173–174). The often bitter conflicts were finally resolved, if not settled to everyone's satisfaction, through a decentralization proposal worked out by the state legislature.

Another form of lay direction of education developed in President Lyndon Johnson's Great Society program. Here, as Paul Peterson (1985) put it, "a rival system of vocational education separate from the public schools" (pp. 200–202) came into being. Manpower training programs, neighborhood youth corps, job corps, comprehensive employment and training centers, and community action programs flourished. In Washington D.C., it was the Department of Labor, not the Department of Education, that administered these programs. On the local level, city halls and departments, community organizations and private firms, rather than public school districts, were the responsible agencies. In these cases, just as in Germany, government came to the aid of civil society; but in the United States, in contrast to Germany, it was nonprofessionals who seized the initiative everywhere.

More lasting forms of school choice emerged in New York and other American cities with magnet schools and alternative schools within public schools. Magnet schools offered specialized curricula of high quality. The alternative school concept came to include tuition vouchers that allowed parents to send their children to schools of their choice, some public, others private. Public reaction to vouchers, however, remains mixed. The chief objections are the perceived destructive effect they would have on public schools and, in the case of parochial schools, the violation of the doctrine of the separation of state and church. The issue, however, is by no means settled. As choice plans come to focus heavily on inner-city schools and are put to the test with voucher plans in Milwaukee and Cleveland, the debate over school choice continues with renewed vigor.

Summary and Conclusion

Looking back over the history of schooling in Germany, what is notable, above all, is the persistent adherence of proponents of both state supervision and of community direction to a belief in the necessity of state authority over education. The role of the state in education is far less questioned than it is in the United States. To be sure, German partisans of school choice ask for greater freedom for private schools from the many state regulations. They plead that public school systems allow alternative tracks and institutions. Cultural pluralism or multiculturalism, they assert, requires diversity of school forms and the rights of parents to choose from among them for their children (Jach, 1991, p. 43). But given the entrenched German legal code, the inflexibility of the school bureaucracy, the centuries of state-governed practice, and the restorative tendencies in German educational policy in the century's last third, it is hard to foresee any changes that would go beyond relatively minor alterations in the existing system. Whatever advances the forces of civil society might score in the so-called third or nonprofit sector, they will take place under strict governmental direction and supervision.

In the United States, community initiatives in education and school choice have always been more vibrant issues than they have been in Germany. Throughout the country's history, parents and taxpayers have asserted their right to freedom from governmental direction of their schools. They fought for local control and opposed professionals who wanted to centralize and rationalize the public school system. American Catholics triggered the most vociferous debates when they tried to win recognition for their religious teachings in the public schools and, later, when they sought to obtain public funds for the maintenance of their parochial schools. Parents who, for varied and opposed reasons, resented the outcomes of the Supreme Court's desegregation decision initiated other bitter and continuing debates.

This live tradition of local control in public education and the strength of private institutions in higher education have given to civil society a far greater voice in educational policy than has been heard in Germany. Civil society thus is likely to hold its own, even advance, in its contest with the state. Neither the defenders of the public school *status quo* nor the advocates of complete school choice are likely to prevail unchecked. The United States is not about to jettison its public school system. At the same time, the labor market, not the school-choice market, will force greater diversity and, with that, increased opportunities for choice among educational offerings. The debate is going to continue with new variations on the theme but essentially along familiar lines.

References

Berg, C. (Ed.). (1980). *Staat und Schule oder Staatsschule?* Königstein: Athenäum.

Blum, V. C. (1958). *Freedom of choice in education.* New York: Macmillan.

Chubb, J., & Moe, T. (1990). *Politics, markets, and America's schools.* Washington, DC: Brookings Institution.

Cremin, L. A. (1951). *The American common school, An historic conception.* New York: Teachers College.

Deutscher, E. K. (1976). *Private Schulen in der deutschen Bildungsgeschichte.* Inauguraldissertation, Johann Wolfgang Goethe Universität, Frankfurt.

Fichte, J. G. (1846). Reden an die deutsche Nation. In I. H. Fichte (Ed.), *Sämmtliche Werke,* vol.VII. Berlin: Veit.

Fuller, W. E. (1982), *The old country school.* Chicago: The University of Chicago Press.

Heckel, H. (1967), *Schulrecht und Schulpolitik.* Neuwied/Berlin: Hermann Luchterhand Verlag.

Heinemann, M. (1974), *Schule im Vorfeld der Verwaltung.* Göttingen: Vandenhoeck and Ruprecht.

Herbst, J. (1989), *And sadly teach.* Madison: The University of Wisconsin Press.

Herbst, J. (1996), *The once and future school.* New York: Routledge.

Herrlitz, H., Hopf, W., & Titze, H. (1993). *Deutsche Schulgeschichte von 1800 bis zur Gegenwart.* Weinheim: Juventa.

Humboldt, W. (1792/1972). Ideen zu einem Versuch, die Grenzen der Wirksamkeit des Staats zu bestimmen. In A. Flitner & K. Giel (Eds.), *Werke in Fünf Bänden* (Vol. I). Darmstadt: Wissenschaftliche Buchgesellschaft [English: The Limits of State Action. Indianapolis, IN: Liberty Fund, 1972].

Humboldt, W. (1809). Der Königsberger und der Litauische Schulplan. In A. Flitner & K. Giel (Eds.), *Werke in Fünf Bänden* (Vol. IV). Darmstadt: Wissenschaftliche Buchgesellschaft.

Humboldt, W. (1810) Bericht an Altenstein über die Finanzgrundsätze der Sektion. In A. Flitner, & K. Giel (Eds.), *Werke in Fünf Bänden* (Vol. IV). Darmstadt: Wissenschaftliche Buchgesellschaft.

Jach, F.-R. (1991). *Schulvielfalt als Verfassungsgebot.* Berlin: Duncker & Humblot.

Jeismann, K.-E. (1988). Preußische Bildungspolitik vom ausgehenden 18. bis zur Mitte des 19. Jahrhunderts. In U. Arnold (Ed.), *Zur Bildungs- und Schulgeschichte Preußens.* Lüneburg: Nordostdeutsches Kulturwerk, pp. 9–38.

Kaestle, C. F. (1973) *The evolution of an urban school system.* Cambridge, MA: Harvard University Press.

Kaestle, C. F., & Vinovskis, M. A. (1980). *Education and social change in nineteenth-century Massachusetts.* Cambridge,U.K.: Cambridge University Press

Kaestle, C. F. (1983). *Pillars of the republic.* New York: Hill and Wang.

LaVopa, A. J. (1980). *Prussian schoolteachers.* Chapel Hill: University of North Carolina Press.

Lilge, F. (1948). *The abuse of learning.* New York: Farrar, Straus & Giroux.

Peterson, P. E. (1985). *The Politics of school reform, 1870–1940.* Chicago: University of Chicago Press.

Ravitch, D. (1974). *The great school wars.* New York: Basic Books.

Ravitch, D. (1983). *The troubled crusade.* New York: Basic Books.

Rudolph, F. (1965). *Essays on education in the early republic.* Cambridge, MA: Harvard University Press.

Schleiermacher, F. E. D. (1814). Über den Beruf des Staates zur Erziehung. In E. Lichtenstein (Ed.), *Ausgewählte pädagogische Schriften* Paderborn: Verlag Ferdinand Schöningh, pp. 18 – 32.

Schmale, W., & Dodde, N. L. (Eds.). (1991). *Revolution des Wissens?* Bochum: Dieter Winkler.

Scurla, H. (1970). *Wilhelm von Humboldt: Werden und Wirken.* Berlin: Verlag der Nation.

Tyack, D. B. (1974). *The one best system.* Cambridge, MA: Harvard University Press.

Tyack, D. B., & Hansot, E. (1982). *Managers of virtue.* New York: Basic Books.

Zedlitz, K. A. (1787). Vorschläge zur Verbesserung des Schulwesens in den Königlichen Landen [Suggestions for improving education in kingdoms]. *Berlinische Monatsschrift, X,* pp. 97–116.

Chapter Eight

Educational Autonomy in a Civil Society: A Model of Checks and Balances

HEINZ-DIETER MEYER

In the education-reform debate we can often discern three rival approaches revolving, respectively, around markets, government, and the family. In the first, the main assumption is that the power of the *market* to enhance the common welfare, as an aggregate result of the individual pursuit of self-interest, can be fruitfully exploited for the purpose of general education. In the second, the assumption is that *government* is the privileged actor in ensuring civility and civic education and maintaining schools free from the strife of groups, religious sects, and the fetters of prejudice. In the third, the *family* is considered the key agent of education on the assumption that parents are the ones most intimately concerned about the well-being of their children and because they hold ultimate authority over their upbringing. In this essay I suggest that the civil society, properly understood, represents a frame of reference that facilitates harnessing the educational powers of all three agents just mentioned. Specifically, I argue that an institutional arrangement that satisfies the different normative implications of civility in the realm of education is one that casts the different agents of education in a relation of checks and balances. This is especially clear if we compare European and American traditions of civil society.

Civil society, properly understood, is a realm of conflicting normative claims delimited by the claim of liberty and freedom from undue government interference on one hand (Mill, 1985; Tocqueville, 1971), and by the claim of community obligation and solidarity on the other (Dahrendorf, 1990; Taylor, 1992; Walzer, 1995). This is, at any rate, suggested by American and European experiences of civil society. In the

American tradition of civil society the emphasis has typically been on unconstrained individuals, free to associate to generate the services they need without government interference. In this tradition government and civil society have often been seen as antithetical. Consistent with this tradition, the emphasis of the intellectually most active groups in the recent education debate has been on voucher schemes and how to harness market forces for the rejuvenation of education. In the Continental European tradition, by contrast, the emphasis has more often been how to engage and employ government (the State) to redress some of the imbalances that develop spontaneously among societal groups and how to use government to carve out and protect spheres of civility within society (Smith, 1986).

Both traditions have their obvious strengths and weaknesses. The kind of civility that civil society needs must be responsive to both, the claim of liberty and the claim of communal solidarity. The maturity of a civil society is not only measured by the extent to which non-governmental actors are engaged in the provision of public goods but also by how wide we draw the circle of goods that are available to all citizens.

In what follows, I want to consider what sort of institutional or policy regimes are best able to satisfy these conflicting claims. To that end, abstract faith *and* abstract distrust in government and in markets must be jettisoned, because, as it turns out, both agents (plus a third one, the family) are needed for education to contribute to and benefit from civil society. I begin with a discussion of the normative implications of the idea of civility in civil society. Next, I consider the potential and the limits of government, markets, and the family as providers of education. I conclude by suggesting that a model of checks and balances, in which all three agents can influence education but also mutually check and balance each other, might be best suited to educational autonomy in a civil society.

Conflicting Meanings of Civility

For the purposes of this chapter I define civil society as the social space where private individuals contribute directly or indirectly, intentionally or unintentionally, to the public good by means of voluntary association.

By associating voluntarily, formerly unconnected and unassociated individuals transform themselves into socially connected ones. They emerge from the sphere of private individuals into public space, which they attempt to order according to shared standards of civility. Civil society thus joins two important dimensions of civility, a normative and an institutional one. The latter has to do with the configurations of institutions that expand the realm of the society of citizens and curtail the influence of potentially or actually opposing forces, such as markets or governments. (I will deal with this aspect in the second part of this chapter.) The former refers to an implicit or explicit normative ideal by which a society's standards of civility are evaluated. Scope and content of this idea differ widely in different times and places. As Norbert Elias (1994) has shown, in its earliest meaning, civil was used to distinguish the warrior from the courtier, martial life and manners from domestic and peaceful ones. When the aristocratic courts gave way to commercial and bourgeois enterprises as the dynamic center of society, the word civil took on a greater variety of meanings, ranging from a willingness to eschew violence as a means of settling affairs between individuals to include fairness, politeness, and tolerance as norms that govern the social intercourse of citizens. As the horizon of the European public expanded to include the peoples of Africa and America, civil and civilized also came to draw a line between primitive and developed, illiterate and literate cultures. All of these meanings remain active when we use the terms civil and civility today. What is less obvious in everyday usage is the fact that the norm of civility contains a crucial and often unacknowledged tension that is at the bottom of much conflict between partisans of different versions of the civil society.

The Libertarian Face of Civility

The great promise of civil society in modern usage is to free the social realm from the unlimited dominance of the political, which is, in the last resort, always a realm of power and of force (whether the Leviathan is manned by the *demos*, a monarch, or an aristocracy) and to carve out a separate sphere of free, civil interaction mediated not by force but by voluntary agreement and association, and inspired by the lights of reason and justice. The underlying idea is that a government that is involved with every social activity—from childrearing to licensing piano teachers—cannot fail to assume a despotic aspect. This is so especially if the bulk of government activities is carried out in the name of justice and the welfare of the people, because no other government mission legitimizes more pervasive meddling in the affairs of every citizen than the welfare of the people. Under such conditions, a people inevitably develop a rather narrow idea of what it is capable of. First the habit and then even the memory of individuals accomplishing great public deeds by associating freely and voluntarily vanishes. It was Tocqueville (1971/1830) who first expressed the libertarian aspect of civil society most succinctly:

> One of the happiest consequences of the absence of government (when a people is happy enough to be able to do without it, a rare event) is the ripening of individual strength which never fails to follow from it. Each man learns to think and to act for himself without counting on the support of any outside power which, however watchful it be, can never answer all the needs of man in society. . . I admit that in fact [a man] often is less successful than the authorities would have been in his place, but, in the total, the general result of all these individual strivings amounts to much more than any administration could undertake; and moreover the influence of such a state of affairs on the moral and political character of a people, would more than make up for all the inadequacies if there were any. But one must say it again, there are but few peoples who can manage like that without a government. Such a state of affairs can only exist at the two extremes of civilization. The savage with nought but his physical needs to satisfy, he too relies on himself. For the civilized man to be able to do the same, he must have reached that state of society in which knowledge allows a man to see clearly what is useful for him and his passions do not prevent him from carrying it out. The most important concern for a good government should be to get people used little by little to managing without it. (p. xi)

This is the young Tocqueville speaking whose political views were strongly influenced by the stark contrast between the political habits of his French compatriots who were apt to expect all public action to emanate from government, and the habits he observed in the United States, where citizens produced great public deeds through voluntary association. The advantages of the latter mode of public action are real and tangible. The public is enriched, not impoverished, if private individuals and organizations are allowed to make arrangements in a matter of great public interest (such as education) rather than forcing them into submission to a busy body bureaucracy. Unlike political society, civil society is the sphere of the rule of example. It does not require lockstep movement based on majority decision, but instead encourages individuals to act on their ideas (and ideals) and put their visions into practice. It facilitates the expression of genuine human affiliations unfiltered by bureaucratic or political mediation. It allows us to contribute to the public good without forcing us to sever our attachments to concrete, and that means necessarily particular people and ends. Every time potentially endless political deliberations are cut short because a group of like-minded individuals have the courage to "put their money where their mouth is," we experience the great blessings of the libertarian side of civil society.

The Communitarian Face of Civility

That aspect of civil society that facilitates Tocqueville's "ripening of individual strength" we may call the libertarian face of civil society. But civility has another meaning too, no less important and sometimes conflicting with the one just alluded to. It means that, as a community, we want certain goods and certain resources to be available to all members within its realm; they deserve them not in recognition of particular merits but as fellow humans, as members of the human fraternity. They are, if you will, the advance credit we give to everyone in our midst, regardless of desert. The scope of these goods that result from a community's commitment to solidarity and *fraternité,* as the French revolutionaries called it, differs from one society to another. It is clearly culturally defined. In most countries, for example, people believe that urban parks are a public good that ought to be accessible to all. In fact, communities go to great length to keep these areas free from the encroachments of urbanity. In a way, we treat them as urban extensions of the outdoors, the forests and plains that are open to all. Yet, as anyone who has enjoyed the parks in great metropolitan cities knows, maintaining them as safe and peaceful retreats from urbanity can be difficult and costly. Erecting fences around these oases of green and calm and charging cost-covering entrance fees would, in many cases, vastly simplify their maintenance and turn a drain on public funds into a wellspring. But to do so would collide so strongly with our sense of civility that we absorb the losses because they are worth the civic gains. The same is true for a host of other goods, from publicly maintained swimming pools, health care, and highways, to education. Civility in this sense is about inclusion of all into the fold of the fraternal community, about our sense that to live together in one society requires that certain goods must be available to all members, irrespective of their status, wealth, beliefs, or whatever else may distinguish them as persons.

In practice, the inclusive impetus of civil society is often most strongly counteracted by the dynamics of capitalist markets. Not surprisingly, among the scholars who exhibit the least appreciation of this aspect of civility and civil society (although often great champions of the libertarian side) we often find economists who believe that the market provides the ideal mechanism to structure virtually all relations between individuals in society. Milton Friedman, for example, is the author not only of education voucher proposals but also of the idea that public parks ought to be maintained through tolls collected at the gates to their fenced in environs. In the book in which he introduced the idea of educational vouchers, Friedman (1962) also discussed the issue of using market mechanisms to maintain public parks. Friedman believes that fenced-in parks that charge entrance fees at toll booths are, in principle, a good idea, because the costs of park maintenance are shifted to their actual users. The sole reason the idea cannot be put into practice is, according to Friedman, because "to maintain toll collectors at the gates or to impose annual charges per window overlooking the park would be very expensive and difficult" (p. 31). For Friedman, the main obstacle to privatizing public parks are pragmatic, never mind civility. In contrast, Arthur Okun (1975) has shown that in a capitalist society that aspires also to be a democracy, the market must be blocked from many exchanges that are economically efficient and plausible, but that would undermine the idea of democracy. Thus, we do not sell voting rights on the open market (even though there would be many interested buyers and sellers), nor do we allow people to buy their way out of army duty, because doing so would violate our sense of equality and civility.

These examples, and there are many others, illustrate that civility often requires deliberate efforts to negate and neutralize the effects of wealth, status, and a host of other attributes that distinguish us as persons but that we deem irrelevant for civil society membership. Considering schooling in this light makes clear that the extent to which civility prevails in a given society is not only defined by the degree to which government leaves the organization of education to voluntary associations. It is also defined by the extent to which a community has been able to neutralize and negate the influence of educationally irrelevant factors in channeling access to education. Just as we don't want to exclude people from the pleasures of a stroll in a city park because they may not be able to pay their share of the upkeep, so we don't want do exclude people from becoming literate, numerate, and learned in the essentials of civic and political participation because they lack the income to pay their share of the real costs of such schooling.

The libertarian dimension requires that civil society be protected from the encroachments of government. The communitarian face requires that civil society be protected from the encroachments of the market. Both requirements sometimes coincide and enhance each other. But they probably just as often clash. Fencing in New York City's Central Park and charging a $20 entrance fee would, in one fell swoop, lower the park's notorious crime rate (a very civil concern) as well as the tax burden on all New Yorkers. But it would also turn the park into an exclusive resort of the-well-to-do, and make New York a less civil place. Liberalizing drugs, to take another example, would, in one legislative act, drain a source of organized and unorganized crime and, theoretically, limit the harmful effects of drugs to those who choose to use them. Yet, again, as a community we hesitate to take this step because we feel that over-the-counter heroin would very often amount to collectively condoned self-destruction. I cite this last example not because I am necessarily convinced that the public consensus against liberalizing drugs is wise but to show that, as a community, we often absorb great losses for the sole reason that we consider the alternative—fenced in parks, over-the-counter heroin—to be uncivil. While interest groups can play a constructive role in civil society, organizations that merely pursue the collective self-interest of a private enterprise unmediated by concerns of civility and justice are mere lobbyists. Fortunately for our main interest, basic education (literacy, numeracy, and the civic basics) is located at a far less controversial point along this continuum between liberty and community. It is part and parcel of the Western tradition of education that a people, in Jefferson's words, "cannot hope to be ignorant and free," even though in some cases it took decades of struggle against private interests to make the leveling of taxes and other private sacrifices for the purpose of education compulsory.

Government, Markets, and Families as Agents (and Obstacles) of Education in Civil Society

One implication of the distinction between a libertarian and a communitarian dimension of civil society is that governments as well as markets constitute potential encroachments on civil society, threats to its autonomy. This means that civil society is inherently a realm of tradeoffs and compromise between similarly basic claims of civic autonomy and communal inclusion. Paradoxically, however, markets and governments are also among the main tools we have to protect ourselves from these encroachments. In this section I want to address the question of how civil society can be defended against overreaching governments and the imperialism of markets. In this context, we must also consider the role of the family. The answer is only superficially paradoxical: by institutional arrangements that allow governments, markets, and the family to check and balance each other. To that end, a contrast of American and European traditions of civil society is useful.

As pointed out previously, in most Anglo-American conceptions civil society and government are seen as antithetical. In this view, government is seen as an actor of last resort and civil society is believed to be strong where government is limited, and vice versa. The idea of government as a residual force of which the less the better has become one of the few articles of faith in this tradition (which last made its appearance on the American scene in Newt Gingrich's "Contract with America"). In contrast, a positive view of the civilizing role of government has been much more strongly embraced in the Continental European tradition hailing from Rousseau and Hegel. The latter especially did not share Locke's trust in the ability of free associations to produce a well-ordered civil society because freedom to associate and shape public welfare would inevitably be used more effectively by the strong rather than the weak (Smith, 1986). To redress the inevitable asymmetries was the chief task of the state. And as the young Tocqueville pointed out in the quote above, societies that are able to carry out significant portions of their public activities without government are the exception rather than the rule, to be found, as he puts it, "at the extremes of civilization." Most countries in Europe have occupied a midpoint on that continuum. For these societies, government (the State) has often been an actor of first resort in their efforts to make strides towards civility.

Government as Agent of Civil Society. When considering the European and American forms of civil society building, two motives can be distinguished that led men and women to enter the stage of civil society: patrician and plebeian. Civil society organizations of patrician origin are readily recognized. Universities, hospitals, institutions of social reform of all sorts, schools and academies, and prisons have often been the result of initiatives of men (less often women) of independent means, able to dedicate significant amounts of money to a worthy cause. The private universities in the United States, which so wonderfully demonstrate that excellence in science and scholarship can be pursued successfully without resort to the protective cover of the state, would have been impossible without the largesse of a large number of superbly wealthy patrons (Hall, 1982; Levine, 1988). The same can be said for many other organizations and foundations in the United States as well as other countries. Their existence is important and necessary and has, in large measure, given flesh and bone to that otherwise abstract term civil society. However, another source of civil society initiatives has often emerged from the other end of the social class spectrum, that is in initiatives of the laboring classes. The organizations and initiatives started by groups from these quarters have been more typical and culture-forming for the civil society in Western Europe than in the United States (although by no means absent in the latter), and more contentious, quarrelsome, and more militant than those from the patrician quarter. But, on the whole, they have been no less civil. Here we find labor unions and a host of other labor organizations (worker cooperatives, friendly societies, savings and self-help organizations, cooperative consumer organizations, workers' education societies), farm organizations, and, more recently, environmental and other social movement organizations of all kinds (Gauchet, 1989).

I emphasize the difference between these two kinds of civil society actors perhaps a bit too strongly. Still, in a historical and comparative perspective, the difference seems important. Too often has civil society been associated exclusively with the efforts of those who had already achieved secure standing in its midst while discounting those who had to wage sometimes long struggles to be included (Marshall, 1992). If inclusion is an important dimension of civility, history shows that time and again it only came as the result of collective struggles of those theretofore marginalized and excluded. In this respect I believe that Tocqueville (1969) got it wrong when he likened civil associations in Europe to nothing "but a right to make war on government" (p. 194)— even though that was, no doubt, one of their distinctive features.

But apart from its historical and comparative interest, there is a more general problem involved here, concerning the role of the state. The fact is that the plebeian groups took a markedly different stance toward the state than the patricians. While the latter could proudly do without government, the former both fought the state and claimed its assistance. The fight was typically a fight for inclusion, often for civil rights to be uncoupled from property rights (Dahrendorf, 1990). But it was just as often a fight for protection and assistance, a fight for privileges that the unpropertied classes would not be able to enjoy but for the state's active aid. A locus classicus for this role of government as grudging promoter of civility is Marx' (1967) analysis of the struggle for the shortening of the working day.

Next to laws regulating working conditions, public education is perhaps the key case in this category. Before the state got involved with mass education, the children of the laboring classes had access to schooling only by attending charity or parochial schools. And although it must be remembered that these institutions provided astonishing numbers of lower- and middle-class children with basic education (Stone, 1964), access to education remained even under the best conditions tied to the accident of time and place. Under such conditions the right to basic education could effectively be implemented only if it was guaranteed by the state. But even in this century and as recently as a few decades ago, the government played an important role in promoting universal, secular, and free education. In the United States this refers especially to the fight to extend education to all children, indifferent of race. In Germany, access to higher education was until the 1960s tied to socioeconomic status. It is hard to see how these struggles, which had to overcome resistance from entrenched prejudice as well as vested interests, could have been fought without rallying the forces of government. Any advocate of civil society will always view these experiences and struggles with mixed feelings, proud that they were fought and concerned that they led to a dramatically increased involvement of government in education. This sort of ambiguity, however, is inherently tied to action in the civil society. If we accept that securing equal access to education was an important item on the agenda of civil society, it is hard to see what a realistic alternative to state involvement might have looked like.

The Market as Agent of Civil Society. Markets, like governments, can be obstacles as well as agents of civil society in education. With its ability to shift great amounts of decision making from the command centers of the Leviathan and diffuse it across a myriad of individual agents, the market can clearly be a powerful ally of civil society (Lindblom, 1977). The advantages of opening up the system of public education to market forces seem vast indeed. The promise, as first extolled by Friedman (1962) and by Chubb and Moe (1989) is that competition, entrepreneurialism, flexibility, and the reduction of the decision load on overburdened government agencies will revitalize education and make it more responsive to the demands of diverse groups and individuals (see also Cooper & Randall, chapter 9, this volume). So far, so good. But the pursuit of public interests through free and voluntary association of private individuals is not only threatened by the stifling weight of bureaucracy. It is equally endangered by the paralyzing effects of extreme gaps in market power. Since Tocqueville (1969) warned in "Democracy in America" that a new aristocracy of industry might undermine the social basis of democracy (pp. 555–560)—not to mention Marx's ringing denunciation of the unequal effects of capitalism—the case against the corrosive effects of an unconstrained market has lost little of its validity. If the ability to found and support private associations is limited to a few wealthy citizens, the result will be a civil society in name only. The market can be an ally of civic associations by stimulating bottom-up entrepreneurialism and putting the requisite information in the hands of every concerned individual. By vastly expanding the scope of material goods available to individuals, it also provides the basis for physical and material comfort—not an uncivil concern. But while the market may support civil society, it does not replace it. An unconstrained market is as detrimental to civil society as unconstrained government. Schools need walls (Walzer, 1983). Although they are inevitably embedded in the institutional frameworks built by markets and governments, they must also be buffered and shielded from coercive effects of both. To harness both markets and governments for the end of civic education thus requires using them to check and balance their potentially coercive and corrosive effects. This is especially obvious if we consider the role of the family in education in a civil society.

The Family as Agent of Civil Society. In some proposals for a market-based education, the abstract faith in the market that would tolerate no constraints for the sake of civility has combined with a sort of abstract faith in the family as ultimate authority of education. The argument, which provides the key rationale for many voucher plans, begins with the idea that parents love their children, and of all possible authorities to shape education they are the most likely to consistently seek the good of the young (Coons & Sugarman, 1978). From there it follows that parents ought to be the ultimate arbiters of their children's education, a mission in which they should not have to compete with forces that often are far more powerful, such as a secular school culture maintained by a secular governmental monopoly in education (Coons, 1985, p. 509).

It is certainly true that parents' ability to shape the moral climate in which their children grow up is severely limited by a bureaucratic government committed to a value-free neutrality in schools and the commercialism of media and a consumer culture targeting increasingly younger audiences. But this does not mean that the school system is best which allows for the most immediate translation of parental will into educational policy. As in other domains of politics, the translation of the *will of all* into the *general will* is a vexing problem that cannot be solved by merely equating the two. Of the many pertinent objections I will mention only two. First, when it comes to their own offspring, people are at their most selfish. In a conflict over resources, the concern for our own children will always trump every other concern. It is hard to see how a civic constitution of education could emerge from the aggregation of selfish wills. Secondly, at any given point in time, the sum of parental will includes a significant portion of parents whose will consists in neglecting or abusing their children, keeping them out of school for the sake of profitable employment, or, if they are rich, sending them into schools held out by their own money. For theoreticians in love with the elegance of market models this does not constitute a serious problem. They are likely to point out that those parents who are, at a given point in time, neglecting the best interest of their children, can be divided into two groups: those who will alter their behavior given appropriate incentives and those who will not do so under any conditions. The first group, so the argument continues, is likely to respond to the incentives of market pressure, the second group is not going to respond to any pressure. But while shape up or ship out is a good principle in many kinds of market transactions, in education those forced to ship out remain entitled to a general education. Whereas defenders of theoretical parsimony can ignore them, practitioners of education (teachers, administrators, and policymakers) cannot. They must act in the here and now to ensure every child's educational civic minimum, without knowing who is likely to ultimately respond to market pressures and who isn't. And in a civil society the standards of their actions must be civil, applied to children of crack-addicted single mothers with the same unscrupulous thoroughness as to children of middle-class families or overworked parents straining to hold on to their minimum-wage jobs while raising a family.

However, education policy as an extension of parental will fails not only at the margins of the socioeconomic spectrum. It is flawed also when considering the solid-middle class family with enough time and resources to take charge of their children's education. Because they are motivated by love for their children, they are likely to side with the latter and to extend the benefit of the doubt to them rather than the classmate with whom they had a fight, or the teacher with whom they had a disagreement over a grade. The particular attachment of parents to their own children's happiness is their great strength, but for a sound educational policy it also constitutes a problem. Such a policy can obviously not be a mere sum of the various parental particularisms. Making the will of parents the ultimate authority in education would be possible only at the price of turning teachers into parents' mere servants. And although there is a strong tendency in the American political tradition to do just that (Waller, 1932), it is very much an open question if the country if well served by it. The subservient status of teachers conflicts obviously with the fact that, in modern societies, teachers are and must be professionals. Like other cases of professional–client interaction (doctors and patients; architects and customers), the proper form for the interaction between parents and teachers is negotiation, compromise, and hopefully, trust. It is not one of master–servant, employer–employee. This, however, would be a necessary corollary of a policy that tries to make parental will the ultimate authority of education.

Finally, advocates of choice must deal with the very different meanings of choice in the field of education and in that of consumer goods. Unlike breakfast cereals, where one crunch says it all, a given choice in education is something to chew on for years. Extreme fickleness that concludes after 3 months that a school is bad for one's child may be justified in extreme cases. In the aggregate, such fickleness would be a highly effective self-fulfilling prophecy.

Parents who want their children's education to be governed by nothing but the closest possible approximation to their own will and values should definitely have the opportunity to find appropriate arrangements (i.e., home schooling, private schools, etc.), provided the children are also taught the civic minimum. But as long as there are parents who are barred from this sort of deep involvement with their children's education, be it from indifference, ignorance, or plain lack of time, parental will is likely to be only one of several competing influences on schools and their work.

Education Between Liberty and Solidarity

Education in a mature civil society will be responsive to the imperatives of liberty as well as solidarity. It will be autonomous, shaped and pervaded by educational imperatives. To that end, it will incorporate the demands from governments, markets, and families, but also balance them against each other. The emerging institutional arrangement has the best chances to fend off the tyranny of non-educational spheres over education. As Pascal (1961) defines it in Pensée 244, tyranny is the "wish to obtain by one means what can only be had by another." It is to desire power "outside of its own sphere." Schools that are mere arms of government will, ultimately, be just as tyrannical as schools that are dominated by private market interests, or that are extensions of parental will. Civilizing education is the art of harnessing the constructive civilizing elements of those three agents, while checking their coercive ones.

Often these coercive effects of education parade as positive goods. Recall Max Weber's critique of the rationalization of education (Weber 1946, p. 240–244) in which he warned that a society where all positions and offices are accessible only based upon standardized forms of education, human experiences and abilities that do not readily translate into educational certificates are increasingly devalued. Such a society is in danger of producing a standardization of character, a narrowing of human diversity that is or can be the very opposite of education. Criticism of the narrowing and even deformation of character in the name of education is also expressed by contemporary writers, as in this critique of aspects of the French system of elite education:

> Given that this enterprise of hothouse cultivation is carried out on adolescents who have been selected and who have selected themselves according to their attitude toward the school, in other words, according to their *docility*, at least as much as their academic ability, and who, shut up for three or four years in a protected universe with no material cares, know very little about the world other than what they have learned from books, it is bound to produce forced and somewhat immature minds that . . . understand everything luminously and yet understand absolutely nothing. (Bourdieu, 1989, p. 91; italics in the original)

A thoroughly rationalized society in which all desirable positions depend on education certificates inevitably grants an inordinate amount of power to an exclusive caste, the men and women at the top of the education hierarchy—be they ministers and civil servants, or philosopher-scholars, as in the case of the Chinese mandarin caste. In a sociological sense, mandarins can be defined as a class of political rulers whose power is based on their exclusive mastery of a canon of knowledge. The problem inherent in mandarinism is that knowledge, rather than being a tool for liberation becomes a tool for oppression. Where mandarins are the gatekeepers for all advanced positions of influence and power, the state is effectively in their hands. In its homelands, China and Japan, mandarinism has long been criticized for turning a country's school years into "examination hell,"—a coercive process in which students spend a large part of their youths in drills and rote learning and are forced to neglect all other aspects of their lives and character development. As Rohlen (1983) puts in his incisive critique of Japan's high schools: "What Americans might regard as the lunatic fringe—students memorizing whole English dictionaries or doing seven hours of preparation a night for a year—actually sets the pace in this sort of competition [of the university entrance exams]. Moderation is a losing strategy as long as entrance examinations measure the gross absorption of knowledge and the perfection of problem-solving and test-taking skills" (p. 106). But moderation might well be the hallmark of education in a civil society—a state where the multiple and inevitably competing influences on education have a chance to check and balance each other.

Trans-Atlantic Learning

Inevitably, different nations come to emphasize different dimensions of civility in the course of their political and social development. Inevitably, they become one-sided in their pursuit of justice and democracy. Perhaps we are at a point where Americans and Europeans can hope to engage in a new and more profound dialogue about the future of civil society. The libertarian dimension of civil society has been pursued and institutionalized in the United States. The communitarian dimension has been institutionalized in Western Europe. People on both sides have reason to look across the Atlantic for a more complete sense of how to advance civility and education.

References

Berger, P. L., & Neuhaus, R. J. (1996). *To empower people. From state to civil society.* 2nd ed. (M. Novak, Ed.) Washington, DC: AEI Press.
Bourdieu, P. (1989). *The state nobility. Elite schools in the field of power.* Palo Alto, CA: Stanford University Press.

Chubb, J. E., & Moe, T. (1989). *Politics, markets, and the organization of schools.* Washington DC: Brookings Institution.

Coons, J. E., & Sugarman, S. D. (1978). *Education by choice. The case of family control.* Berkeley: University of California Press.

Coons, J. E. (1985). Intellectual liberty and the schools. *Journal of Law, Ethics and Public Policy,* I, 495–533.

Dahrendorf, R. (1990). *The modern social conflict: An essay on the politics of liberty.* Berkeley: University of California Press.

Elias, N. (1994). *The civiliźing process.* Oxford, UK: Blackwell.

Friedman, M. (1962). *Capitalism and freedom.* Chicago: The University of Chicago Press.

Gauchet, M. (1989). Tocqueville, Amerika und Wir. In U. Rödel (Ed.), *Autonome Gesellschaft und libertäre Demokratie* (pp. 123–207). Frankfurt: Suhrkamp.

Hall, P. D. (1982). *The organization of American culture, 1700 - 1900. Private institutions, elites, and the origins of american nationality.* New York: New York University Press.

Levine, L. W. (1988). *Highbrow–lowbrow. The emergence of cultural hierarchy in America.* Cambridge, MA: Harvard University Press.

Lindblom, C. E. (1977). *Politics and markets.* New York: Basic Books.

Marx, K. (1967). *Capital, Vol. I.* New York: International Publishers.

Marshall, T. H. (1992). *Citizenship and social class.* London and Concord, MA: Pluto.

Mill, J. S. (1985). *On liberty.* London: Penguin. (original publication 1859)

Okun, A. M. (1975). *Equality and efficiency. The big tradeoff.* Washington, DC: Brookings Institution.

Pascal, B. (1961). *Pensées,* (J.M. Cohen, Trans.). Baltimore: Penguin.

Rohlen, T. (1983). *Japan's high schools.* Berkeley: University of California Press.

Smith, S. B. (1986). Hegel's critique of liberalism. *American Political Science Review,* *80*(1), 121–139.

Stone, L. (1964). The educational revolution in England, 1560–1640. *Past and Present,* No. 28, pp. 41–80.

Taylor, C. (1992). *Multiculturalism and the politics of recognition: An essay. With commentary by Amy Gutman.* Princeton, NJ: Princeton University Press.

Tocqueville, A. (1969). *Democracy in America.* New York: Basic Books.

Tocqueville, A. (1971*). Journey to America.* New York: Anchor Books.

Waller, W. (1932). *The sociology of teaching.* New York: Wiley.

Walzer, M. (1983). *Spheres of justice. A defense of pluralism and equality.* New York: Basic Books.

Walzer, M. (1995). The concept of civil society. In M. Walzer (Ed.), *Towards a global civil society* (pp. 7–28) Providence, RI: Berghahn.

Weber, M. (1946). From Max Weber: Essays in sociology (H.H. Gerth & C. Wright Mills, Eds. and Trans.). New York: Oxford University Press.

Chapter Nine

Vouchers: Still (Largely) Untested and Why

BRUCE S. COOPER
E. VANCE RANDALL

The idea is simple enough. Provide parents the means, such as vouchers, to choose any school, public or private, that will best meet the educational needs of their children. The response, however, to this uncomplicated concept has been anything but simple. School vouchers—government grants to parents or guardians who can select a school of choice for their children—were stopped by a clever set of actions so effective as to suggest a conspiracy of politicians, interest groups, university scholars, and policy experts. We maintain, however, that vouchers were stymied not by a calculated conspiracy of individuals and groups, but by a *conspiracy of coincidences*. It was the particular combination of the following three major developments that were effective in slowing and even stopping the major voucher movements:

1. Polarization of Left and Right. The voucher issue so divided the liberal and conservative actors that little real dialogue, compromise, and political strategies to support vouchers were possible. Vouchers were scuttled in large part by a united and strident anti-voucher lobby on the liberal Left, separating it widely from vouchers' conservative sponsors.

2. A Divided Right. The drive for vouchers also suffered from the lack of a unified voice of support on the Right. Religious and libertarian conservatives withdrew support of the voucher plans that did not also include a total separation of education and government control, whereas the more mainstream, business-oriented neoconservatives pushed hard for vouchers. These neoconservatives had simultaneously to fight their

ideological opponents on the Left and their comrades on the far Right (see Bast & Harmer, 1997; Dewey, 1997).

3. An Emerging Radical Center. As if to fill the leadership void, an "extreme center" (Cooper, 1992) of moderates from both Left and Right, public and private schools, successfully captured the choice issue, enacting a host of new reforms: magnet schools for racial integration, charter schools for school site autonomy, school site budgeting and management, outsourcing or contracting schools and even whole districts out to private, for-profit firms (e.g., Edison Project and Alternative Education Inc.), and securing large, private donations to subsidize public schools (e.g., the Annenberg Challenge). These milder forms of choice were release valves for pressures to seek radical privatization. By making changes at the margins, these reforms deflected arguments for vouchers while keeping the monopoly of the public school system firmly intact and fundamentally unchanged.

In the final analysis, the liberal left faction closed ranks, the right was badly fractured, and a radical center grabbed center stage with an array of moderate choice plans which attenuated the need for family choice through vouchers. This chapter has two major purposes: First, it describes how these three major developments occurred; second, it explores what the future may hold for the voucher movement.

The Politics of Stopping Vouchers

Few will doubt the power of the liberal left in opposing vouchers. Their arguments, well rehearsed, are readily available to anyone who even suggests the dreaded "V" word, and these defenses of public education and drives against privatization of schools are strong and cogent. Vouchers would certainly threaten the public school system as it is currently constituted. Vouchers would remove the nearly exclusive ownership and hegemony of the "one best system," and few of us know exactly what would happen to the public school system. We would certainly see a massive shift of power and control of education from government institutions (public schools) to private entities such as parents and families.

The Liberal Left and the Education Establishment

The liberals and the education establishment have seized, with great skill, some high ground with their argument. Their anti-voucher position is based on four major propositions: (a) that public education embodies the ideals of American democracy, unity, and social progress; (b) that public schools hold out the greatest hope for equity and equal educational opportunity for all, especially the poor, the disadvantaged, the less able and challenged, the immigrant, and children of color; and (c) that private venues of education have insufficient capacity and quality adequately to educate 51,683,000 children (U.S. Department of Education, National Center for Education Statistics, 1996) and d) that publically aided religious schools are unconstitutional if religiously affiliated (which most are). These four arguments—American ideals, equity and equal educational opportunity, the limited capacity and constitutionality of private religious schools—have virtually shut down the voucher movement.

The liberal-left bases its voucher attack on four closely related objections. These are: identification of public schools with the American way, equity issues, market capacity, and parents as rational consumers.

Public Education and the American Way. At the heart of the objection to using the market, rather than the government, to allocate resources and make educational key decisions is the prevailing belief that only the government can be trusted to guarantee every child an equal educational opportunity. Cookson (1992) stated well the argument for the public monopoly of government schools and against vouchers or any other privatization schemes:

> Despite all the criticisms directed at them—and the criticisms are legion— public schools have survived because they fulfill a basic requirement of democracy. In

principle, free public education promises every child an equal educational opportunity. This promise has been violated repeatedly, but not because the ideal is flawed. It has been violated because, in a highly stratified society, schools have limited capacities to bring about greater social equity. If the public school system were to lose its authority and mission, it would wither and collapse, leaving in its wake an educational wasteland, not an educational wonderland as the free market advocates claim. (p. 97)

Equity Issues. When Chubb and Moe (1992) proposed direct grants to schools, based on parental choice, Bill Honig, California's superintendent of public instruction, reacted against any form of private support or choice, whether parochial aid, vouchers, magnet schools, or open enrollment plans. He argued that choice could lead to illegal support for religious schools, for private elitist schools or even for off-the-wall "cult" schools at taxpayers' expense. In his opinion, parental choice leads to even greater social inequities, mitigating against a major social goal of reducing social inequality through participation in a school system regulated by the government.

The Weak-Market Argument. With the provision of vouchers to parents, will enough new and diverse schools open to meet the increasing demand? Will consumers of educational services really have much choice, depending on the amount of the voucher and the willingness of schools to admit them without raising tuition and cutting out the poor? Will children with special needs and from disadvantaged backgrounds find appropriate schools on the open market? These are important questions about the capacity of the marketplace to provide educational goods and services in a manner that is fair and meets the needs of consumers.

Cookson (1992) criticized vouchers and other radical choice schemes on their own economic terms: that is, education as "businesses," to use the lingo of the Right. How ironic it is that, in the age of huge conglomerates and multinationals, schools should be asked to become mom-and-pop educational stores, struggling along from year to year entirely dependent on the whims of the marketplace. At the very time when big business is consolidating its holdings and becoming increasingly international, it is suggested that schools be run according to business principles that were discarded and discredited more than 50 years ago (p. 96).

Furthermore, critics note the great danger in converting the valued education of children into a heartless, unpredictable market that pits personal, individual interests against the greater public good. Cookson (1992) warned that "if the consumership coalition succeeds, then we will have entered a new era of American education, an era in which self-interest and competition will pit student against student, and family against family, in the struggle for educational survival" (p. 97). Richard Elmore (1986) maintained that "educational policy in the United States is, for the most part, based on the premise that the individual interests of parents, students, and educators should be subordinate to broader public policy objectives" (p. 2). These critics contend that the individualism and narrow self-interests of the marketplace would replace primary concerns for the community and the larger public interest.

Parents as Rational Consumers. Amy Stuart Wells and Robert L. Crain (1992) questioned whether parents can really "play the market" effectively to ensure their children an adequate education. With vouchers, everyone presumably would be "in the market" and the competition for seats in the better schools would likely increase. Would parents have adequate access to information and would they be able to evaluate this information about educational options in the best interests of their children? Given the many tough decisions about choosing appropriate schools, would parents make the "right" choice for their children? Wells and Crain thought not. They based their analysis of parental choice on "rational choice theory of consumer behavior." With vouchers, would parents act "rationally, in a goal-oriented fashion, to maximize their educational utility by finding the 'best' school for their children" (p. 66)? Wells and Crain held that parents base their choice of schools less on "objective" results and more on the social, economic, and racial make-up of schools. Parental choice, according to critics, may preclude adequate education, equity, inclusion, and student success. Wells and Crain concluded: "Only through inclusive, regulated programs such as these can we achieve anything close to equal educational opportunity through parental choice in education" (p. 81).

The Divided Right

Besides polarization along the Left–Right spectrum, voucher plans suffered from another coincidental event, a divided voice on the Right. This group has sponsored and supported vouchers for more than 45 years since the concept was quietly suggested by economist Milton Friedman in 1955. However, a raging debate goes on within the Right, as typified by a fascinating issue of *Policy Analysis* from the CATO Institute entitled, "Vouchers and Education Freedom: A Debate." This issue featured Bast and Harmer (1997) defending vouchers as a necessary step toward disestablishing public education. At the same time, Douglas Dewey, head of the National Scholarship Center in Washington, D.C., advocated a strict libertarian position and viewed vouchers as an anathema. Vouchers are seen as a kind of seduction of education, an eroding force in the march away from independence and personal freedom and right into the clutches of government control. Shocked and dismayed, Bast and Harmer (1997) explained that

> As school choice approaches its hardwon moment of political success, its proponents have been surprised to meet opposition from members of the very group that gave birth to the idea: conservatives and libertarians . . . Persons once thought to be natural allies of the movement have instead become its vocal critics, even to the point of publicly campaigning against school choice referenda and legislation. (p. 4)

The far Right's objection to vouchers grows from a libertarian view of the role of government and the effects of state intervention on individual liberty. Dewey (1997) based his objections to vouchers on five neoconservative tenets, revolving around definitions of liberty and the dangers of government controls.

Weakens Personal Sacrifice. Dewey stated the religious and libertarian Right's position, seeing any government role as seductive and dangerous, as having a harmful effect on personal sacrifice and voluntarism, and as weakening the private sector. Dewey (1997) explained:

> The remnant [population who pay for their own children's education] is not, after all, the private schools themselves but the parents who believe that they, not the government, are responsible for their children's education. The whole message of the welfare state is to disdain sacrifice, to prefer today's creature comforts to abstract notions like liberty and great grandchildren. Vouchers say to the remnant parents, "stop sacrificing!" when sacrifice is the essence of strong families and the hallmark of a free people. (p. 42)

Increases School Dependence on Government. Vouchers will do just that. Succinctly, Dewey (1997) explained that "vouchers would improve and enhance the dominance of government schools in communities where government schools are 'reasonably' satisfactory" (p. 29). The "twin pillars" of government's authority are the use of tax money for schooling and the compulsory education laws; vouchers correct neither.

Steps Toward Government Control and Take Over. Dewey called upon evidence from other nations to bolster his conviction that the more dependent private schools become on government largesse, the more these schools come to resemble government schools. In a survey of 35 nations, Estelle James (1991) found that "government controls over private schools are found even without subsidies. However, heavy controls invariably accompany subsidies, particularly over teacher salaries and qualifications, price, and other entrance requirements" (p. 374; see also James, 1990, 1994). Evidence from abroad, then, suggests that vouchers in the United States would bring government controls of private schools. These controls would ultimately destroy the unique character and effectiveness of private schools. James (1994) explained that "large private sectors in developed countries are heavily subsidized, heavily controlled, and in fact, these forces lead [private schools] to behave very much like the public sector" (p. 782).

Loss of School Mission and Meaning. One of the great fears of the religious Right is that government will insinuate itself into the life and spirit of their schools and remove their institutional souls. One example: In November 1995, Republicans in the House passed a pilot voucher program for the nation's capital, which was delayed by Senator James Jeffords (Rep.Vermont). As explained by Dewey (1997), at the House/Senate Conference Committee meeting a compromise bill emerged requiring

> that all participating private schools submit written assurance that no student receiving voucher would be required to "attend or participate in a religious class or religious ceremony without the written consent of the such student's parent." That is a stab at the heart of what makes private education desirable: its mission. The mantra of government schooling is that since we cannot all agree on one mission, we will have no mission. To accept the notion that it is reasonable for children to be permitted to attend a school while opting out of its mission is to accept the premise of mission free government schooling. (p. 39)

A second provision of the Washington, D.C. voucher bill was equally scary for the religious Right and others concerned about the mission of private education. The legislation stated that none of the voucher money could serve a school's religious mission. Because the proposed D.C. voucher covered anywhere from half to all the school's costs, about $3,000 per student, this regulation meant that schools "would have to certify that most of their curriculum was religion free, that is to say, mission free" (Dewey, 1997, p. 39). Vouchers, then, for those in religious schools, threaten the fundamental religious mission of the school and may prompt some private school leaders to reject students with vouchers.

Can Destroy Existing Independent, Religious Schools. Finally, some critics on the Right fear that vouchers would have the opposite effect of that which was intended: that instead of expanding and strengthening the nonpublic sector, vouchers would actually destroy the private schools in the United States. Here the mainstream Right and the hard Right are in sharp disagreement. The former seems willing to sacrifice a few independent schools by offering government subsidies for the many who would benefit from widely available choice under a voucher plan. Bast and Harmer (1997) state this utilitarian tradeoff quite well:

> An accurate understanding of the current system makes it plain that while the interests of the 12 percent in private schools or the 1 or 2 percent who might be hurt by a voucher plan are important and must not be overlooked, it is cruel indeed to overlook the calamity facing the 88 percent now trapped in government schools. Our first concern should be saving the millions of children now put at risk in government schools. And once that becomes our first concern, we understand the need for a plan to get from here to there, and the vital role that vouchers play in the movement for complete separation of school and state. (p. 24)

The Radical Middle Steals the Show

The last hope of substantial support for vouchers is the moderate Right, joined by some disenchanted liberals, and well-organized religious groups such as the Roman Catholic church. They find public schools unacceptable but are not easily convinced that total privatization with unregulated markets is the real answer. This group is deeply concerned about the apparent failure of public schooling, is interested in some forms of privatization, but refuses to embrace any privatization plan that would abandon the public school system. Thus, their interests are in reformation of the current educational system rather than the re-creation of another type of educational system that would just throw the baby out with the bath water. These reform efforts can be placed into five categories: choice within public school sector, choice at the margins, outsourcing, private subsidies for public education, and the overregulated voucher.

Choice Within the Public Schools. The most attractive, middle-of-the road reforms are those that introduce private-like changes without altering the basic control, funding, and involvement by the government. In fact, when most commentators and authors discuss choice in education, these observers are typically talking about the troika of choice, markets, and competition within the public education sector. They do not usually mean vouchers or other more radical forms of privatization such as Chubb and Moe's direct funding of public and private schooling through parental choice.

Whereas magnet schools, charter schools, alternative schools, open enrollment plans, and schools-within-schools all involve some parental choice, mild intrasystem competition, and the semblance of a market, these reforms are very much within the box of public, government-controlled schooling. Support for within-the-system choice runs a mile wide and an inch deep. According to Dougherty and Sostre (1992), although these soft forms of privatization have made such choice reforms more palatable to more mainstream and liberal groups, they have also made the coalition vulnerable and the possibility of more radical reforms less likely. These authors state: "The unusual coalition of conservatives, liberal policy analysts, urban educators, black and white parents, and the Catholic Church has put choice on the national [and state] agenda, but it also makes the movement very fragile" (p. 37). Thus, "the movement may be shattered by the deep fissures it carries within it, especially the division between those who favor government support for private school choice and those for whom only public school choice is acceptable" (p. 25).

Choice at the Margins. Charter schools in the United States and the City Technology Schools, or CTCs that are high schools in Great Britain, are examples of the work of the extreme center in action. Both types of schools are founded by private individuals and operated and managed privately, but receive full operational resources directly from the government. Hence, charters and CTCs are mixed models of school reform. As such, they are both an example of the viability of government–private sector cooperation and are hybrids that suffer from all the weaknesses of trying to live in both the private and public sectors. In both Britain and the United States, these quasi-public, quasi-private schools simply take their place among the variety of other government-controlled schools but do little, from the conservative perspective, to disconnect government control of education through the distribution of education dollars directly to parents and children.

Outsourcing Schools and Districts. Another moderate form of privatization is to contract out the operation of an existing public school: that is, public ownership and public funding, but private managerial know-how. Although the Edison Project is now running 78 schools, 12 of which are charter schools, efforts by groups like Alternative Education Inc. (AEI) to take over the management of an entire school system, the Hartford, Connecticut, public schools, were a disaster, nearly landing AEI in bankruptcy. The Hartford Board of Education still had control over the funds and made much of the general policy. The involvement of AEI in running a few dozen schools in Baltimore also ended in failure with the teachers union forcing the firm to operate within the same parameters as the public system.

Private Subsidies for Public Education. The radical center has been active in attracting private money into public schools. The best example is the Annenberg Challenge, a grant from Walter Annenberg to school systems to change processes and improve performance. This approach to school reform has several shortcomings as an alternative to vouchers: First, one wonders why the nation's second-largest government monopoly (public education comes just behind the health care system in expenditures) requires donations from the free enterprise system. Is it good practice to subsidize monopolies, as it encourages them to continue operating at low levels of efficiency and quality?

Second, the infusion of these dollars has a strange effect on the local and regional support system for privatization. In New York City, for example, the Manhattan Institute was a noted neoconservative think tank with close ties to the New York City public schools. When the Annenberg Challenge arrived, the Manhattan Institute joined the Annenberg board, and started raising $150 million. In so doing, the Institute became part of the education establishment, and was much less likely to lobby for total privatization and vouchers.

The Overregulated Voucher. Finally, the radical center has sought a voucher that is acceptable to its constituency: the coalition of centrists

who favor modest change but are attempting to balance choice and competition with issues of equity, acceptability, and pragmatism. Vouchers
crafted by the extreme center are so heavily regulated and controlled that
they cease to look like vouchers and become something else. It may be,
as Friedman (1955) called it, a "welfare voucher" or a form of "market
socialism."

Douglas D. Dewey (1997) explained what happened in California
when Proposition 174 failed and advocates for vouchers, including mil-
lionaire John Walton, tried to design a more popular version.

> Among the flaws, the plan included a gauntlet of qualifying requirements for
> voucher-redeeming private schools, including accreditation; teacher credentialing;
> and vaguely defined standards for hiring, admissions, enrollment, and curricula.
> And to ensure that the public trust would not be violated, the Walton Plan granted
> full authority to qualify voucher-redeeming private schools to the state superinten-
> dent of public instruction! (p. 32)

In effect, then, the strength of the radical center in the school reform effort is its ability to appear to get things done without threatening the
status quo in any fundamental way. These reforms drew their leverage-
from dissidents, reformers, middle-of-the-roaders, and the drive for privatization, not to mention the belated support from the teachers unions
and other education groups that figured it was easier to join and co-opt
the movement than to fight it. And once these moderate forms of privatization began, the unions and other privatization opponents could say,
"Look, we're already privatizing, offering choice, and prodding schools
into reform. Vouchers are now unnecessary, divisive, and likely to fail
politically. So why raise the issue?"

The Critics and the Political Process

This analysis now puts the pieces together: the interests, values, and
needs of diverse constituents with the political balancing process of trying to legislate educational reform. All of this happens within such a

broad spectrum of political beliefs about education reform and with the move to the Right. The results, in terms of legislating vouchers, have fallen short in all but a few, limited places.

We argue that with the move to the Right, made real by the regimes of Presidents Reagan and Bush, and continued in Gingrich's Congress and in a number of the states, the groups have now shifted to a point where the school reforms being tried are more conservative in nature. These include public school choice such as open enrollment, magnet schools, charter schools, and experiments with radical decentralization (site-based management, decision making, and budgeting). All of these types of reforms change the public system without altering the power structure or threatening its existence. And, in most cases, these privatization-like efforts have acted as release valves for the pressures to sell the school, move to vouchers, and thus to separate education from government ownership and control.

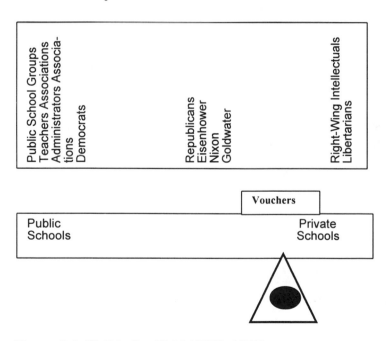

Figure 9.1: Shift to the Right (1950–1970).

Figure 9.1 shows the array of political forces from Left to Right, with their relative postures on issues of education reform. From 1950 to 1980, virtually all but a very small number of Libertarian and ultraconservative critics favored government-run education. Certainly, Republican presidents like Eisenhower, Nixon, and even as late as Gerald Ford, hardly attacked the notion of public or government education. True, the public schools in the 1950s themselves were more conservative in comparison to the post-1960s: students repeated or heard prayers regularly and repeated the Pledge of Allegiance daily. Corporal punishment was permissible, and students as minors had weak to limited rights of free speech and expression.

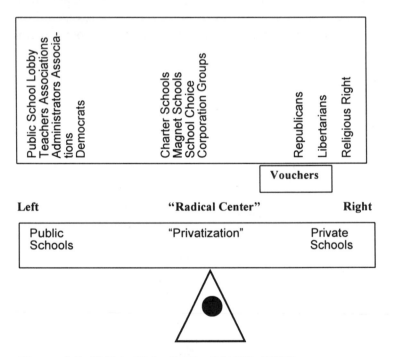

Figure 9.2: Shift to "Privatization" (1971–2000).

Friedman's 1955 voucher suggestion was hardly noticed as the public school system struggled to clean up its own problems, including such court decisions and laws as the *Brown v. Board of Education decisions* (1954, 1955) ordering the desegregation of the nation's schools; *Serrano v. Priest* (1971), a case in California that declared illegal the inequalities resulting from uneven distribution of the dollar value of local property, citing the equal protection clause of the 14th Amendment of the U.S. Constitution; and the rights of the handicapped, that required the least restrictive environment and equitable treatment for challenged children from ages 3 to 21.

Perhaps public educators were so busy trying to solve these monumental racial and social problems that they hardly noticed all the intellectual chatter about freedom, markets, choice, and competition. Thus, prior to the 1980s, as shown in Fig. 9.1, virtually all groups—left, right, and center—stacked up on the public school side (left) of the fulcrum. Between 1981 and 1992, roughly the Reagan and Bush years, however, the combined effects of such reports as *A Nation at Risk* (National Commission on Excellence in Education, 1983), the internationalization of educational comparisons (with the United States falling behind Japan, Germany, and other modern nations in achievement)—a wakeup call, not unlike the launching of Sputnik in 1956—all worked to prod conservatives to question the government's monopoly over public education.

Figure 9.2 shows the new alignment, with Republicans, some moderate Democrats, some religious groups (particularly the religious Right groups), and some mainstream business and commercial associations (U.S. Chamber of Commerce, Business Roundtable), and even academics beginning to challenge the wisdom of continuing the government dominance over education. After all, some said, that the active effort to fix the nation's schools from Truman through Nixon had produced very little improvement in American education, or so people thought. However, the choice movement of the 1980s, leading to open enrollment, magnet schools, and school-site management, had taken the edge off the privatization efforts. At the same time, members of the hard Right fought among themselves concerning the wisdom of keeping any government role in education at all.

Figure 9.2 also shows the rather narrow, divided band of politicians and educators even interested in vouchers. Only under very restricted circumstances—small numbers of children and no religiously sponsored schools—did the voucher experiments in Milwaukee, New York City, and Cleveland even get off the ground. It is unclear at this point, however, whether any states will adopt a voucher (South Carolina came within two votes of passing a voucher bill in the state legislature), or whether major cities such as Baltimore, Detroit, Chicago, or Washington, D.C. will create a voucher plan in a desperate attempt to solve their educational crises (Calvert Institute, 1997). Perhaps the success of the burgeoning charter school movement, adopting tougher standards to raise the quality of education, and other in-house reforms will attenuate the need for vouchers. In addition, credible research on voucher experiments in Cleveland, Milwaukee, and New York City are just beginning and many questions remain unanswered.

The Future Is Now

What will the future bring? Surely the conspiracy of coincidences of political action will break down and changes will occur. The voucher concept is too simple, logical, and real not to take full root somewhere. Thus, given our discussion in this chapter, we make the following ten predictions, any combination of which can pave the way for making a major voucher initiative a reality.

The Collapse of Radical Center Reforms. One thesis of this analysis is that the milder forms of privatization—such as public school choice, magnet schools and charter schools, and outsourcing school management—were effective at defusing, displacing, and delaying the drive for stronger medicine, such as vouchers. What happens if charter and magnet schools are too limited, weak, and ineffective to solve the major problems of the education of the urban poor in the United States? What will be the consequences if these public-sector choice options do not solve the educational and related social problems? The embrace of public-choice options by the liberal Left has raised the stakes on school reform to even higher levels. Will the extreme centrists join with some of their more right-wing comrades and give vouchers a try? Could happen.

The Left Loosens Up. Another development is also possible. What happens if National Education Association and American Federation of Teachers, the National Associations of Elementary and Secondary School Principals, and other groups begin to represent educators from charter schools, and even a few schools taking vouchers? Will these groups begin to lighten up in their constant attack on vouchers and give them a chance?

Albert Shanker, before his death, was beginning to favor choice; and educators of color, working in inner cities, may respond to their constituents and support vouchers for the poor and disadvantaged. In an effort to have some voice and control over the inevitable appearance of voucher plans in several states and major cities, will these public school associations and groups want to have some role, input, and influence on the specifics of voucher plans? Would they join the voucher movement much as they have done with the charter school movement in numerous states? Thus, once the liberal Left school-establishment groups issue fewer objections to vouchers, the spread of ideologies ranging from Left to Right may narrow sufficiently to make a political compromise feasible and real choice experimentation with vouchers possible.

The Right-Wing Coalesces. As the CATO Institute papers by Dewey (1997) and Bast and Harmer (1997) indicate, the Right is beginning to realize that internecine battles only weaken its voice and destroy its basic program. For these groups on the Right, will vouchers usher in the dream of less government and more family control? It depends on the nature of the voucher plan. But the hard Right spokespeople still maintain that vouchers are the "camel's nose" in the tent of government control over private and religious schools. Those nonpublic schools trying to remain independent (refusing to take vouchers) will be under enormous pressure because families can take their chit to another private school, greatly reducing their costs. Once the Right stops the in-fighting, this group can have enormous influence, as the Reagan, Bush, and Gingrich years indicate.

The General Shift to the Right Continues. We have shown how the strengthening of the neoconservative position in U.S. politics has made some privatization possible and has put vouchers within reach. Should this trend continue and spread, the voucher option will become a more and more mainstream idea and acceptable to wider and wider audiences. In New York City, when the Roman Catholic cardinal offered to take 1,000 public school kids to relieve overcrowding in the New York City public schools, the city's mayor, Rudolph Giuliani, accepted immediately and offered, in an instinctive moment, to pay for the tuition out of city funds. When the civil liberties groups went ballistic, His Honor thought again and helped to raise the money privately. All of a sudden, at the suggestion of a Catholic cardinal, a moderate Republican mayor in the nation's largest city school system was raising private money (much of it from Jewish donors), to send African American Protestant public school students to Catholic schools free of charge.

Urban Education Failures Continue. Much of this discussion is premised on the belief that large, monopolistic urban public systems cannot improve themselves. To save the cities, to give the poorest, most disenfranchised children in the United States the same opportunities as the middle class, vouchers may be the only hope of really shaking up the urban school systems and establishing pockets of excellence. As Doyle, Deshryver & Munro (1997) explained: "Arguments about economic efficiency have not carried the day. Neither have arguments about religious liberty or simple morality. What remains is an argument not yet widely made. Good schools are the lifeblood of the city. Save the schools and we save the cities. Lose the schools and we lose our cities" (p. 29). Vouchers may help our cities most, thus extending the opportunity for poor children to attend schools with strong, cohesive religious values, such as many urban Catholic and Protestant schools exhibit.

The Legal–Constitutional Barriers Come Down. The courts have issued some startling decisions on church–state issues of late. First, in Wisconsin, the state supreme court issued a stunning ruling June 10, 1998 that the voucher plan, The Milwaukee Parental Choice Program of 1995, was constitutional (*Jackson v. Benson,*1998). The *Jackson* decision was appealed and the U.S. Supreme Court refused to review the case, letting it stand. Recall the reversal of the *Aguilar v. Felton* (1985) decision banning public school teachers from helping parochial school children on the premises under the Title I/Chapter 1 federal program, something of a breakthrough. In *Agostini v. Felton* (1997), the U.S. Supreme Court overturned *Aguilar* and found that the use of this type public resource to help students at the private school neither (a) established religion, (b) prohibited the free exercise of religion, nor (c) "entangled the Church and State."

Vouchers: Starting Small, Growing Larger. The snowball thesis is also possible. Much like the spread of charter school legislation from a single state in 1991 to 33 states in 1998, so too might voucher laws take off. Perhaps this growth explains in part the vigorous opposition to voucher plans in Milwaukee, Cleveland, and New York City by the liberal Left. In June 1998, Congress passed a final version of an education savings account bill that would let families use tax-free savings to pay for books, computers, tutors, and other K–12 school costs, including tuition for private schools. Families, relatives, or even corporations could put up to $2,000 a year into a tax-free account for education, a strategy perhaps for getting the middle class on board. However, President Clinton has vetoed the bill.

Already, vouchers are in action: In Milwaukee, 1,600 poor children receive a subsidy averaging $3,600 to attend private, nonreligious schools; Cleveland provides aid of up to $2,500 to parents of about 2,000 public school pupils from impoverished families who can select a private or religious school; Minnesota has now expanded an existing income tax deduction for private school tuition and other expenses (in the public schools) to provide tax credits of up to $1,000 per child for families with modest incomes for textbooks, home computers, transportation, summer school, and tutoring—a voucher by another name; New York City went the private voucher route, raising money to send 1,000 public school students to Catholic schools; and in May 1998, the Houston School District approved a plan that allows failing students in low performing schools "to attend a district-approved private school at the District's expense ("Houston School District OKs Private School Plan," p. 13).

The Research and Data Appear to Be Supportive. Part of the shortcomings with voucher research is that there have not been sufficient numbers in enough locations to test their effectiveness. Walberg and Bast (1993) explain that "the definitive test of education choice has not been conducted" (p. 117). Will they work? Studies in Milwaukee, Cleveland, and New York City underway, by Greene, Howell, and Peterson (1997) and others, indicate that they might not only develop stronger academic performance but also build human virtues. Glenn (1992) asserted even eight years ago that It has become clear through experience and recent research that schools operated by religious organizations and other groups can be at least as successful as the state in developing civic virtue" (p. 62).

Social Justice and Equity. What would happen if all children had vouchers, in some form, and could act on them? By denying the poor and disadvantaged the same opportunities to secure an adequate education as the wealthy and advantaged, a social injustice occurs. A sense of fairness dictates that a child's chance for learning and the exercise of parental choice in the upbringing of children should not be a function of family wealth. Coons (1992) argues for family subsidies, not as an economic imperative (although efficiency might increase) and a stimulant to growth (although school productivity might indeed rise) but as a human and moral issue. He writes, "Shifting educational authority from government to parents is a policy that rests upon basic beliefs about the dignity of the person, the rights of children, and the sanctity of the family; it is a shift that also promises a harvest of social trust as the experience of responsibility is extended to all incoming classes. So far, that part of the message is not making it in the current great debate about schooling [and vouchers]" (p. 193).

Thus, in a truly equitable society, the role of government would be to create, sustain, and expand equal educational opportunities for all, and not to fight against the expansion of such choices. The middle and upper classes will always buy their way out of trouble and into a school of their choosing. It is the poor who need assistance from the government to ensure social justice, not by restricting the market and educational choice, but by making the marketplace truly equitable.

The Political Economy of Education Is Restructured. Ultimately, can public education be that much different from the private economic sector? The true role of government might better be to break up monopolies in education, not create and protect them, just as such authorities have done in virtually every other field of social and economic endeavor. Vouchers would be one way to privatize and de-institutionalize education, following somewhere behind the radical changes in the commercial and industrial sectors. Would the school market respond, producing new options? In turn, would the proper role of government be to protect and expand the market, giving start-up grants to new market entries, so that every child would have a wide choice of schools and school types to attend? Holland does this. Any 36 families can open a school and the government subsidizes the start-up costs and the tuition.

Finally, one wonders whether a state-run education system (even though it is ostensibly local and democratic) can survive in a nation or a world that is becoming more capitalist, global, competitive, entrepreneurial, and decentralized. We think not. Education vouchers, then, are inevitable as the coincidences change. It is now just a question of when, where, in what form, and under what circumstances.

References

Agostini v. Felton, 118 S. Ct. 40 (1997).
Aguilar v. Felton, 473 U.S. 373 (1985).

Bast, J. L., & Harmer, D. (1997). The libertarian case for vouchers and some observations on the anti-voucher separationists *Policy Analysis, 269*(2), 4–28.

Brown v. Board of Education, 347 U.S. 483 (1954).

Brown v. Board of Education, 349 U.S. 294 (1955).

CATO Institute (1997, March 12). Vouchers and education freedom: A debate. *Policy Analysis*, 269, 2, 78–89.

Chubb, J. E., & Moe, T. M. (1992). The ideology of consumership and the coming deregulation of the public school systems. In P. W. Cookson, Jr. (Ed.), *The choice controversy* (pp. 83–99). Newbury Park, CA: Corwin.

Chubb, J. E., & Moe, T. M. (1994). The forest and the trees: A response to our critics. In E. Rasell & R. Rothstein (Eds.), *School choice: Examining the evidence*, Washington, DC: Economic Policy Institute, pp. 219–240.

Cookson, P.W. Jr. (Ed.) (1992). *The choice controversy*. Newbury Park, CA: Corwin.

Coons, J. E. (1992). School choice as simple justice. *First Things*, *22*(15), 193–200.

Cooper, B. S. (1992 August 5). School reform meets the 'radical middle', *Education Week XI, No. 40,* 76.

Dewey, D. D. (1997). Separating school and state: A prudential analysis of tax-funded vouchers. *Policy Analysis, 269*(2), 29–48.

Dougherty, K. J., & Sostre, L. (1992). Minerva and the market: The sources of the movement for school choice. In P.W. Cookson, Jr., (Ed.), *The choice controversy.* (pp. 24–45). Newbury Park, CA: Corwin.

Doyle, D. P., Deshryer, D. A., & Munro, D. P. (1997, August). *Reforming the schools to save the city: Part I: Toward a new common school for Baltimore*. Issue Brief Vol. 1, No. 1. Baltimore: Calvert Institute.

Elmore, R. F. (1986). *Choice in public education*. Madison, WI: The University of Wisconsin, and New Brunswick, NJ: Rutgers University—Center for Policy Research in Education (CPRE).

Friedman, M. (1955). The role of government in education. In R.A. Solo (Ed.), *Economics and the public interest* (pp. 127–134). New Brunswick, NJ: Rutgers University Press.

Glenn, C. L. (1992). Who should own the schools? *Equity and Choice*, *9*(1), 59–63.

Greene, J. P., Howell, W. G., & Peterson, P. E. (1997, September 18). Cleveland shatters myth about school choice, *The Wall Street Journal*, p. 23.

Houston school district oks private school plan. (1998, June). *School Reform News*, 2, 6, 11.

Jackson v. Benson, No. 97-0270, 1998 WL 301189 (June 10, 1998).

James, E. (1990). Private education and redistributive subsidies in Australia. In W. Gormely (Ed.), *Privatization and its alternatives* (pp. 101–121). Madison: University of Wisconsin Press.

James, E. (1991). Public policies toward private education: An international comparison. *International Journal of Educational Research, 15*(5), 131–41.

James, E. (1994). The private-public division of responsibility for education. In *International encyclopedia of education* (2nd ed. pp. 78–85) Oxford, UK: Elsevier Science.

National Commission on Excellence in Education. (1983). *A nation at risk.* Washington, DC: Author.

Serrano v. Priest, 487 P.2d 1241 (Cal. 1971).

U.S. Department of Education, National Center for Education Statistics. (1996). *The condition of education*, 1996. Washington, DC: Author.

Walberg, H. J., & Bast, J. L. (1993). School choice: The essential reform. *Cato Journal, 13*(1), 101–121.

Wells, A. S., & Crain, R. (1992). Do parents choose school quality or school status? A sociological theory of free market education. In P. W. Cookson, Jr. (Ed.), *The choice controversy* (pp. 65–82). Newbury Park, CA: Corwin.

Chapter Ten

Expanding the Third Sector in Education?
A Critical View

MANFRED WEISS

The fiscal stress and the growing legitimization problems of state institutions that many countries are facing have led to an increased interest in alternative ways of providing public services.

As a result, the nonprofit sector (third sector, voluntary or independent sector) has received special attention as an alternative to both state and market provision. This development is also reflected in a growing research interest. Different disciplines have contributed to the theoretical foundation of the nonprofit sector. Microeconomic theories, which were introduced more than a decade ago by Henry Hansmann and Burton Weisbrod, are of particular relevance.

In explaining the existence of nonprofit organizations in the school sector the heterogeneity thesis and entrepreneurship theories developed and empirically tested by Estelle James (1993) deserve special attention. The central underlying assumption is that in developed countries the size of the third sector in education is directly related to differentiated demand and nonprofit supply, stemming mainly from cultural heterogeneity, especially religious heterogeneity. "On the demand side, differentiated tastes about ideology lead people voluntarily to opt out of the public system even when space is available, to secure the kind of education they prefer. On the supply side, private schools are a convenient institution for diverse non-profit-maximizing religious organizations to use in their competition for a larger market share of 'souls'" (James, 1993, p. 574).

Empirical tests of the heterogeneity and entrepreneurship theory provide mixed results. Whereas James (1993) found some evidence for the explanatory power of conceptual models based on that theory in cross-national analyses, a recent comparative study by Anheier (1997) did not find a relationship between multicultural heterogeneity (degree of ethno-

161

linguistic variety) and the quantitative importance of the nonprofit sector in education.

The limitations of the heterogeneity and entrepreneurship theory (and other economic theories) become particularly evident when looking at the long-term development of the third sector in education. As plurality and cultural diversity have significantly increased in many Western societies in the last two or three decades, according to the theory this trend should be noticeable (with a certain timelag) in a corresponding expansion of the third sector in education.

Statistics on the development of the proportion of primary and secondary private school enrollments in Organization for Economic Co-Operation and Development (OECD) countries do not reveal a clear trend (see Tables 10.1 and 10.2 for details): In some countries the third sector expanded (e.g., Australia, Denmark), in others the enrollment rate remained constant or even declined (New Zealand, Spain).

Even though a differentiated quantitative analysis of this pattern cannot be provided here, the assumption that reality does not follow a single theory appears to have sufficient face validity. Some countries show anomalies according to heterogeneity and entrepreneurship theory: Their plural and multicultural character is not reflected in a strong third sector. Unless we content ourselves with idiosyncratic explanations (which historians might favor), other theories have to be considered, theories that sufficiently take into account the mediating influence of the specific institutional context of societies. This context, which manifests itself (inter alia) in legal and financing regulations, can restrict or foster the demand and supply-driven development of the third sector as hypothesized by heterogeneity and entrepreneurship theory (see tables 10.1 and 10.2 at the end of this chapter).

To explain third sector differences found in international comparisons, institutional theory has received special attention in recent years. Following—and in part extending—the work of Esping-Andersen (1990), the implications of different welfare state concepts for the formation, function, and state of the third sector have been expounded and partly tested empirically (e.g., Anheier, 1997). This theoretical approach in its basic version distinguishes between a *liberal* and a *conservative-*

statist welfare state concept. A more differentiated typology developed by Anheier (1997) additionally includes a *social democratic* and *corporatist* model.

In the liberal and social democratic model, the state and the third sector are regarded as competitors, as alternative mechanisms for meeting collective needs. In the liberal model with its corresponding market orientation (represented e.g., by the United States), state interventions are limited, the nonprofitsector can freely develop and is mainly privately funded. The social democratic model is characterized by a strong social commitment of the state (high social expenditures) which at the same time restrains private activity in the nonprofit sector (e.g., Sweden). In the case of the statist situation, a strong state position coincides with limited social commitment and a restricted scope of action for nonprofit organizations (e.g., Japan). In contrast to this, the corporatist model is characterized by a close cooperation between government and religious and secular associations. The third sector is more or less an integral part of the state system, often funded to a significant extent from public sources and subject to extreme regulations and intensive control (e.g., Germany).

This typology developed by institutional theory provides a better understanding of third sector differences between countries. It also allows a more differentiated answer to the question of when the third sector can be expected to be superior in stimulating innovations and improving system performance in education. This question will be addressed using Germany as an example.

The Private School Sector in Germany

The corporatist concept of third sector in education is laid down in Article 7 of the Federal Constitution. According to Section 1, "the entire school system is under the supervision of the state." This also applies to private schools to which the Constitution explicitly refers in Article 7, Section 4. It guarantees a right to private schooling. By establishing Article 7, Section 4, on the one hand the legislators clearly reject a state monopoly on schools with the aim of creating the basis for a diverse school system. On the other hand they want the state to retain responsibility for the whole school system, and for that reason they defined criteria that private schools have to meet in order to be recognized as "substitute" schools *(Ersatzschulen)* with a legal right to state financial aid. These schools must be equivalent to state schools, that is, not inferior in terms of their educational goals, facilities, and staff qualifications. Furthermore, these schools may not discriminate against students on the basis of parental income (see, for details, Weiss & Mattern, 1991). The state is legally obliged to officially recognize a substitute school if it meets the criterion of equivalence. This state recognition does not, however, automatically imply that substitute schools are entitled to award certificates and credentials (e.g., to confer the *Abitur,* the right to university entrance) like state schools. They are entitled to do this only if they are state-approved, and in practice this means that a high degree of conformity with state schools is a precondition. It is evident that meeting the criteria laid down in Article 7, Section 4 and the private schools' interest in acquiring state approval leaves little room for significant deviations from the mainstream; in other words, private schools resemble state schools to a large degree.

The constitutional context reflecting the corporatist third sector concept in Germany outlined above is important for understanding the status and role of the German private school sector and the prospects of strengthening its role discussed in the following sections.

Statistics on the German Private School Sector

In international comparisons the German corporatist third sector concept in education is reflected in a proportion of private school enrollments that is significantly below the OECD average (17%). In 1994, in the old Federal Republic, some 460,000 students attended private schools in the general education sector. They represented about 6% of the total school population in this sector. In the new *Laender* only 1% are enrolled in private schools—in other words, unification has reduced the nationwide percentage.

The comparison of the development of enrollment rates in the private and public sector between 1985 and 1994 shows that in the private sector the increase amounting to 12.3% was about twice as high as that in the public sector. This difference is in part due to the fact that the various schooltypes are not equally represented in both sectors. If we restrict the comparison to the *Gymnasien*, the dominant schooltype in the private sector (in 1994 almost 45% of the private school students in the former Federal Republic attended this schooltype), it becomes evident that the public sector experienced a 4% decline in enrollments in the period under consideration, whereas the enrollments in the private sector increased by 5%. Although private schools have become more attractive in Germany, there is, however, no boom, as is sometimes claimed by the media.

Of course, these figures only reflect realized educational demand; the latent aspirations are significantly higher: According to surveys (Rolff, Bauer & Klemm,1994, p. 53), almost one fifth of the parents in the old *Laender* want their children to attend a private school. The main reason for this mismatch can be found in the frequent lack of a local private school supply rather than in deterrent fees.

When compared according to providing body, the largest group of private schools (general and vocational) turns out to be denominational schools, which enroll about three fourths of all private school students (50% Roman Catholic, 25% Protestant); roughly 10% attend Rudolf Steiner (Waldorf) schools, and the remaining 15% are enrolled in non-denominational vocational schools, boarding schools and international schools. With the exception of some types of alternative schools that were initiated by parent groups, third sector schools in Germany are not the result of civil society activities.

The relatively small proportion of students enrolled in private schools is surprising in view of the substantial public financial aid substitute schools receive. Significant public funding is another characteristic of a corporatist third sector concept. Nationwide public funds on the average cover about 85% of the recurrent costs. For private schools without boarders in the general school sector student fees are only of minor importance: denominational schools charge either no fees at all or only a small amount of no more than 100 DM per month. Rudolf Steiner schools charge an average of 250 DM per month, socially graded according to parental income. Considerably higher fees are paid at international schools (1000 DM per month) and especially at private nondenominational boarding schools, where fees range from 2000 to 3500 DM per month.

Expanding the Third Sector: A Promising Path?

Strengthening the third sector seems to be a promising strategy in view of the increasing pluralization of German society and its corresponding differentiation of educational preferences, the unsatisfactory quality standards of the public school system, which the Third International Math and Science Studies (TIMSS) plainly uncovered (Baumert, Lehmann, & Lehrke, 1997), and the situation of fiscal austerity in education (Weiss, 1998). Will this strategy lead to greater efficiency in the educational sector, foster community building in schools, and stimulate pedagogical innovations as expected by its proponents? Or will it result in a more segregated educational system as claimed by critics? These questions will be addressed in the following section.

The Impact on Costs and Effectiveness. Shifting educational production to third sector institutions is recommended to cope with public budget constraints. Notwithstanding the fact that private provision cannot be enforced by the state, the expected relief of public budgets is quite uncertain. Because private schools would strive to acquire state approval, substantial public subsidies would accrue. If these schools provided educational services at the same costs as public schools, private contributions to their financing would be necessary, that is, an expanding third sector would lead to a greater privatization of costs. This could be avoided if private schools operated at a lower cost than public schools. In this case, even their full subsidization would relieve public budgets without increasing the private cost burden. A lower cost level of private schools is often asserted or tacitly assumed; reliable cost comparisons are, however, missing (Weiss, 1988). With regard to the most important cost item, teacher salaries, there are no significant differences between public and private schools. The cost advantage of private schools resulting from lower administrative costs and a more intensive use of voluntary work is offset by diseconomies of scale due to their smaller size. From a macrolevel perspective, further cost disadvantages can be expected to accrue in the course of a significant shift of educational production to third sector institutions, because this would make a planned coordination of school supply aimed at an economical utilization of resources increasingly difficult.

Because no sectoral achievement comparisons are available in Germany, any conclusions concerning the impact of an expanding third sector on system performance must be speculative. The specific attractiveness that some alternative private schools (such as Waldorf schools) enjoy might be regarded as an indicator of high performance. Until now there have been, however, no empirical studies that convincingly demonstrate that the success of these schools is rooted in the specific treatment students experience rather than in the favorable ensemble of contextual circumstances (highly motivated students, high parent involvement) as a result of selectivity and self-selectivity. There is also no evidence for the often stated improvement of public schools when they are exposed to the competition of more efficient private schools on local educational quasi-markets.

The Ambivalence of Value Communities. The selectivity mechanisms that became effective in the third sector have ambivalent consequences. On the one hand, value communities develop that—as we know from school-effectiveness research—positively affect school climate and reduce conflict potential. This is generally recognized as a major advantage of choice schools, particularly in the private sector. On the other hand, by creating value communities through selectivity and self-selectivity private schools inevitably tend to become monocultures, settings providing few stimulating experiences. Multicultural education, for example, will hardly succeed in a culturally homogeneous school milieu that only permits teaching about cultural differences in an abstract cognitive way, not, however, allowing students to learn about these differences in direct cultural contact.

The homogeneous value community found predominantly in private schools is the result of boundary creation, of excluding diverse voices and perspectives: Only those parents and students come together or are accepted as community members who share the same norms, beliefs, and values, those who do not conform have to find their community elsewhere. This concept of community is an integral part of the school choice paradigm that has become the driving force of school reform in many countries.

It fundamentally differs from the concept of community of difference and dialogue that has been suggested recently by Shields and Seltzer (1997) as a more appropriate conceptualization of the notion of community in schools. It is based on the idea of schools as microcosms or reflections of the wider community, which share its conflicts and commonalities, differences and similarities. Under such conditions a moral community of difference can develop within schools "in which authentic dialogue is the norm and the diversity of beliefs, values, assumptions, and practices is exposed" (Shields & Seltzer, 1997, pp. 432–433). Unity in this case comes from the "celebration of diversity" (p. 436), not from its elimination, which is characteristic of value communities.

Some scholars hold the opinion that the institutionalization of discourse through such a concept of community is necessary for the survival of a pluralistic democracy that is imperiled through progressive fragmentation (e.g., Bryck, 1988; Ottersbach & Yildiz, 1997). Private choice schools with their emphasis on value communities do not provide a context for such a discourse. Their understanding of pluralism is one of a "separate way pluralism" (Preuss-Lausitz, 1995).

Educational Innovation. It is one of the persistent myths that the third sector in education has a monopoly on pedagogical innovations from which the state school system could benefit. This innovatory function was of some relevance for independent schools founded in the wake of reformist pedagogies at the beginning of this century. For the large majority of existing private schools this does not hold true. These are mostly denominational schools which are not known as places of pedagogical innovations. The prevailing milieu in these schools (particularly the Catholic schools) is characterized by a conservative pedagogical orientation and an emphasis on achievement in a traditional sense. Their philosophy is not to secure pluralism of viewpoints but a homogeneity of values. Such a milieu is preferred by parents who complain about the lack of clear and stable values in the public school sector.

Within the group of nondenominational schools, Waldorf schools experienced a substantial increase in attractiveness in recent years, especially among the growing number of well educated, ecologically oriented, middle-class families. The dogmatic understanding of the Waldorf pedagogy finds, however, increasingly less acceptance in educational science (e.g., Ullrich, 1991). In this respect Waldorf schools resemble the majority of alternative (free) schools, which are remnants of the period of antiauthoritarian education in the early 1970s. They operate in a small market niche devoid of any influence on the present reform discussions in education. It is difficult to comprehend why these schools should energize school reform in the public sector.

The opinion that private schools in general have an innovatory function for the public schools because they are (in the perception of private choice proponents) the natural terrain for pedagogical experiments meets with another objection: the limited possibility of generalizing experiences made in specific private school settings. Transferring educational concepts that have been successful in private schools to public schools is often prevented by the absence of the necessary preconditions, for example, parents who are willing or able to become intensively involved in school life and decision-making, which is a constituent element, for example, of the Waldorf school concept. These preconditions can be established more easily at private schools due to their greater autonomy in selecting desirable customers. Whereas this is regarded as a legitimate strategy of private schools, in the public sector any attempt to secure the success of reforms through deliberate client selection would be rated as a severe violation of basic equity principles. In other words: Criteria that are relevant for the evaluation of public school reforms are not applied to the private sector.

Social and Ethnic Segregation. The homogenization of school milieus through client selection is not only questionable from a pedagogical point of view. An even more serious problem is the secondary selection according to social and ethnic criteria often accompanying this process. Empirical evidence suggests that even in those countries where private schools receive the same funds as state schools or significant public financial aid, disintegrating effects and inequalities can be observed for certain social and ethnic groups. For the Netherlands, an OECD report concludes that "free choice has made it easy for Dutch parents to avoid schools with minority children, increasing segregation in some of the larger cities" (Seashore Louis, 1991, p. 29). This finding is supported by the results of a survey of school principals (Karsten, 1994). For France, a significant under-representation of immigrant children at private secondary schools is reported in surveys (Lebon, 1985). A recent study presented by the Institute for National Statistics and Economic Studies (INSEE) found a high social selectivity at Catholic schools.

As regards the situation in Germany, there is no empirical information available from representative surveys. Data for the City State of Berlin suggest, however, that the private school sector evades fulfilling the integration function expected from state schools (Preuss-Lausitz, 1995). Figures for 1993 show that the proportion of foreign students enrolled at private schools (amounting to 8%) is almost 5 points below the proportion of this group in the city's total school population. At Waldorf schools, 3.4% of the students are of foreign origin. Less than 1% of the Turkish school population in Berlin attend these schools. Nationwide (including the new *Laender*) the proportion of foreign students at Waldorf schools was 2.1% in 1994, representing 0.2% of all foreign students in Germany. A closer look at the composition of the foreign student population at these schools shows that only 15% to 20% come from recruitment countries. The figures for comparable school types in the public sector are higher: At primary schools almost every tenth child is from a foreign family, the proportion at *Gymnasien* amounts to 5%. Although at this type of secondary school social and ethnic integration is still insufficiently achieved, the private sector is doing even worse.

It appears that the choice of a private school is largely an option for a school with few children from working-class families and ethnic minorities. This cannot be attributed to the fact that private schools are not fully state funded as claimed by their representatives. It has, instead, much to do with deliberate selectivity practiced by the schools (which the Constitution concedes to them) as well as self-selectivity, that is, the interest of parents choosing a private school to place their children into the preferred social and cultural milieu (of the middleclass). Private schools are in a better position to meet these parental preferences than public schools. This is, however, achieved at the expense of greater social and ethnic selectivity.

Conclusion

The differences in size, structure, and orientation of the third sector that we can observe across countries cannot be explained by a single theory. Recently economic theories have been supplemented by institutional theory, which emphasizes the specific institutional context in which nonprofit organizations are embedded. The corporatist third sector concept existing in Germany manifests itself in a private school sector that is relatively small, subject to state supervision, and publicly funded to a significant extent. Article 7, Section 4 of the Federal Constitution regulating the establishment of private (substitute) schools was introduced with the intention of avoiding a state monopoly and to secure a diverse school system. Actually, however, the restrictive interpretation of the approval requirements laid down in the Constitution act in the opposite direction—a further expansion of the third sector would hardly contribute to greater plurality in educational supply.

New impulses for school reforms cannot be expected from strengthening the role of private schools. At present, in accordance with international experiences, it is the public school sector, partly relieved from bureaucratic control, that seems to stimulate school reform. In Germany, several *Laender* have decided on strengthening the individual school's autonomy by granting a greater scope of action in pedagogical, curricular, organizational, and resource allocation matters, and they have amended their school laws recently. Schools have been enabled to develop specific curricular or pedagogical profiles and thus to become more responsive to their environment. In international comparison, school autonomy in Germany, allowing only moderate deviations from the mainstream, does not appear to be very spectacular. If one takes into account the strong German statist tradition, however, this development has the quality of a shift in paradigm. The process of deregulation and decentralization initiated can be expected to activate an innovative potential in the public school system and bring about greater diversity. This development will bring public schools functionally closer to private schools with regard to meeting differentiated demand. In contrast to these, the public good orientation remains, however, a binding frame of reference for the evaluation of reforms. The politico-administrative system can intervene if these reforms should turn out to have detrimental consequences for the school system as a whole and if they should violate overarching societal interests.

Notwithstanding obvious deficiencies of the public school sector with regard to its integration success, the third sector seems to have a built-in mechanism to increase social, cultural, ethnic, and religious segregation even in a corporatist institutional context. With regard to the process of fragmentation that many societies are currently experiencing, strengthening the third sector would be counterproductive in that this process would be reinforced. This conclusion will not be shared by those who hold the position that schools are agents of family whose primary concern is to please their clients (Chubb & Moe, 1990, p. 184). This position is in accordance with the zeitgeist. A contrary position, which emphasizes the public good dimension of schooling, might regain ground when the fatal consequences of the progressive societal disintegration process become fully apparent.

References

Anheier, H. K. (1997). Der Nonprofit-Sektor im internationalen Vergleich: Ein theoretischer Versuch. In R. Schauer, H. K. Anheier, & E.-B. Blümle (Eds.), *Der Nonprofit Sektor im Aufwind—zur wachsenden Bedeutung von Nonprofit-Organisationen auf nationaler und internationaler Ebene* (pp. 13–56). Linz: Trauner.

Baumert, J., Lehmann, R., & Lehrke, M. (1997). *TIMSS — Mathematisch-natur- wissenschaftlicher Unterricht im internationalen Vergleich*. Berlin: MPIB.

Bryck, A. S. (1988). Musings on the moral life of schools. *American Journal of Education, 2,* 256–290.

Chubb, J. E., & Moe, T. M. (1990). *Politics, markets, and America's schools*. Washington, DC: Brookings Institution.

Esping-Andersen, G. (1990). *The three worlds of welfare capitalism*. Princeton, NJ: Princeton University Press.

Grosskopf, S., Hayes, K., Taylor, L., & Weber, W. (1995, June). *On competition and school efficiency*. Paper presented at the 70th Annual Western Economic Association Meeting, San Diego, CA.

Hoxley, C. M. (1994). *Does competition among public schools benefit students and taxpayers?* (Working Paper No. 4979). Cambridge, MA: National Bureau of Economic Research.

James, E. (1993). Why do different countries choose a different public-private mix of educational services. *The Journal of Human Resources, 3,* 571–592.

Karsten, S. (1994). Policy on ethnic segregation in a system of choice: The case of the Netherlands. *Journal of Education Policy, 3,* 211–225.

Lebon, A. (1985). Second-generation foreigners in France. In R. Rogers (Ed.), *Guests come to stay: The effects of European labor migration on sending and receiving countries* (pp. 135–158). Boulder, CO: Westview Press.

Ottersbach, M., & Yildiz, E. (1997). Der Kommunitarismus: eine Gefahr für das Projekt der pluralistischen Demokratie? *Soziale Welt, 48,* 291–312.

Preuss-Lausitz, U. (1995). Private und Freie Schulen—Besser als die öffentliche Schule? *Die Deutsche Schule, 4,* 447–462.

Rolff, H. G., Bauer, K., & Klemm, K.. (Eds.). (1994). *Jahrbuch der Schulentwicklung* (Vol. 8). Weinheim and München: Juventa.

Seashore Louis, K. (1991). Choice and centralism in Dutch education. *The OECD Observer, 172,* 27–30.

Shields, C. M., & Seltzer, P. A. (1997). Complexities and paradoxes of community: Toward a more useful conceptualization of community. *Educational Administration Quarterly, 4,* 413–439.

Smith, K. B., & Meier, K. J. (1995). School choice: Panacea or Pandora's box. *Phi Delta Kappan, 4,* 312–316.

Ullrich, H. (1991). *Waldorfpädagogik und okkulte Weltanschauung* (3rd ed.). Weinheim und München: Juventa.

Weiss, M. (1988). Kostenkennwerte staatlicher Schulen. Zur Problematik ihrer Verwendung bei Systemvergleichen und der Festlegung der staatlichen Finanzhilfe für Privatschulen. *Recht der Jugend und des Bildungswesens, 3,* 48–55.

Weiss, M. (1998). Ist Bildung noch zu finanzieren? In S. von den Steinen & C. Sulzbacher (Eds.), *Schulentwicklung und Schulsozialarbeit.* Hohengehren: Schneider.

Weiss, M., & Mattern, C. (1991). The situation and development of the private school system in Germany. In H. von Recum & M. Weiss (Eds.), *Social change and educational planning in West Germany* (pp. 41–62). Frankfurt: German Institute for International Educational Research.

TABLE 10.1   Development of Relative Enrollments at Private Primary Schools
in OECD Countries (in Percent)

OECD Countries	1970	1975	1980	1985	1989	1995	75/95
Australia	20	-	20	23	25	26	6*
Austria	3[b]	3	3	4	4	4	1
Belgium	52	52	53	55	56	56	4
Canada	2	2	3	3	4	4	2
Denmark	6[a]	7	9	9	10	11	5
France	14	14	15	15	15	14	0
Germany	1[a]	-	-	2	2	2	1
Greece	7	8	6	6	7[f]	6	-2
Ireland	100	100	100	100	100	100	0
Italy	7	7	7	7	8	8	1
Japan	1	1	1	1	1	1	0
Netherlands	73	70	68	68[d]	69	69	-1
New Zealand	13	9	9	2	3	2	-7
Norway	0	1	1	1	1	1	1
Spain	28	37	36	34	35	29	-8
Sweden	0	0	1	1[e]	1	2	2
Switzerland	-	2[c]	2	2	2	3	1
Turkey	1	0	0	0	1	1	1
UnitedKingdm	-	-	4	5	5	5	1**
United States	12	13	11	11	12	12	-1

Note. a For 1971, b For 1972, c For 1976, d For 1984, e For 1986, f For 1988, g For 1990;
* Basis year 1970. ** Basis year 1980. From: UNESCO-data bank, own calculations.

TABLE 10.2 Development of Relative Enrollments at Private Secondary Schools in OECD Countries (in Percent)

OECD Countries	1975	1980	1985	1989	1995	75/95
Australia	24	27	29	32	34	10
Austria	5	6	7	7	8	3
Belgium	-	64^a	65	67^b	69	5*
Canada	-	7^a	7	6	6	-1*
Denmark	-	11	14	16	15	4*
Germany	-	6^a	7	8	7	1*
Greece	-	9	3	4^c	4	-5*
Ireland	70	70	-	-		
Italy	5	6	6	7	6	1
Japan	14	13	13	15	16	2
Luxembourg	10	8	8	7^b	7	-3
Netherlands	72	72	72	73	76	4
New Zealand	14	13	5	5	5	-9
Norway	-	3	3	5	1	-2*
Spain	46	37	35	32	29	-17
Sweden	1	-	0	1	-	-
Switzerland	-	7	6	6	8	1*
Turkey	-	2	3	4	3	1*
United Kingdom	-	8	9	9	8	0*

Note. a For 1983, b For 1987, c For 1988, * Basis year 1980. From UNESCO-data bank, own calculations.

Chapter Eleven

School Voluntarism, Social Capital, and Civil Society

DANIEL J. BROWN

During the mid-1980s, I became acquainted with a number of public elementary schools rich in volunteers. Although I saw that the donation of volunteers' time constituted a substantial resource for the schools, the existence of so many volunteers presented a paradox for me. My impressions of public education had led me to believe that its raison d'être was to create schools that did not depend much on their communities for support. Ostensibly, they could be independent of their settings and largely free of community constraints. Yet my exposure to these schools showed that volunteer parents contributed actively to programs in public schools and that administrators appeared to welcome them. Was this activity evidence of subversive action designed to undermine the tenets of public education? Or was something else at work? Were these school volunteers actually important or were they simply doing nice things, that is, making insignificant contributions? Were they, in a quiet way, adding something special to the life of their schools?

The use of volunteers in public schools is an example of what has come to be called civil society (Berger & Neuhaus, 1977). The mediating structures, particularly family and neighborhood, are given the job of supplementing the tasks of a governmental agency, specifically a school. On the one hand, the use of mediating structures constitutes a most promising way of addressing some of the problems schools and societies face. On the other hand, they are a necessary but not an entirely certain mechanism to help restore moral society (Himmelfarb, 1998).

In order to understand the merits and limitations of voluntarism in public education, I conducted a Canadian study that investigated what volunteers did, the effects they had, and the ways in which schools responded to them (Brown, 1998). Canada provided an appropriate context for an inquiry into giving behavior in public schools because it is situated between the more traditional old-world European societies on the one hand and the most individualistic society of the new world, the United States (Lipset, 1990).

The initial data were gathered from interviews of 185 principals, teachers, and volunteers. Interviews were conducted in 72 schools found in a variety of contexts in British Columbia, a province in which public revenues for education had been curtailed severely during the 1980s and 1990s. One of the ways schools reacted to the lean years was to rely on voluntarism. Fifty-four were selected from ones known by reputation within their respective 17 districts for their active volunteer programs. Focus was on the exceptional, rather than the status quo, which was represented by 18 unselected schools that provided contrast. The unselected schools were regarded as typical elementary schools within the same districts. The overall emphasis on the selected schools was diminished by secondary data assembled from the extant literature, however. Secondary data were often included in surveys of current levels of voluntarism in public schools and districts from around the world but mainly from the United States. Some of the data were provided by works that have lighted the way for the study of community involvement in education.

In this chapter, I first report on some of the salient results of my study, starting with a sense of the impact of voluntarism on the public schools and the way the schools responded to their many volunteers. The outcome is what I call a *voluntary public school*. I then link voluntarism in public education to cornerstone concepts associated with civil society, particularly the notion of bridging between two classic divisions: primordial institutions such as families and communities on the one hand and modern organizations such as public schools on the other. Once the tentative conceptual framework is set in place, I then turn to the general policy question of how to balance services that rightly ought to be provided by governments and those that could benefit from the personal touch of volunteers. Assuming that voluntarism in public education is a good idea that deserves to take its place among the many policy options for the 21st century, I then sketch certain policies that educational jurisdictions could adopt that would encourage schools to take advantage of the services they can receive via the gift of time. When schools are fortunate enough to benefit in this way, I think of them as *schools with heart*.

Voluntarism in Practice

Schools with volunteers offer many services that schools without volunteers do not. Some of the tasks volunteers perform are mundane ones, such as photocopying and library card cataloging. As one volunteer remarked, "There is no need for the teacher to waste her time doing that. Now she has more time to help the kids." Other tasks were directly instructional, as described by a principal: "We had one of our mothers, who is a constable with the police force, give talks to 80 percent of the classes on her role and the types of things she deals with. I had a lady who gave a demonstration on face painting. We had [Native American] people come in. A father, active in the dance troops, performed for the school. A grandfather did a demonstration of carving." Some events, in which volunteers helped, were mainly social, such as Christmas or Easter parties. Others had a financial goal. Examples were bake sales, hot dog sales, or campaigns to raise money for library books, computer hardware and software, or instructional supplies. Although efforts usually benefited the school, some schools were most generous to external causes. Were these contributions a matter of some necessity rather than just extras? A number of teachers believed that they were, as illustrated by a remark from one: "The volunteers provide more adult bodies in the classroom to meet the individual needs of the children. The children receive a better program because I am able to offer more varied, exciting, and interesting activities. I could not carry out some of my programs without the use of volunteers."

Educators in the sample of elementary schools, particularly those in the selected schools, considered the overall duties accomplished by volunteers to be highly necessary to the education of children in their charge. One head teacher summed up this assessment very clearly: "We couldn't run the school the way we want without volunteers. If we had to do everything ourselves, lots would be left undone." For many teachers, the volunteers were a sine qua non of many services their students were provided with. Yet, the volunteers did not usually appear without some kind of encouragement. The overtures the schools made to the volunteers constitute an important component of voluntarism.

When respondents were asked how the high levels of benevolence came about in their schools, they noted frequently that the principal was either responsible for the initiation of the program of volunteers (in cases when the school was perceived to be hostile or noncommittal to volunteers before the principal arrived), or that the initiative of the principal had increased the level of participation. Why and how would principals engage the people in their neighborhoods as benefactors? The most common justifications were ones such as, "The bottom line has to be the children." One principal suggested that many of his contemporaries had a desire to control the personnel in their schools. In contrast, his orientation was "You need to trust people. I become the facilitator—the guy who removes the roadblocks. I liken my role to being a parent. You must give up control for influence."

Principals who were committed to benevolence worked long hours in their schools and communities to achieve it. Over and over, interviewees enunciated the words, "make them welcome" when they referred to their prospective volunteers. Some spoke of the "attitude of the school" and others stressed a "school climate" that favored benevolence. They used recruitment methods such as written communications sent to students' homes, gatherings at schools, and personal contact in order to ensure that parents in particular were aware of the request to donate their time to their children's education. Whereas principals played mainly an administrative role, the persons who made the direct requests were often committed teachers and enthusiastic volunteers. These willing workers made contacts and offered encouragement to the people they thought might give their time. Whereas selected schools were successful at recruiting volunteers, many unselected schools were not.

This depiction of voluntarism in practice sounds very positive. That is because the responses in the interviews were overwhelmingly supportive of volunteers and the contributions they made to schools. Were there any drawbacks to the use of volunteers? Although minor, some problems required the attention of school personnel: a few volunteers did not maintain confidentiality about students, some offered transportation in unsafe vehicles, and some had questionable motives toward children. Support staff unions occasionally objected to regular volunteer help. And the placement, training, and supervision of volunteers added to the workload of school personnel. Although teachers strongly supported the use of volunteers, they acknowledged these difficulties. Principals in particular watched for and addressed the challenges as they arose. The following case illustrates both the volunteers' participation and the active role of the principal where problems were minimal.

Sawmill School enrolled 84 children in kindergarten to grade seven with five teachers. It is located in a small, rural community that has modest, well-maintained homes and a sense of isolation although it is within 15 minutes travel of a larger town and less than an hour and a half of a small city of 250,000 people. At Sawmill, there were 8 to 10 regular volunteers and 45 others. Some brought toddlers with them. Others were grandparents and uncles. Benefactors made a quilt with the help of students and teachers. It was raffled for $700. Two more quilting bees were planned. Donations from teachers and others were converted into coinage for a money tree that was raffled for $500. Pancakes were served on Winnie-the-Pooh's birthday. At Christmas, poinsettias were sold, wreaths made, children given stockings, and a turkey dinner was provided for all students at lunch time. Benevolence thrived in other ways. Older students phoned the homes of absentees in the safe arrival program and Community Night saw the school kilns opened to pensioners and others. The reaction of the students was seen to be very positive. They became accustomed to the presence of their parents. A volunteer recalled her son's request, "Stop in at recess and say 'Hi,' Mom!" She observed that "they notice when you're not there." Much of this social capital was crafted deliberately by the principal. He established the parents' advisory council and initiated an open door policy in which parents were welcome to come to the school at any time. This change (from a previous understanding that parents were not welcome) was designed to give community members a sense of ownership and make the school "a place where the kids want to go." Linkages with the rest of the community were also a priority of the principal. All teachers lived in the small town. The principal chaired the local recreation association, which held summer and winter programs for adults and school-aged students, and was active in bowling, curling, hockey, softball, and the summer swim regatta. When discussing the role of school personnel, he claimed, "You're one with the community" and described the school–town closeness as "familial."

Granted Sawmill School is small and rural, features often associated with a familial atmosphere, but the same sense of solidarity was evident in the other selected schools that were much larger and located in suburban or urban neighborhoods. Unlike many conventional schools, particularly those referred to as unselected in the sample, they were marked by significant numbers of volunteers. The next section offers a more general description of this special kind of school.

What Is a Voluntary Public School?

A voluntary public school is one that is mainly supported by public funds but receives a substantial amount of its resources in the form of gifts. This definition clearly excludes schools that are strictly public (such as those with no gifts of time, dollars, or goods), and those that are strictly private (those not in receipt of any public aid). The meanings of *mainly* and *substantial* are deliberately left vague, except that most of the resources originate from public revenues via taxation whereas some of the support comes from gifts. *Resources* is taken to mean the total supply of public money, volunteer time, and other donations on which the school depends. Private resources that emanate from exchanges are not included in the definition; voluntary public schools may or may not gain support via fees, lotteries, or the sale of services. Apart from their general sources of support, voluntary public schools also share some particularly notable characteristics.

A voluntary public school receives many gifts. Some, such as tutorial time, aid student learning directly; other gifts assist in learning indirectly, as with teacher clerical support and student transportation; still other donations help with special events. A few persons associated with the school give much; many give a little; many more give none. Although the value of the voluntary school's gifts is modest compared to its public funding, the total monetary equivalent is likely many, many millions of dollars when aggregated across the United States and Canada. The school's benefactors tend to be mothers who are employed part-time or not at all outside the home. Some patrons are single parents, senior citizens, or college students. They give in order to receive personal benefits (such as a sense of fulfillment or employment skills), out of duty to the younger generation, or because they enjoy the sociability of participation.

A voluntary public school is noted for its student achievement supported by the learning norm (students should apply themselves to their studies) and its solidarity between benefactors and children supported by the caring norm (students should give time to others). Its students are linked to their communities and correspondingly, certain community volunteers are linked to their schools. The school is at least partly familial thanks to the presence of parents. Although it receives gifts of physical and financial capital, the school is most strongly marked by its social capital, that is, the network of relations that support its students, school personnel, and community members.

A voluntary public school may be found in any neighborhood. It may be located in wealthier circumstances where parents participate almost automatically; it may be found in a poorer neighborhood or in a context of varying ethnicities where barriers of language and tradition have been overcome so that community members donate their time actively. It may be situated where parental work and family lives do not permit much time for volunteering and it may be located in urban, suburban, or rural settings.

The principal of the voluntary public school makes extensive efforts to locate prospective patrons through various media. Teachers and volunteers are among the most active recruiters. The school offers incentives to donate time: personal benefit, sense of obligation, and potential friendships. Once volunteers are on hand, the school's administrators match them to the tasks to be performed. Donors of time are usually trained on-the-job by teachers and later thanked formally or informally for their contributions. Administrators ensure that volunteers are made welcome in the school. They expend extra effort seeking gifts, and work to build relationships with others outside their school building.

Voluntary Support Staff

Cooperation of support staff and teachers sustain the voluntary public school. Support personnel willingly work alongside benefactors; teachers perceive the contributions positively because the donors increase teachers' ability to instruct and they, on balance, appear to reduce work loads. The home and school organization assumes key responsibilities for the administration of volunteers and establishes fund-raising priorities with school personnel. Although a voluntary public school would not normally receive external assistance designed to attract benefactors, it may be connected to a district program that is intended to increase the numbers of volunteers who give their time to schools.

Where can the voluntary public school be placed with reference to the bureaucratic or communitarian models of schooling? The school retains many of the elements of the bureaucratic model (Bidwell, 1965). Its basically hierarchical structure (with layers of administrators, teachers, and support personnel) is the same as most public schools. It is lodged in a school district organization set up to deliver a state mandated curriculum and to provide most of the resources needed by the school. Instructional and subject matter expertise largely resides with the teachers. Standardized administrative procedures address uniform tasks, such as grouping students and monitoring their progress. Many universalistic expectations of children are upheld. However, some aspects of the bureaucratic model are discarded. Rather than having a sharp separation between school and community, the school blurs the distinction considerably, particularly with the infusion of members of students' families. The services of these people are welcomed and their presence emphasizes the acceptance of at least some of the values of the community that the school serves. Rather than have all the resources of the school provided by taxation, aid also comes from gifts freely given. Consequently, the neighborhood context of the voluntary public school takes on a greater importance than the bureaucratic model would imply.

The voluntary public school may also be compared with the communitarian model that gives rise to the communal school (Bryk, Lee, & Holland, 1993). There are many features that the two types of schools have in common. The voluntary public school may be considered to be a small society in which school personnel, students, parents, and other community members participate. Certain norms are emphasized and the lives of participants are more integrated through the construction and affirmation of norms that make up social capital, particularly for the young. However, the school is not fully a communal school, partly because it retains some public (and therefore bureaucratic) elements. It is not simply an extension of its community; integration is by no means complete. Boards of public education and school district administrators have their say. Nations, states, or provinces assume a governing role and exercise their mandates on a range of functions such as evaluation and employment. Most of the resources needed to sustain the voluntary public school come from outside its neighborhood. It is still a formal organization and not a primary group. It is not strictly a creature of its context.

Thus, the bureaucratic and communitarian models may be used to understand the voluntary public school—but only partially. Actually, the school fits largely under the model of overlapping spheres (Epstein, 1990). If the distinction between family and community is removed and the influence of peers set aside, then two spheres remain, school and community. The voluntary public school exhibits a bridge between these two institutions—one a formal organization, the other an entity with primary group characteristics. Existing neither as a citadel in a foreign land nor as a simple extension of localism, the voluntary public school apparently resolves the tension between the public and the private and between formal and informal social structures. Its generalization of labor and community participation make it communal but its embeddedness within a larger organization and its external funding permit a degree of separation. Resources and controls come from two sources. In order to demonstrate the significance of the major binary division between the private and the public, the next section provides the foundation for understanding the nature of the two institutions that make up modern societies, one communal, the other organizational, and how they relate to school voluntarism.

Bridging Gemeinschaft and Gesellschaft

All of social space may be divided into two parts. One of the earliest thinkers who wrote about this bifurcation was Ferdinand Tonnies who observed that there were two basic forms of human association. He labeled the first one *Gemeinschaft*. It is close to the concept of community in that it exists in nonutilitarian relationships. It refers to bonds such as those formed within families and friendships which exist as "ends in themselves" (Tonnies, 1940). Actions within this realm are governed by love, understanding, and custom, directed by what Tonnies called the "natural will." In contrast, there is *Gesellschaft*. This term is ascribed to calculated relationships. All things, including people, are viewed as means to ends, hence, contracts are based upon results alone. The roles most closely associated with Gesellschaft are those of some businessmen or politicians who appear to care little for the people with whom they deal. Actions in this realm are guided by measures of wealth or power based on the "rational will." Tonnies's elegant statement of what I call the two social galaxies remains the conceptual basis of more current thought.

The distinction between Gemeinschaft and Gesellschaft closely resembles the difference between primary and secondary groups. Litwak and Szelenyi (1969) emphasized the tasks performed within primary groups, which are face-to-face, permanent, affective structures. They consider secondary groups to be wholly instrumental. For instance, the nuclear family undertakes tasks that require few adults whereas extended kinfolk help with commitments that are long-term but not usually face-to-face. Friends provide close bonds with long-term involvement, whereas neighbors do everyday jobs such as aid in the socialization of the young. Litwak and Szelenyi insisted that these primary group roles are neither interchangeable nor can secondary groups substitute for them.

Although Litwak and Szelenyi described the two social galaxies, the most compelling depiction and exposition of them may be Coleman's (1990). He saw the construction of primordial institutions (families, clans, communities, and religious organizations) as based on simple relationships between two persons at a time, such as father and son or king and vassal. These relationships are self-sustaining and extend like building blocks to larger structures. Community thus grows from principal relationships between persons and forms a natural social environment. In contrast, modern corporate actors (such as businesses, governments, and schools) are not self-sustaining but dependent upon third parties (e.g., the roles of customer, server, and owner of a business). Unlike simple relationships, these complex relationships do not require binary personal obligations and expectations as mechanisms for social success. Rather, they invoke complicated maneuvers to attain the satisfaction of all three parties and thus, the continuation of complex relationships is much more involved than simple ones. Modern corporate actors provide a social environment analogous to the constructed physical environment in which human beings live.

Elements of school voluntarism may be seen in light of Coleman's understanding of the two social galaxies and how they function. Using his nomenclature, much of voluntarism emanates from primordial institutions such as families. The relationships are mostly simple and exist between volunteer and student or teacher. Roles are diffuse rather than strictly delineated. Givers identify with schools. Schools become somewhat familial. Students receive a measure of care. To some degree, community is constructed as persons work together on common aims. But voluntarism also takes place with a modern corporate actor, the school, which is based on complex relationships. The school takes actions to encourage benevolence; it also reconstitutes its structures by sharing control so that it augments its resource flows. The school is further embedded in a network of other modern corporate actors that affect its behavior. As described, the alliance between the primordial and modern corporate actors sounds quite harmonious and positive for communities and schools, but that is not the relationship advanced by the foregoing writers.

The thinkers who have analyzed the two social galaxies have stressed two themes. One is that there is extreme tension between these two realms of social interaction. The authors speak of antithetical conditions, allegiance to the two worlds, and their outright incompatibility. This conflict stems largely from the divergent functions they perform (Nisbet, 1962). Individuals often find themselves adrift between the two galaxies, their lives pulled toward both at once. The other theme is that there has been a unidirectional shift over the last 500 years from the dominance of primordial institutions to the near-supremacy of modern corporate actors today, although the authors note that aspects of primary groups or primordial institutions persist (Coleman, 1990).

Unlike the pattern in general society that indicates the near-supremacy of modern corporate actors, voluntarism provides the school with an interinstitutional bridge between primordial structures and the large corporate actors. School voluntarism in particular can foster a remarkably cooperative relationship between the family and community on the one hand and school on the other. Rather than increasing the segmentation of children's lives, benevolence augments the social capital available to children by multiplying the time they spend with members of their communities. The child is claimed. Unlike many public schools, voluntary schools may have succeeded in reversing a social trend evident for five centuries, at least temporarily. As one volunteer in my study said:

(Benevolence) makes the school more open. It makes new parents feel more comfortable. Having parent volunteers in the school gives parents, who cannot come to help, a sense of security because they know that there are familiar parents present to help with their children. By including members from the local community hall (who no longer have children attending the school) in special school events, there is a bridge between the school and the community.

The *intergalactic bridge* is not a one-way link between the hearth and the outside world. It is not used to describe the public school's role as a catapult from private life within Gemeinschaft and primary groups to the public business of Gesellschaft or secondary groups. Rather, the bridge is a pathway crossed and recrossed by many persons in both the school and community. Naturally, the supports of the bridge are the benevolence of the hearth and the response of the school. As individuals traverse this bridge, they pose questions regarding the relationship between the services they perform and the ones for which the public in general ought to bear responsibility. How should the balance be struck?

Government and Voluntarism

According to Coleman (1990), modern corporate actors have assumed control over many services once offered by primordial institutions. For example, the provision or support of health, education, and welfare services by various levels of government is the status quo in North America and many countries worldwide. Governments have displaced the provision of services by primordial institutions—a shift that one writer calls the "crowding hypothesis" (Weisbrod, 1988). Some time ago, Tocqueville (1966, p. 487) warned about the United States, "The more government takes the place of associations, the more will individuals lose the idea of forming associations and need the government to come to their help." He was referring to what is now called social capital and spoke against its depletion. But social capital has not vanished; it exists especially in parts of society where modern corporate actors do not dominate. Still, social capital is affected by governmental action, particularly the ability for individuals to make decisions on matters that affect one's work or personal life. Control of resources has drifted from natural persons to corporate bodies. Coleman (1990) offered an arresting description of this problem:

Thus a person living in a large city, working for a large firm, belonging to a large union or professional association, and having some interest in political affairs receives many benefits in the form of money, services, and other resources, but at the cost of having little control over those events which interest him. The individual in modern society has surrendered control of many of the activities of daily life to those corporate bodies that service him." (p. 459)

As corporate actors, governments have positive intentions but their efforts are sometimes ineffective. They constitute a poor substitute for primordial institutions which are much more closely controlled by individuals. When services are not provided as desired, people begin to see governmental provision as unattractive. Lack of viability may stem from the diverse demands that citizens make upon governmental agencies that really are just suited to providing uniform services. Viability breakdown may also occur when the cycle of accountability (say from elector to politician to bureaucrat) is too large, rather than small enough to link pairs of natural persons—for instance, mother and daughter (Coleman, 1990).

Governmental institutions are also facing a crisis caused by a paucity of resources. This difficulty stems mainly from the desire to reduce public debts. Additionally, economic downturns reduce resource availability because tax revenues available for public spending are lowered. Budget reductions, accompanied by continuation of the desire to maintain services, enhance the call for volunteers and gifts of all kinds (Kramer, 1987). Perhaps as a consequence of the inability of governments to provide many services, voluntarism has blossomed across a broad spectrum of society, including public safety, justice, the arts, recreation, religion, health care, transportation, agriculture, welfare, business, the environment, and the military. One estimate suggests that 20% to 30% of all volunteer programs are associated with the public sector (Brudner, 1990). In fact, even as the public finds governments ineffectual, volunteers are deeply involved in the coproduction of services with governments. Is voluntarism as a means to provide services just a romantic ideal? Some think not:

> Voluntarism evokes so many negative feelings and connotations that it is important to underscore the fact that much of the new interest in voluntarism is not in restoring a situation in which the wealthy bestowed charity on the grateful poor, but in sustaining and strengthening patterns of what might better be called self-help. (Glazer, 1988, p. 136)

The image of lady bountiful is replaced by one of many hands making light work. Sorokin (1954) endorsed the inability of public efforts to substitute for direct giving:

> Real sympathy, a warm heart, unquestioning friendship, all-forgiving love—these free gifts of good neighbors can hardly be granted by official agencies. These gifts are in the long run possibly more valuable than any number of dollars or material goods supplied. In this role the social functions of good neighbors are perennial and immortal. Their forms may change; their substance remains unchangeable. (p. 16)

Such positive assertions about voluntarism should be tempered, however. First, voluntarism sometimes serves just as a fill-in for actions where governmental services and markets leave off. That means there may not be sufficient capacity to sustain the needs of millions of people through benevolence alone. Second, benevolence is susceptible to favoritism, and so there is a risk that some in need will not benefit. Thus, voluntarism is not wholly complementary to the provision of services by other means (Himmelfarb, 1998; Salamon, 1987).

A discussion of voluntarism as it applies to all government services is beyond the scope of this chapter. However, it is fitting to mention its role in addressing the problem of equality of educational opportunity. John Rawls (1971) observed that social justice is achieved through equal opportunity; as such, justice must involve support for the least advantaged. In the context of education, his ideas place all persons on the same footing; family influences on a child's opportunities are discounted. He envisioned a central authority to carry out the redistribution of wealth. This view of justice was challenged by Robert Nozick (1974), who argued that justice constitutes entitlement or benefit. In contrast to Rawls, Nozick asserted that people should benefit from the results of their own labors and not be compelled to give to others. How, then, do policy-makers find compromise and balance justice as equality with justice as benefit? In education, the implication is that schools should manifest both egalitarian and entitlement principles in order to be properly just. Is there a pragmatic way out of the conflict? Wise (1979) suggested that schools should get on with the job of education whereas governments should ensure equity. If that is the case, then voluntarism is seen as a local matter and governments have the responsibility for the redistribution of wealth on the large scale. Somehow, the particular must be balanced with the universal. The next section contains some suggestions.

Policies for School Voluntarism

Voluntarism, defined as the transfer of resources from one actor to another with no certain return, and a concurrent positive interest on the part of the giver for the welfare of the recipient, constitutes a phenomenon that has the potential to become a powerful force within public education. This potential leads naturally to the contemplation of policies to augment voluntarism, policies that are directed at increasing the number of voluntary public schools. Recall that voluntary public schools are mainly supported by public funds but receive a substantial amount of their resources in the form of gifts. This section describes some interventions designed to increase benevolence and thus address the problems of resources and control faced by public education today, as well as enhance learning and the creation of much-needed social capital. An increase in benevolence is desired to transform public schools from citadels into institutions in which parents and community members are welcomed. Fundamentally, the schools may be altered so that they serve the interests of natural persons more readily than they do today.

What could nation-states, states, and provinces do to enhance school voluntarism? The history of action to increase benevolence is extensive. The Parent Teachers' Association was founded in 1897 in the United

States and is now its largest voluntary organization. A significant advance was made by the Public Education Association when it received a grant from the Ford Foundation to establish the National School Volunteer Program. Seventeen large cities started or enhanced programs in this way in 1964. The United States Department of Education maintained an office of volunteers for two years from 1970 to 1972. Today, the leading organization in support of school voluntarism is the National Association of Partners in Education, a nonprofit society (Michael, 1990). There are also reform projects under way that involve benevolence. Most noteworthy is the Institute of Responsive Education's League of Schools Reaching Out in the United States, a national strategy involving a cross-section of schools that is designed to enhance parental involvement and increase the academic and social success of children. Its support comes from foundations (Davies, 1991).

Actions by states to increase voluntarism have been modest. One of the earlier efforts was the establishment of an Office of Citizens' Affairs in North Carolina during 1970–1971. Its aim was to place an adult for each 13 children in primary classrooms. The Florida Education Act of 1975 is regarded as the lighthouse effort, however. It provided training for volunteers and matching funds for school volunteer programs (Hill, 1980). The survey undertaken by Michael (1990) revealed that among the states, Florida maintained the strongest legislative commitment to volunteers, having included estimates of 2,000 schools in programs with 140,000 volunteers.

It would not be difficult for nation-states, states, and provinces to establish programs to encourage voluntarism. But new programs are not regarded favorably in times of retrenchment or debt reduction. If there are not millions in spare cash in the public coffers, what can be done? Voluntarism may be enhanced through the normal resource allocation channels. If only 1% of all available revenues was made available to school districts as funds for voluntarism, the boards and schools could deploy them to amplify the amount of donations already being received, perhaps by a factor of two to four. For instance, if every school had a part-time volunteer coordinator (a person indigenous to the neighborhood), the amount of benevolence could be magnified. It means that the allocation of public funds could be used to generate private resources. It also implies that school finance may be conceived as three-tiered with provision at the national, district, and school-site levels. If states and provinces were to offer basic funding for educational equity, districts were to add some dollars, and neighborhoods were asked to contribute a further reasonable percentage to school operations, then the benefits of voluntarism could be realized by most public schools. Persons who conceive of public education as fully public may find this proposal shocking. That is partly because public schools have seldom asked for direct help. Yet, if elected officials and educational administrators pointed out the public obligation to support schools through voluntarism, the public's view of the institution would change. As one teacher in the study said, "We need to be honest, . . . we need their help in educating their kids." People of all predispositions would offer their help to public schools.

It may be expected that persons who hold strong egalitarian views or those whose power is threatened may speak and act against proposals that embody voluntarism, despite its generally beneficial outcomes. Yet, these difficulties may be overcome because benevolence achieves certain aims deemed to be very positive for schools. These aims include a union of schools with their neighborhoods and communities—a desirable condition that was ignored until recently. Thus, educational finance, which has been directed toward the elusive goal of student equity for 100 years, can accommodate another goal—the enhancement of community. The implementation of some or all of these specific policies toward fostering benevolence in education would result in bonds between schools and neighborhoods within a framework of governmental support.

The state can pay the bills but it can't love a school. What kind of educational institutions do we want for our children at the start of the millennium? Can they be schools with heart?

Acknowledgment

Portions of this chapter are taken from Brown (1998).

References

Berger, P. L., & Neuhaus, R. J. (1977). *To empower people: The role of mediating structures in public policy.* Washington, DC: American Enterprise Institute.

Bidwell, C. E. (1965). *The school as a formal organization. In J. G. March (Ed.), Handbook of organizations* (pp. 972–1022). Chicago: Rand McNally.

Brown, D. J. (1998). *Schools with heart.* Boulder, CO: Westview Press.

Brudner, J. L. (1990). *Fostering volunteer programs in the public sector.* San Francisco: Jossey-Bass.

Bryk, A. S., Lee, V. E., & Holland, P. B. (1993). *Catholic schools and the common good.* Cambridge, MA: Harvard University Press.

Coleman, J. S. (1990). *Foundations of social theory.* Cambridge, MA: Belknap Press.

Davies, D. (1991, April). *Testing a strategy for reform: The League of Schools reaching out.* Paper presented at the annual meeting of the American Educational Research Association, Chicago.

Epstein, J. L. (1990). *School and family connections: Theory, research, and implications for integrating sociologies of education and family.* In D. G. Unger & M. B. Sussman (Eds.), Families in community settings: Interdisciplinary perspectives (pp. 99–126). New York: Haworth Press.

Glazer, N. (1988). *The limits of social policy.* Cambridge, MA: Harvard University Press.

Hill, C. P. (1980). *A comparative study of formal volunteer programs in educational settings.* Unpublished doctoral dissertation, University of Utah, Salt Lake City.

Himmelfarb, G. (1998). Democratic remedies for democratic disorders. *The Public Interest,* 131, 3–24.

Kramer, R. M. (1987). Voluntary agencies and the personal social services In W. W. Powell (Ed.), *The nonprofit sector: A research handbook* (pp. 240–257). New Haven, CT: Yale University Press.

Lipset, S. M. (1990). *Continental divide: The values and institutions of the United States and Canada.* New York: Routledge.

Litwak, E., & Szelenyi, I. (1969). Primary group structures and their functions: Kin, neighbors, and friends. *American Sociological Review,* 34, 465–81.

Michael, B. (Ed.). (1990). *Volunteers in public schools.* Washington, DC: National Academy Press.

Nisbet, R. (1962). *Community and power.* New York: Oxford University Press.

Nozick, R. (1974). *Anarchy, state and utopia.* New York: Basic Books.

Rawls, J. (1971). *A theory of justice.* Cambridge, MA: Harvard University Press.

Salomon, L. M. (1987). Partners in public service: The scope and theory of government-nonprofit relations. In W. W. Powell (Ed.), *The nonprofit sector: A research handbook.* (pp. 99–115). New Haven, CT: Yale University Press.

Sorokin, P. A. (1954). *The ways and power of love.* Boston: The Beacon Press.

Tocqueville, de A. (1966). *Democracy in America.* (G. Lawrence, Trans.; J. P. Mayer & M. Lerner, Eds.). New York: Harper and Row. (Original work published 1835)

Tonnies, F. (1940). *Fundamental concepts of sociology* (C. Loomis, Trans.). New York: American Book Company.

Weisbrod, B. A. (1988). *The nonprofit economy.* Cambridge, MA: Harvard University Press.

Wise, A. E. (1979). *Legislated learning: The bureaucratization of the American classroom.* Berkeley: University of California Press.

Chapter Twelve

Balancing the State, Markets, and Civil Society in Education Reform:
Trends and Issues in England and the United States

WILLIAM LOWE BOYD

Recent school reform efforts in England and the United States have many parallels. Both have combined opposing impulses: more centralization (an increasing role for the central government, as well as state governments in the USA) and more decentralization or devolution (i.e., more decision-making powers and choice to schools and parents). Both countries, but especially England, have seen centralization more than offset devolution, contrary to claims the two were to counterbalance each other. For example, in both nations, national curriculum standards and testing have become issues raising fears for freedom, diversity, and local control. Consequently, both countries have growing reactions against centralization.

Significantly, the policy debate in both nations has focused mainly on the "state" and "big government" versus market forces and individualism, while neglecting until recently the role and importance of the "civil society" in education and social reform. The imbalance between structural and normative issues caused by this neglect has become increasingly apparent as problems in the moral order of society have become more salient. This paper discusses these developments and reflects on the prospects in England and the United States for a more balanced approach to educational reform.

Framing the school reform debate as a choice between the advantages of markets or of the public sector, obscures the most fundamental issue. This question, as Strike (1997, p. 20) argues, is how can we "have schools that are educative communities that serve both the public and private functions that schools need to serve"? It seems unlikely that this goal can be reached via the mainstream reform debate. School reform is usually framed in narrowly economic and technocratic terms (developing human capital and economic competitiveness); humanistic values, democracy and community are neglected or pushed to the periphery. The overwhelming concern of business leaders and policy makers is with improving the workforce and economic competitiveness. Moreover, as Kahne (1996) has powerfully demonstrated, mainstream policy analysis adds to the problem: It is so technocratic that it lacks both the vocabulary and the inclination to examine important questions of democracy, community, and social justice:

> Currently, policy analysts emphasize a different agenda. Assessments of educational quality focus on individual rather than group achievement and on standardized and meritocratic notions of equality. Indeed, policy analysts lack the vocabulary, the conceptual frameworks, and the technical procedures needed to consider systematically and articulate concern for these alternative ideals. Important questions regarding the relation between schooling and the promotion of democratic communities are not the subject of systematic analysis. . . . Despite the respect Dewey commands among educators, those assessing educational policy generally ignore the social concerns of democratic communitarians. (Kahne, 1996, p. 246)

While economic issues command center stage, countries such as U.K. and the United States certainly share a growing concern about the breakdown of families, traditional values, civility and civic participation (Himmelfarb, 1994). However, until recently this has been very much a secondary concern in education policy and, importantly, one rarely addressed by major reform policy initiatives. What kind of role do schools have in this social sphere? Can schools be more successful in moral and character education? How should schools teach citizenship and democratic values? What is their relationship to the "civil society," that is, the independent "third sector" of voluntary associations (e.g., families, clans, churches, civic organizations) that "mediates between our specific individuality as economic producers and consumers and our abstract collectivity as members of a sovereign people" (Barber, 1998, p. 4)? To what extent should schools be communities unto themselves or part of the larger polity and national community? (For a discussion of this question, see Davies & Guppy, 1997.)

Conventional discourse pitting market-oriented reforms versus "big government" solutions usually skirts these normative issues or addresses them rhetorically rather than substantively. Recent developments in England and the United States, however, suggest growing discontent with both of these polar alternatives. Debates in both nations increasingly attempt to introduce local government, local communities, voluntary associations, and parents as important actors in more effective school reform.

This chapter begins by outlining the debate about alternative approaches to school reform. Then it illustrates these issues by reviewing developments in England and the United States. Finally, it considers the implications for community and democracy in schools and society.

Approaches to School Reform

In response to the changing world economy (e.g., the decline of traditional industries in developed nations and the rise of the knowledge or information industries), debates have focused on the best way to achieve greater economic competitiveness and better educated workforces to meet the new demands to "work smarter." This issue has been seen mainly in structural terms: Can we devise policies to "restructure" government school systems to make them more effective or, as some contend, are they so bureaucratic, monopolistic, and ineffective that they must be fundamentally transformed or even replaced by a privatized, market-driven system? Initially, these debates pitted "top-down" approaches to education reform against "bottom-up," school-based approaches. As evidence began to emerge suggesting that elements of both approaches were needed, much of the debate shifted to how best to combine and balance these opposing approaches. But the normative issues associated with the voluntary sector or civil society and with family and community norms, responsibilities and relationships in education were generally neglected until recently.

Initially, the debate asked, should we try to fix school systems via top-down approaches (such as national standards and testing, mandates, and accountability schemes) or via bottom-up, approaches at the school level (e.g., professional development, 'capacity building" and the 'self-managing school')? Gradually, a third option began to emerge: Should we use strategies combining both of these approaches, in the belief that they need and will complement each other? At the same time, some have argued for more radical approaches to try to transform or replace government school systems via the introduction of market forces, school choice, and privatization. Ultimately, policy makers sometimes have combined elements not only of the top-down and bottom-up, but also the fixing and transforming strategies.

The approach of combining strategies recognizes that each strategy may have weaknesses as well as strengths. Rather than either top-down or bottom-up, reformers increasingly agreed with management theorists, such as Peters and Waterman (1982), who claimed that excellent companies are characterized by "simultaneous loose-tight properties." That is, they are "both centralized and decentralized" (p. 15) and distinguished by "the co-existence of firm central direction and maximum individual autonomy" (p. 318). In this view, the firm central direction sets the key values and parameters that guide activity, but the sphere of activity has an openness that encourages individual initiative and creativity. Analysis of education policy initiatives, effective schools, and effective management practices suggests that the optimum approach in school reform also might be characterized by "simultaneous loose-tight properties (cf. Fullan, 1994). However, as elaborated below, the British and American experiences suggest that achieving balanced "simultaneous loose-tight properties" is a very elusive quest. The tendency, as in Chicago's well-publicized school reform efforts (Smylie, Kahne, & Shipps, 1997), is to tilt back and forth, between looseness (devolution) and tightness (centralization).

Of course, the goals of education reform and the debate surrounding it are more complicated than this quick overview suggests. For instance, as Davies and Guppy (1997) note, national curriculum and testing schemes may be advocated not just to improve student achievement and workforce competitiveness—goals of economic conservatives—but also (and especially in nations experiencing growing diversity due to immigration) in pursuit of "cultural literacy" (Hirsch, 1988) and national unity—goals of cultural conservatives. Thus, in both Britain and the United States, differences in goals between economic conservatives and cultural conservatives have led to major differences in the direction of policy (Ball, 1990; Jenkins, 1995; Strike, 1997). While economic conservatives and libertarians favor markets and a minimal state, cultural conservatives wish to use the state to impose their version of what the national culture should be. In Britain under Margaret Thatcher, the latter impulse was dramatically in ascendance.

As it turns out, attempts to use national curriculum and testing schemes, whether for economic or cultural goals, have proved to be quite controversial in Britain and the United States. Above all, such efforts draw governments into decision-making on very sensitive policy questions, politicizing a wide variety of curriculum and assessment issues, many of which previously were quietly handled by educational experts. Thoughtful observers agree that there are dangers to freedom in such government involvement (Black, 1994; Strike, 1997) and Stephen Arons (1997) goes further, asserting that it opens up a "short route to chaos."

Beyond further politicizing education, the other great danger in getting national governments involved in determining curriculum and testing schemes is that this power may be abused for political purposes (Arons, 1997; Strike, 1997). As Arons argues, it can lead to the enactment of what counts as "official knowledge," to the detriment of freedom in, for instance, the pursuit of scientific knowledge or the expression of minority or contrary views. With the advent of the National Curriculum in England, for example, the far-reaching powers of the Secretary of State for Education sometimes have been used to micromanage the curriculum. Among the controversies this caused, prior to New Labour taking control of government in May 1997, one arose from an edict that the study of British history would not include recent decades. Critics alleged this policy was intended to preclude debates about the Thatcher government's record in school classrooms often staffed by teachers hostile toward Thatcherism.

The power of economic globalization and the standardization that it brings in many domains, not just education, have produced a much noted countervailing response: the rise of "tribalism" and identity politics, as diverse immigrant, ethnic, religious, and national and sub-national groups seek to assert and protect their distinctive cultures, traditions, and rights (Barber, 1995; Davies & Guppy, 1997). In education, this has led to controversy between cultural conservatives and the champions of minority interests but, nevertheless, to at least partially successful efforts to establish multiculturalism, anti-racism and diversity in the curriculum. Efforts to design and implement national curriculums now must contend with these sensitive matters. Here, groups on the political left and right find a cornucopia of disputes. To the extent that multiculturalism finds support, those running schools and making policy must contend with a new multicultural vision of "nation building" not the "melting pot" but the "mosaic," the "view that national polities ought to be communities of communities, with schools playing a vital role in this reconstruction" (Davies & Guppy, 1997, p. 443).

Problems of Social and Cultural Disintegration

With the explosion of the internet, satellite television, videos, movies, and multinational mass marketing, issues of culture and multiculturalism have escalated. We truly now live in a global "electronic village." At best, this is a mixed blessing because the great breakthroughs in communication and the flow of information have been accompanied by a worldwide flood of images and ideas from Hollywood, MTV, and Madison Avenue. This blitzkrieg of marketing and consciousness-altering images and ideas is endangering indigenous cultures and socializing the youth of the world to the crass ethic of hedonism and non-deferred gratification celebrated around the clock on MTV (Barber, 1995). Post-socialist nations once characterized by "collectivization" find themselves being pulled to the other extreme via "commodification." All of this raises serious questions of values and philosophy. Although the flow of information over the internet is a boon to education, learning requires at least a modest commitment to deferred gratification, which is an increasingly endangered ethic.

As Kymlicka (1995) notes, "Globalization has made the myth of a culturally homogenous state even more unrealistic, and has forced the majority within each state to be more open to pluralism and diversity." This important effect of globalization challenges the old paradigm of public education as a "neutral" vehicle for national unity based on majority values. Tensions mount as public education's universalistic "one-best system" tries to accommodate cultural diversity without betraying its "common school" philosophy. Can the "center hold" in public education when, as Alan Wolfe (2000, p. A22) observes, "America is engaged in an experiment in moral federalism, as state and local governments take sides in the country's culture wars." Whose version(s) of moral standards shall the public schools adopt? Irving Kristol summed up the current social and political situation in the United States as follows:

> The current breakup experienced by the American family is having a profound effect on American politics, as well as on American society. One can go further and say that the social problems we are confronting, problems either created or exacerbated by our welfare state, are making the welfare state a cultural issue as well as an economic one. The Christian Right understands this, as does the secularist left. The "culture wars" are no political sideshow. Today, and in the years ahead, they will be energizing and defining all the controversies that revolve around the welfare state. (Kristol, 1996, p. A16)

One can vigorously debate about the extent to which it is the welfare state or the capitalist state that has created or exacerbated the social problems confronting us, but there is no doubt that they are there. With soaring divorce and illegitimacy rates, the lives of families and children are increasingly imperiled. The neglect of children, especially poor children, in America is appalling. The burgeoning senior citizens' lobby can vote, but children can't. As a result, Sylvia Hewlett (1991) notes that, "We spend nine times as much on the elderly as on children, and twice as much on military pensions as on AFDC [Aid for Dependent Children]. We underwrite multiple bypass surgery for prosperous seventy-year-olds but fail to find the money to provide prenatal care for poor women." As James Garbarino (1995) sees it, we are now raising children in a "socially toxic environment" polluted by the combined effects of poverty, the breakdown of families and communities, the neglect of children, the glamorization of violence in the movies and television, soaring levels of actual violence and crime, including the proliferation of guns and shootings, drug and alcohol abuse, and the threat of AIDS. Similarly, Steinberg (1996) argues that school reform is limited by forces lying "beyond the classroom."

Another problem is the increasing concentration of the poor, the underskilled, and underemployed in the inner cities of large metropolises. The American version of this, compounded by racism and an exodus to the suburbs of the middle class and of employment opportunities, has produced an "underclass" that William Julius Wilson (1987) calls the "truly disadvantaged." With the rapid disappearance of opportunities for unskilled labor, social conditions in the inner-city ghettoes have plummeted to acute levels of squalor and despair (Wilson, 1996).

Finally, this summary of negative trends must also include the breakdown of the sense of commonweal, of community and caring, as too many citizens in our highly secularized and "de-moralized" societies (Himmelfarb, 1994) narrowly pursue their economic self-interest, assert rights without a sense of responsibility (Etzioni, 1993), and retreat from communal activities into solitary television viewing (Garbarino, 1995; Putnam, 1995). In a widely cited article, this marked decline in civic participation and communal involvement, and its troubling implications for democracy, were captured metaphorically by Robert Putnam (1995), who asserts that many Americans are now, in effect, "bowling alone," rather than participating as members of clubs and associations.

Given the magnitude of the problems outlined here, one can rightly ask how much the schools can reasonably be expected to contribute to their solution. Still, the tendency to see the schools as vehicles for the resolution or at least amelioration of social problems is deeply imbedded in the public's mind. While this is a misguided attitude that sets the schools up for failure, it is still true that schools, because of the strategic place they occupy in society, can in fact contribute to the reduction—if not solution—of many social problems.

Developments in British and American Education Policy

Although school reform policies in Britain and the United States have become increasingly similar, the politics behind them have differed. Until 1994, school reform policies in the United States generally enjoyed broad, bipartisan support. By contrast, British school reform was highly controversial during the long ruling Conservative governments of Margaret Thatcher (1979–1990) and John Major (1990–1997), with Conservatives (the Tories) and the opposing Labour Party very much at odds. In the past, one would have assumed there would be sweeping changes when the Labour Party took control of the national government, as it finally did in May 1997. Despite the heated ideological differences between the parties, however, the Labour Party—in its reincarnation as "New Labour" under the leadership of Tony Blair—surprised even its own members by retaining most of the Tory policies established in the far-reaching Education Reform Act of 1988 and subsequent related Acts.

The United States also experienced some surprising developments. In the November 1994 election, the Republicans gained control of both houses of Congress for the first time in 40 years. Because the Right wing of the Republican party gained control, many features of President Clinton's (Democratic Party) policies were challenged. The bipartisanship characterizing education policy over the prior ten years suddenly disappeared, as the moderate Republicans who had provided this support became less influential. As an immediate consequence, the "Goals 2000: Educate America Act," passed in March 1994, came under intense attack and faced threats of being dismantled (as did the U.S. Department of Education itself). Ironically, the Goals 2000 Act actually constituted one of the most striking examples of American bipartisanship in education policy. It represented a culmination and enactment, through the leadership of Democratic President Bill Clinton, of many aspects of Republican President George Bush's "America 2000" education strategy, which had been announced in April 1991.

Background: Parallels in Education Policy

In many ways, the major political parties in Britain and the USA parallel each other: Conservatives and Republicans have much in common, as the strong friendship between Thatcher and Reagan demonstrated. Likewise, Labour and the Democrats are inclined toward similar philosophies, although socialism never has played the role in the Democratic party or the USA that it has in Britain. But, beginning in the mid-1970s, the decline of public faith in the welfare state and the growing ascendance of the conservative belief in individualism, competition and market forces forced both the Labour and Democratic parties to rethink their philosophies and try to reinvent themselves to compete more effectively for middle class voters. Indeed, the "scale and speed of the "new Labour" cultural revolution, under the leadership of Tony Blair, had many in the Labour Party "shell-shocked." This prompted some to ask, "Is Labour now too right-wing?"

The trends described above, along with a sustained "discourse of derision" (Ball, 1990) in the media, eroded the legitimacy of "progressive education" policies in both Britain and the USA and changed the focus of the policy debate. Although this process of derision was not as dramatic in America as that portrayed in Britain by Ball (1990), the effects were quite similar. This can be seen readily by comparing Ball's (1990,

p. 45) analysis with that by Clark and Astuto (1986) of American developments. Clearly, ideology and debate over education policy developed in both countries along a number of parallel lines, despite many significant differences in historical, social and political context.

Thus, the parallels between the school reform efforts of the Thatcher and Major governments in Britain (and their continuation, in large part, under Blair's "New Labour" government) and those of the Reagan, Bush, and Clinton governments in the United States were extensive and, after 1991, increasingly so due to the thrust of President Bush's "America 2000" education strategy and President Clinton's continuation of this approach in his "Goals 2000: Educate America Act."

Some of these similarities came from conscious transatlantic borrowing of policies. For example, Britain's Secretary of State for Education, Kenneth Baker, made a whirlwind visit to the United States, saw some of our magnet schools, and this led to the idea for the creation of City Technology Colleges (CTCs). Similarly, the idea of school-business compacts or partnerships, especially the example of the Boston Compact, got extensive attention in Britain. More recently, aspects of Britain's Education Reform Act (ERA) of 1988 (especially its National Curriculum and assessment provisions) were strongly echoed in "America 2000" and "Goals 2000."

Major Policy Issues

With this brief background of parallels in education policy between Britain (more specifically, England) and the United States, let us turn to the major policy questions each country faces. In broad terms, the issues they confront revolve around (1) how much the government or the market should shape education policy, and (2) the proper relationship between the central government and local or regional governments, communities, voluntary organizations, and parents.

England. Under the conservative governments of Thatcher and Major, the education system in England was radically reformed, from top to bottom, in a most dramatic (and for those living within it, traumatic) fashion (Stearns, 1996). Despite the widespread discomfort of educators, and numerous research studies reporting negative or questionable effects of many of the changes (e.g., Fitz, Halpin, & Power, 1995; Gipps, 1995; Whitty, 1995), the British public liked most of the reforms. This led to New Labour's acceptance of most of these policies. Indeed, in assessing New Labour's education policy, Power and Whitty (1999) found much more that aligns with the neoliberal policies of the Thatcherite "new right" than with either the "old left" or the "third way" policies that Tony Blair has claimed to be at the philosophical heart of New Labour. Power and Whitty (1999, pp. 538–540) note, for example, that "quasi-markets remain the principal means of distributing resources," that the "deficit view of LEAs seems to be as strong . . . as under the Conservatives," that choice and diversity continue to be key elements, and that, rather than ending selection of students by ability, this practice is being "extended through the increasing number of 'specialist schools.'"

While both the Conservatives in the U.K. and the Republicans in the USA share many views and values, they differ dramatically in their attitude toward a strong central government. This difference illuminates important dimensions of the politics of both nations. In the United States, Republicans favor the 'least government possible' and wish to see as many aspects as possible of the federal role returned to the states and local governments (or simply left undone). The government most feared by Americans is the Federal government. This view has become even more salient with the recurrence of what Hofstadter (1965) called the "paranoid style in American politics," and also the rise of the Christian Coalition as a very important political force supportive of the Republican Party. For members of the Christian Coalition, there is little difference between being 'pro-family' and 'anti-government,'" and to be 'pro-family' in a Christian way is at the center of their belief system. The increasing important of religion in American politics, incidentally, highlights another important difference between Britain and United

States: If religion is not 'dead' in Britain, in comparison to the role it plays in the USA, it is far less visible as a force in public life.

In stark contrast to the Republicans' deep faith in local government, the Tories—and especially the Thatcherites—seemed to mistrust local government and, consequently, dramatically increased the powers of central government, especially in education policy. From the Tory point of view, local councils and LEAs in England and Wales too often had been under the control of the Labour Party. As Conservatives see it, Labour governments (at whatever level) tend to be wasteful, big spenders, and also political impediments to the realization of Conservative goals—especially, the dream of a simultaneous restoration and renewal of traditional British society, one that this time is embedded in an 'enterprise culture.' Hence, it follows that strategies to weaken local government were a leading motif of the Thatcherites.

Thus, the Tories accompanied measures for devolution in education with extensive and, many contend, overriding central controls that Republicans would find unthinkable. For example, critics argued that the Tory education policies (especially local management of schools [LMS], centrally controlled funding formulae, and the undermining of the LEAs) had reduced, if not destroyed, the democratic local governance of education. Of course, Conservatives would rightly contend that these critics ignored the democratic input of locally elected and appointed "school governors" and school staff to the governance of each state school under LMS.

The United States. The evolving politics of American education are best seen by examining developments associated with the "Goals 2000: Educate America Act" and the quest for agreed-upon national standards that it launched. This Act codified a strategy know as "systemic school reform" in the United States. The Act sought higher student learning outcomes for all children by encouraging our fifty states to voluntarily (1) adopt rigorous standards and curriculum frameworks related to the eight national education goals, (2) link them to a strong testing or performance assessment system, and (3) establish "opportunity to learn"

(OTL) standards specifying the minimum resources and opportunities that schools should provide to give all students a fair chance to learn the more challenging curricular content upon which they would be tested. For the intellectual work behind this, see Smith and O'Day (1991), O'Day and Smith (1993) and Clune (1993). The idea of "opportunity to learn" standards quickly proved to be controversial, on political as well as pedagogical grounds, and was essentially "dead on arrival" as a political matter.

The "Goals 2000" Act was the product of a long policy development process which began about 1986 with the work of the National Governors Association. The initial idea revolved around achieving agreement on six broad "national education goals," which was accomplished in 1989 under the leadership of the Republican President, George Bush. This process enjoyed broad bipartisan support from Republican as well as Democratic governors and legislators, although President Bush ran into opposition from the Democratically controlled Congress over the specifics of his related "America 2000" reform strategy, most notably because his plan called for public funds for private schools.

Under Democratic President Clinton, the "America 2000" plan was repackaged as "Goals 2000" (without funds for private schools) and passed with bipartisan support. However, as noted earlier, this bipartisanship evaporated in the heat of the stunning Republican electoral victory in November 1994. With the Republicans in control of both Houses of Congress for the first time in 40 years, and the Right wing of their party in ascendance over the moderates, war was declared against "big government" and what were perceived to be the many inefficient and unnecessary government programs and agencies the Democrats had created.

Like the splits within Britain's Labour Party over how to deal with comprehensive versus selective schooling, the Republicans have divisions within their ranks over national standards and comprehensive or 'systemic' school reform. Corporate business leaders, whom Republicans tend to count as their own, very much see the need for national standards and systemic reform, but many rank and file Republicans are suspicious of these efforts.

Since the November 1994 election, the Goals 2000 Act has been increasingly demonized by right-wing Americans (Sharpe, 1995), some of whom, as noted earlier, have revived the "paranoid style in American politics." For example, Sharpe (1995, p. A6) reports that "some parents were circulating rumors that Goals 2000 was connected to a United Nations cabal and were discussing how school inoculation programs could result in injections of mind-controlling substances." At its most extreme, the paranoid style is epitomized by the recent growth of paramilitary, anti-government 'militias' and survivalist groups.

Although the Act is replete with references to the voluntary nature of states' participation in the program, the perennial fear of federal control of education (e.g., in selecting curriculum, controlling standards and testing, and using the coercive potential of federal funds and regulations) has plagued the program.

However, the effort to set "national" if not federally controlled education standards for curriculum and testing is continuing in the United States, principally through the activities of national associations and state governments. Yet, even at this level of activity, problems have mounted. Not only have (non-federal) attempts to codify standards for history and English language and literature proved highly controversial, but now even the supposedly value-free domain of math standards has exploded with controversy (Kronholz, 1997).

Having seen the federal "Goals 2000" effort largely sidetracked, as an alternative President Clinton sought approval for a program of national testing of all fourth grade students in reading and all eighth grade students in mathematics. Republicans strongly resisted this plan, because the federal government was to be involved in the creation of the tests. Rather than more standardization and centralized control, the Republicans countered with a plan for federally funded school vouchers, to enable parents to choose the type of school they wish their children to attend. Exemplifying our divided government's penchant for "gridlock," Congress failed to enact either plan.

Toward a More Balanced Approach

The frequent standoff in Congress, between advocates of big government solutions and champions of market choice, illustrates the need for a
more balanced and middle-ground approach to policy. If government
control of the curriculum can threaten freedom, insufficiently regulated
market choice in education can undermine equality. Democracy and
community are vulnerable in both cases. Note that Giddens (1998) sees
the "third way" not as a "middle-ground" approach, but as one that is
"beyond left and right." Strike's (1997) penetrating analysis of these
issues suggests directions for solutions:

> The policy making community has tended to see the point of vouchers and charter
> schools as the creation of quasi-markets in education. However, the motivation of
> those who have sought to create charter schools and of the parents who have sent
> their children to them often seems more communitarian in character. That is, people
> start charter schools because they have a distinctive picture of the character of a
> good education that they are unable to pursue within the confines of most public
> schools. Thus they seek a less regulated environment and a community of the like
> minded. (pp. 12–13)

> [T]he standards movement and systemic reform abet the tendency to conceptualize
> schooling as a government service to be efficiently provided to clients. Parents and
> students are thus not likely to be seen as community members, citizens, participants,
> or owners of the education to be provided. While inefficiency is no virtue and effi-
> ciency is no vice, we should consider whether the framework in which questions
> about efficiency are asked poses the issues in a wrong or misleading way. Possibly
> in an educational system in which there is a stronger sense of community and own-
> ership, efficiency will be easier to achieve. Perhaps we need to focus more on what
> makes schools good communities and less on what makes them efficient organiza-
> tions. (pp. 19–20)

In the competition between curriculum standards and testing on the one
side and school choice and market forces on the other side, the "standards" approach has captured the most attention of policy makers in recent years in both England and the United States. The assumption of the

"systemic" reformers has been that "high stakes" testing of the required standards would force students and teachers to perform at higher levels. Although some evidence of improvement exists, other results indicate real limits on how far (and how fast) high pressure testing can succeed by itself, especially with the most disadvantaged students most in need of improvement. For example, Prestine's (2000) preliminary findings about the implementation of the state of Illinois' new Learning Standards are revealing. She found that some schools whose students have long achieved high test scores made no effort to implement the new standards and still obtained higher test scores than less advantaged schools that made major efforts to implement and teach to the new standards.

In both England and the United States, expectations for success via testing have been based in part on optimistic assumptions about the ability of schools to replicate the practices associated with unusually effective schools. But the presumed knowledge of "what works" derived from the "effective schools" research has often been oversold by advocates and critics looking for a "quick fix." Indeed, the "school effectiveness" movement is now facing mounting criticism. Too often, it has become an oversimplified recipe that underestimates the severe social conditions in which inner city schools operate, legitimates blaming schools and educators for failing schools, and neglects the fiscal, professional, and community development needs of such schools and their neighborhoods (Power & Whitty, 1999; Slee & Weiner, 1998). Evidence of this shift in thinking is seen not only in Britain (Mortimore & Whitty, 1997; Slee & Weiner, 1998), but also in the United States. For example, even some conservative commentators such as Pearlstein (1999) have objected to the sweeping assumptions of the Heritage Foundation's "No Excuses" campaign (Carter, 1999) which argues that there is no excuse for failing schools now that we know "what works."

Of course, few would argue that schools do not matter, or that they cannot make a very important difference in the lives of children. But they seldom can overcome all adverse circumstances by themselves. Something more is needed, and that something is increasingly defined as not only the involvement of parents but also of a revitalized community and civil society that provides the supportive "social capital" needed to help children succeed. This idea is attracting increasing support from both the political left and right in Britain and the United States. For instance, an editorial assessing the first six months of Labour's education policy in 1997 stated that:

> One of the most exciting developments is the recognition that many aspects of life not directly related to matters educational have a bearing on pupils' achievement. The White Paper emphasizes the importance of nutrition and school meals. Jack Straw's policies at the Home Office reflect the expectation that parents are responsible for socializing their children. Homework clubs and after-school schemes are springing up everywhere. (*Times Educational Supplement*, October 31, 1997)

The Labour government seemed to be trying to balance its interventionist stance with strong efforts to engage a wide range of parents, community groups, and even football clubs to motivate a dramatic improvement in pupil achievement, especially among less advantaged groups. Indeed, the partnership theme highlighted in the White Paper is exemplified by Labour's "Education Action Zones," an initiative that Power and Whitty (1999) and Halpin (1999) view as the closest (but still incomplete) approximation to a "third way" in education policy. The public, private and voluntary sector relationships envisioned as part of the education-business partnerships in Education Action Zones represent Giddens' (1998) notion of how to "make things happen." As Halpin (1999) notes:

> [This] requires the state to take on new roles. In particular it must underplay its function as monopolistic provider of welfare services and strengthen its capacity to create the necessary regulatory frameworks within which public, private and voluntary sectors cooperate. This entails providing as well the necessary infrastructures to ensure that socially excluded groups can act as full citizens and thus take greater control over the nature and direction of their own lives. (p. 354)

Similar kinds of efforts to involve parents, community groups, and associations in improving education are also seen in the United States. A wide range of "community connections" projects and movements are in progress, especially in our large urban school districts where our most disadvantaged students tend to be concentrated. One important example of this is the coordinated, school-linked services movement, which focuses on ways for service agencies to cooperate in mounting a coordinated and comprehensive, rather than fragmented and piecemeal, approach to serving the needs of "at risk" children and their families (Dryfoos, 1994). A key method is often the use of "case managers," who look after the overall needs of children and families and facilitate a coherent response to these needs on the part of cooperating, specialized service agencies. How these collaborative models, involving disparate agencies and organizations, are managed or governed and linked to schools, and the degree to which there is provision for democratic, community involvement are challenging and problematic issues in the coordinated services movement (Crowson & Boyd, 1996).

In the community connections sphere, a variety of alternative models and theories of schools and community relationships exists. For example, numerous scholars have used the concept of "sense of community" to explain or highlight social differences between schools. In a seminal work, Coleman and Hoffer (1987) argued that, in contrast to modern-day American public schools, Catholic schools tend to be based around functional communities where school members share the same place of worship and interact with each other both in and out of the classroom and in and out of the school. They made the point that urban Catholic schools are able to attract large numbers of non-Catholic families by offering a "value" community supportive of their beliefs and expectations about schooling and child rearing. For the school and its members, the result is a network of mutually reinforcing social relationships—a well of "social capital" to be tapped for the purpose of attaining meaningful educational goals (see Brown, this volume).

The use of faith-based organizations as a means of tapping into powerful networks of social capital is a growing policy trend in the United States. In 1995, the Clinton Administration issued guidelines for religious expression in public schools, to curb overzealous interpretations of our Constitutional separation of church and state. Such interpretations had intimidated educators and led to a common view that public schools had to be "religion free" zones. The U.S. Department of Education now has a section of its internet web site devoted to guidelines on "Religion and Schools" [www.ed.gov/inits/religionandschools] and the February 2000 issue of its Community Update publication featured a front page story entitled "Faith Communities Partner with Public Schools to Help Children Learn." During 1999, both major presidential candidates endorsed the idea of government and faith-based organizations working together to combat social ills, and the topic is the subject of an important new book by Charles Glenn (2000).

In England, the principal religions have long enjoyed state funding for their "maintained" schools. Beginning in 1998, for the first time a few Muslim, Sikh, and Seventh Day Adventist schools were approved for funding. As Britain has become an increasingly multicultural nation, a broadly representative task force of citizens and religious leaders was convened to determine the fundamental values the population now shares. Composed of 150 people, the National Forum for Values in Education and the Community succeeded in defining a shared set of common values and ethics that could be used for the purposes of moral education and unity in Britain (Tate & Talbot, 1997). Relatedly, Professor Bernard Crick was appointed chair of an Advisory Group on Education for Citizenship and the Teaching of Democracy (see Halliday, 1999 for a critical appraisal). In 1998, this body presented its initial report on a framework and guidelines for effective education for citizenship and democracy (QCA, 1998).

Concerns about the declining quality of citizenship and public participation, and about violence and shootings at schools in the United States have led to efforts similar to those in Britain. In 1998, citing the nation's poor civic health, the National Commission on Civic Renewal released its report, "A Nation of Spectators" (Blair, 1998). To fight apathy, reduce violence, and foster good citizenship, the report advocated teaching character education and service learning in schools. In May 2000, another group, the National Alliance for Civics Education was formed to combat political apathy and cynicism (Hoff, 2000). This alliance plans to campaign for effective civic education in schools. These are just two examples of the mounting interest in programs in conflict resolution and civic and character education.

Conclusion

The increasing emphasis on civic education, community connections and partnership programs in England and the United States is a promising development in educational and social policy, but these programs clearly have a very long way to go to achieve their goals. In England, while the Education Action Zones (EAZ) have strong potential for the enhancement of education and community development, they face numerous problems. Observers worry, for example, that they are inadequately funded; that developments within them may collapse when funding ceases; that the partnerships are likely to be imbalanced, with business interests dominating; that they are experiments with "other people's children"; and that they could lead to increased inequality between disadvantaged areas (Halpin, 1999; Power & Whitty, 1999). In principle, EAZs should promote new forms of local democratic practice and accountability. Early observations, however, suggest that old forms of practice are hard to escape in planning and public meetings. David Halpin (personal communication, June 20, 2000) reports that "Deliberation on issues [in community meetings] tends to be largely one-way and focused on contributions by officers. It also seems that both strategic and operational decisions are sometimes made at venues other than the [EAZ forums], and that forum meetings are often used as an opportunity to report on matters resolved elsewhere."

The scale of social problems and needs in communities with longstanding concentrations of disadvantage is a daunting obstacle. For example, in Philadelphia, Pennsylvania, the sixth largest school district in the United States, Superintendent David Hornbeck led a major effort at systemic reform for 6 years, from 1994–2000. With support from the

Annenberg Foundation and other donors, 150 million dollars of extra money was raised and invested in Hornbeck's visionary "Children Achieving" program of standards-based reform, which was supported by a tightly connected and exemplary program of coordinated, school-linked services. Yet, after modest improvements in student achievement and other indicators, Hornbeck resigned in June 2000 in the midst of a budget dispute, citing inadequate funding and support (Christman, forthcoming).

From this and other examples, it is clear that major success on a large scale in educating disadvantaged children is very difficult to achieve and requires a high degree of sustained effort and support. The success stories most often involve a few schools or smaller school districts, rather than our largest districts. "Going to scale" with these successful models is still a major problem. Yet, more comprehensive approaches hold more promise than policies that focus heavily on either testing accountability or choice pressures, or on either government-driven or market-driven reforms. More comprehensive policies can enlist and combine the respective strengths of government, market, and civil society involvement in improving and revitalizing public schools and the communities they serve. In a balanced involvement of government, markets, and civil society in education, each ideally can compensate for the shortcomings of the others. The voluntary and informal networks of the civil society (e.g., parent groups, neighborhood associations, community and faith-based organizations) are critical in providing vital social capital for the oversight and support of children. The relationships embedded in these networks can help generate trust, establish expectations, and create and enforce positive norms that facilitate the success of schools in their twin tasks of promoting both academic and citizenship goals (Driscoll & Kerchner, 1999). The major challenge therefore is to achieve and maintain the partnerships and political conditions necessary for balancing and sustaining the normative and structural features required for successful comprehensive reform efforts. See also Hill, Campbell, and Harvey's (2000) persuasive analysis and recommendations concerning the need for sustained, comprehensive approaches to urban school reform, including what they call a "community partnership" strategy.

References

Arons, S. (1997) *Short route to chaos: Conscience, community, and the re-constitution of American schooling*. Amherst, MA: University of Massachusetts Press.

Ball, S. J. (1990). *Politics and policy making in education: Explorations in policy sociology*. London: Routledge.

Barber, B. R. (1995). *Jihad vs. McWorld*. New York: Times Books.

Barber, B. R. (1998). *A place for us: How to make society civil and democracy strong*. New York: Hill and Wang.

Black, P. J. (1994, Summer). Performance assessment and accountability: The experience in England and Wales. *Educational Evaluation and Policy Analysis*, 16, 2, 191-204.

Blair, J. (1998, July 8). Decrying nation's poor 'civic health,' group urges schools to take action. *Education Week*, vol. 17, no. 42, p. 15.

Carter, S. C. (1999). *No excuses: Seven principals of low-income schools who set the standard for high achievement*. Washington, DC: The Heritage Foundation.

Christman, J. B., Corcoran, T., Foley, E., & Luhm, T. (forthcoming). Philadelphia's Children Achieving initiative: The promise and challenge of systemic reform in urban school districts. In J. G. Cibulka & W. L. Boyd (Eds.), *Reforming urban school governance: Responses to the crisis of performance and confidence*. Westport, CT: Ablex/Greenwood.

Clark, D. L., & Astuto, T. A. (1986, October). The significance and permanence of changes in federal educational policy. *Educational Researcher*, 15, pp. 4-13.

Clune, W. (1993b). Systemic educational policy: A conceptual framework. In S. H. Fuhrman (Ed.), *Designing coherent educational policy: Improving the system* (pp. 125-140). San Francisco: Jossey-Bass.

Coleman, J. S., & Hoffer, T. (1987). *Public and private high schools: The impact of communities*. New York: Basic Books.

Crowson, R. L., and Boyd, W. L. (1996), Structures and Strategies: Toward an Understanding of Alternative Models for Coordinated Children's Services. In J. Cibulka & W. Kritek (Eds.), *Coordination among schools, families and communities: Prospects for educational reform* (pp. 137-169). Albany, NY: SUNY Press.

Davies, Scott, & Guppy, Neil. (1997). Globalization and educational reform in Anglo-American democracies. *Comparative Education Review*, 41, 4, 435-459.

Driscoll, Mary E., & Kerchner, Charles T. (1999). The Implications of Social Capital for Schools, Communities, and Cities. In Joseph Murphy & Karen S. Louis (Eds.), *Handbook of Research on Educational Administration*, second edition. pp. 385-404. San Francisco: Jossey-Bass.

Dryfoos, J. G. (1994). *Full-service schools: A revolution in health and social services for children, youth, and families.* San Francisco: Jossey-Bass.

Etzioni, A. (1993). *The spirit of community: Rights, responsibilities, and the communitarian agenda.* New York: Crown Publishers.

Fitz, J., Halpin, D., & Power, S. (1995). *Opting into the past? Grant maintained schools and the reinvention of tradition.* Paper presented at the annual meeting of the American Educational Research Association, San Francisco, April 21.

Fullan, M. G. (1994). Coordinating top-down and bottom-up strategies for educational reform. In R. F. Elmore & S. H. Fuhrman (Eds.), *The governance of curriculum.* Alexandria, VA: Association for Supervision and Curriculum Development.

Garbarino, J. (1995). *Raising children in a socially toxic environment.* San Francisco: Jossey-Bass.

Giddens, A. (1998). *The third way: The renewal of social democracy.* Cambridge, UK: Polity Press.

Gipps, C. (1995). National curriculum assessment and reporting in England. Paper presented at the annual meeting of the American Educational Research Association, San Francisco, April 21.

Glenn, C. L. (2000). *The ambiguous embrace: Government and faith-based schools and social agencies.* Princeton, NJ: Princeton University Press.

Halliday, J. (1999, March). Political liberalism and citizenship education: Towards curriculum reform. *British Journal of Educational Studies*, *47*, 1, 43-55.

Halpin, D. (1999, July-August). Utopian realism and a new politics of education: Developing a critical theory without guarantees. *Journal of Education Policy*, *14*, 4, 345-361.

Hewlett, S. A. (1991). *When the bough breaks: The cost of neglecting our children.* New York: Basic Books.

Hill, P. T., Campbell, C., & Harvey, J. (2000). *It takes a city: Getting serious about urban school reform.* Washington, DC: Brookings.

Himmelfarb, G. (1994, Fall). A de-moralized society: The British/American experience. *The Public Interest*, No. 117, pp. 57-80.

Hirsch, E. D. (1988). *Cultural literacy: What every American needs to know.* New York: Vintage Books.

Hoff, D. J. (2000, May 17). Civics alliance forms to combat youths' political apathy, cynicism. *Education Week, 19*(36), p. 5.

Hofstadter, R. (1965). *The paranoid style in American politics and other essays.* New York: Knopt.

Jenkins, S. (1995). *Accountable to none: The Tory nationalization of Britain.* London: Penguin Books.

Kahne, J. (1996). *Reframing educational policy: Democracy, community, and the individual.* New York: Teachers College Press.

Kristol, I. (1996, September 9). The feminization of the Democrats. *Wall Street Journal,* p. A16.

Kronholz, J. (1997, November 5). 'Standards' math is creating a big division in education circles. *Wall Street Journal,* pp. A1 & A6.

Kymlicka, W. (1995). *Multicultural citizenship: A liberal theory of minority rights.* New York: Clarendon Press, Oxford University Press.

Mortimore, P., & Whitty, G. (1997). *Can school improvement overcome the effects of disadvantage?* London: Institute of Education.

O'Day, J. A., & Smith, M. S. (1993). Systemic reform and educational opportunity. In S. Fuhrman (Ed.), *Designing coherent educational policy: Improving the system.* San Francisco: Jossey-Bass.

Pearlstein, M. (1999, December). School daze: If copying great schools were a simple process, many more would have been duplicated by now. *Twin City Business Monthly.* [http://www.amexp.org/tcbm/tcbm1299.htm]

Peters, T. J., & Waterman, R. H., Jr. (1982). *In search of excellence: Lessons from America's best-run companies.* New York: Harper & Row.

Power, S., & Whitty, G. (1999, September-October). New Labour's education policy: First, second or third way? *Journal of Education Policy,* 14, 5, 535-546.

Prestine, N. (2000, June 9). *Organizational and administrative responses to standards-based reforms: Critical determinants for implementation.* Talk given at Pennsylvania State University, University Park, PA.

Putnam, R. D. (1995, January). Bowling alone: America's declining social capital. *Journal of Democracy, 6*(1), 65-78.

QCA (1998). *Initial report of the advisory group on education for citizenship and the teaching of democracy in schools* (part 1). London: Qualifications and Curriculum Authority.

Sharpe, R. (1995, August 30). Federal education law becomes hot target of wary conservatives. *Wall Street Journal*, pp. A1 & A6

Slee, R., & Weiner, G., with Tomlinson, S. (Eds.). (1998). *School effectiveness for whom? Challenges to the school effectiveness and school improvement movements.* London: Falmer Press.

Smith, M. S., & O'Day, J. (1991). Systemic school reform. In S. Fuhrman & B. Malen (Eds.), *The politics of curriculum and testing.* London: Falmer Press.

Smylie, M. A., Kahne, J., & Shipps, D. (1997, October/November). *Asserting the center: Recentralization in Chicago's decentralized school system.* Paper presented at the annual conference of the University Council for Educational Administration, Orlando, FL.

Stearns, K. (1996). *School reform: Lessons from England.* Princeton, NJ: Carnegie Foundation for the Advancement of Teaching.

Steinberg, L. (1996). *Beyond the classroom: Why school reform has failed and what parents need to do.* New York: Simon & Schuster.

Strike, K. A. (1997, April 16). Centralized goal formation and systemic reform: Reflections on liberty, localism and pluralism. *Education Policy Analysis Archives, 15,* 11, 1-24. [Available on the Internet at: http://olam.ed.asu.edu/epaa/v5n11.html]

Tate, N., & Talbot, M. (1997). Shared values in a pluralist society? In R. Smith & P. Standish (Eds.), *Teaching right and wrong: Moral education in the balance.* Stoke on Trent: Trentham Books.

Times Educational Supplement. (1997, October 31). Editorial: *Half a year onward.* (Internet edition). London, England.

Whitty, G. (1995, April). *School-based management and a national curriculum: Sensible compromise or dangerous cocktail?* Paper presented at the annual meeting of the American Educational Research Association, San Francisco.

Wilson, W. J. (1987). *The truly disadvantaged: The inner city, the underclass, and public policy.* Chicago: University of Chicago Press.

Wilson, W. J. (1996). *When work disappears: The world of the new urban poor.* New York: Knopf.

Wolfe, A. (2000, March 29). Uncle Sam Doesn't Always Know Best. *Wall Street Journal*, p. A22.

Chapter Thirteen

Beyond the Nation-State:
Educational Contention in Global Civil Society

KAREN MUNDY
LYNN MURPHY

The past decade has seen a remarkable rise of interest in the role of civil society in processes of educational change. To date, however, this interest has primarily focused on the involvement of nongovernmental actors in national and subnational educational arenas, where civil society is defined both as a "realm of conflicting normative claims" and as a "social space, where private individuals contribute . . . to the public good by voluntary means" (Meyer, chapter 8, this volume).

In this chapter, we depart from the more common focus on national and subnational definitions of civil society to explore the contribution of international nongovernmental actors to educational change at a transnational or global level. Scholars of international relations have defined international civil society as "the realm of international institutions, including the informal norms and practices of state officials and private citizens operating across state boundaries; international regimes created by explicit agreements among states; international nongovernmental organizations; and formal international agencies" (Murphy & Augelli, 1993, p. 76). They have also begun to argue that an increasingly strong and complex array of international nongovernmental actors and organizational forms is developing into a powerful force for greater global civility, democracy, and transformative social change (Lipschutz, 1996; Rosenau, 1997; Smith, 1997; Smouts, 1999).

In what follows, we begin with a brief introduction to the literature on transnational advocacy and global civil society and to the notion of an emergent global arena of educational contention and change. Drawing on interviews with leaders in nongovernmental organizations, which we conducted by telephone or in the head offices of respective organiza-

223

tions (and cite by a coded informant number) we then analyze the actors and ideological processes involved in a recent and powerful example of global nongovernmental advocacy and contention, the Global Campaign for Education, which was launched by Oxfam International, ActionAid, the Global March on Child Labor, and Education International (along with several smaller nongovernmental organizations) in 1999. This campaign is distinctive not only because it highlights an urgent need for global resources to meet the basic educational needs of all the world's children but also because it focuses on the rights of children to publicly provided, free and equal education. It draws on many of the strategies and themes used by other contemporary transnational advocacy networks, and directly targets the reform of global institutions and governance structures.

Transnational Advocacy Networks and Global Civil Society

In previous periods, political scientists have had a very limited view of the potential for international nongovernmental organizations (INGOs) (which are defined broadly as including all voluntary, nonprofit organizations not directly linked either to the state or to the market, whose operations are jointly managed from centers in several countries) to shape the structure of world politics. Because INGOs have so often been dependent on resources provided by nation-states and marginalized in the decision-making structures of large intergovernmental bodies, they were not viewed as capable of launching independent normative claims, but rather were seen as delivering global goods otherwise neglected by governments and intergovernmental institutions.

Today's assessments of the significance of INGOs and transnational social movements have been changed by the enormous structural transformation of world politics that occurred in the last quarter of the 20th century. Shaped by processes of economic, political, and cultural globalization, there now exists a global political system within which far-reaching decisions are made by such centers of power as states, multilateral institutions, and international corporations, and managers of financial capital. Yet the realm of civil society (including most forms of popular democratic participation and societal compromise) has remained largely territorially grounded in increasingly hollowed-out welfare states (Castells, 1997; Held, 1995; Rosenau, 1992, 1997).

In this context, researchers have become increasingly interested in the growth in "the number, size, professionalism, and the speed, density and complexity of international linkages among [INGOs]" over the past three decades (Boli & Thomas, 1999; Keck & Sikkink, 1998). Such issue areas as women's rights, the environment, peace, development, and human rights have seen remarkable coalitions of non state actors emerge as advocates of major social and political change in what Keck and Sikkink (1998) described as "transnational advocacy network" Today there are transnational nongovernmental coalitions fighting Third World debt (Jubilee 2000 Coalition, 1999), the World Trade Organization, and other forms of social injustice related to processes of globalization (Lynch, 1998). These networks of INGOs have been able to gain significant public attention, often leveraging change at national and international levels without significant financial and electoral resources. And their impact has been cumulative: nongovernmental actors increasingly interact, use similar strategies and repertoires for action, and mobilize around overlapping collective action frames (Boli & Thomas, 1999; Keck & Sikkink, 1998; Smith, 1997).

Many scholars go so far as to argue that this new breed of international activism is fulfilling the promise of "global civil society"(Commission on Global Governance, 1995; Gordenker & Weiss, 1996; Lipschutz, 1996; Lynch, 1998; Otto, 1996; Smouts, 1999). Most would agree, however, that assessing this promise depends on both careful empirical case studies and more precise attention to competing definitions of global civility. For example, liberal theory tends to link the idea of civility to the construction of a pluralist society where a certain degree of civility and consensus permits the functioning of formal, institutionalized democracy (Tocqueville, 1969; Putnam, 1993). Neo-Marxist and critical theories view civil society as the sphere in which hegemony and the compromises of the capitalist state are constructed and potentially opposed (Cox, 1996; Jordan & van Tuijil, 1998; Lynch, 1998;

Murphy, 1994; Offe, 1985; Smith, 1997; Tarrow, 1998). Both groups of theory suggest the importance of studying different dimensions of transnational advocacy efforts: their potential to enhance global civility and democracy, and their capacity to advocate for fundamentally transformative social change and to engage in counterhegemonic contention.

For the purposes of this chapter, we conceptualize global civil society as an emergent semiautonomous political space in which popular organizations come together to participate in existing institutions of global governance and to advocate the construction of new ones. In order to show how education has become the focus for recent transnational advocacy efforts in this emergent political space, we focus on two phenomena: the *mobilizing frames* or ways in which global educational problems and solutions are being articulated and used to legitimate and motivate collective action among the INGOs; and the *repertoires of contention,* the strategies and practices that are being developed by INGOs to leverage educational change. Both concepts are drawn from recent work on transnational social movements (Clark, Friedman, & Hochstetler, 1998; McCarthy, 1997; Smith, 1997; Tarrow, 1998). Finally, we draw from different definitions of civil society to suggest the extent to which these initiatives have helped to build global civil society.

Education in the International Arena

International initiatives in the field of education have a complex and dynamic history. The work of John Meyer and his colleagues (1997) has shown us how nearly universal the Western culture of mass schooling (including the components of curriculum, the organization of the classroom, the popular acceptance of schooling as a feature of the child's life course, etc.) has become. Other scholarship suggests that a significant "international architecture" of educational norms and practices developed directly out of the programs and policies of intergovernmental agencies like the Organization for Economic Co-Operation and Development (OECD), the World Bank, UNICEF, and UNESCO in the period between 1945 and 1990 (Jones, 1988, 1992; McNeely & Cha, 1994; Mundy, 1998, 1999).

Recent international educational initiatives build on this history, but they also bring together two key dimensions of global change. The first is the erosion of the post-World War II aid regime, which has contributed both to mounting efforts among international actors to bolster North - South development assistance and to the development of increasingly sophisticated coalitions of international nongovernmental actors. OECD governments today have dramatically reduced their commitment to international development assistance, leaving international organizations and actors engaged in development to seek new ways of legitimating and supporting their work.

The second dimension of change has occurred across the public policy arenas of nation-states. For both rich and poor nations, the 1980s ushered in an era of economic restructuring that contributed to a profound questioning of the capacity of governments to continue to expand social services, including education (Deacon, Hulse, & Stubbs, 1997; Gummett, 1996; OECD, 1988, see chapter on Education). A new policy agenda" emerged across social policy fields. In the field of education, this has translated into new policies and policy debates that emphasize the redemptive capacity of educational investments in the context of global economic competition, while suggesting a more limited, regulatory role for the state in educational provision. The new menu of educational reforms focuses on ways of financing education and increasing its efficiency, emphasizing such measures as privatization, public choice, decentralization, the use of national testing, cost recovery, and encouragement of NGOs as service providers (Carnoy, 1995; Colclough & Manor, 1993; Hinchcliffe, 1993; Mundy, 1998). International organizations have promulgated and diffused these ideas to developing countries, where an era of high debt and painful economic adjustments have contributed to declining primary enrollments and deteriorating school systems (Reimers & Tiburcio, 1993; Samoff & UNESCO, 1994; World Bank, 1988). The net impact has been a fairly radical and widespread departure from the expansive model of national educational provision implied in the commitments to free, equal, and publicly provided education that characterized the constitutions and public policies of virtually all 20th century welfare states.

The 1990s saw both of these dimensions of global change brought together around mounting international interest in basic education. The movement began in 1988, when senior managers at UNICEF, UNESCO, and the World Bank came together to sponsor a World Conference on Education for All (EFA), which convened in Jomtien, Thailand. Their official aim was to expose the deterioration of worldwide access to education in the poorest of developing countries, and get governments in both the North and South to sign on to a concrete program of action aimed at solving this crisis. They also hoped to use a new emphasis on education as a way of combating their own individual fiscal and legitimacy crises (Black, 1996; Chabbott, 1996; Mundy, 1998; Rauch, 1995).

To some extent, both World Conference objectives were met. At the level of global agenda setting and intergovernmental and governmental discourse, a wide number of subsequent international conferences, commitments, and declarations did indeed reflect what the World Conference on EFA coordinator Wadi Haddad described as "an expanded vision of basic education and a renewed commitment to ensure that the basic learning needs of all children, youth, and adults are met effectively in all countries" (Hodgson, 1998). Beginning with the Rio conference on the Environment in 1992, EFA was taken up as a major theme in all the United Nations sponsored world conferences and summits of the 1990s, as well as by the OECD and nongovernmental organization (NGO) networks on human rights and women and child survival. International resource allocations were also affected, with bilateral and international sources of funding for basic education rising by an additional $3 billion to $4 billion between 1990 and 1995 (Bennell & Furlong, 1997; Colclough & Lewin, 1993).

At the same time, however, the World Conference introduced a framing of global educational needs that actually derogated the major post-World War II international formulations of the right to publicly provided education (Hodgson, 1998; Tomasevski, 1999). For example, the final declaration of the World Conference on EFA included no reference to the right to free, publicly provided education and called for the use of

NGOs as educational service providers. Post-Jomtien basic education programs launched by international donors maintained this framing by introducing such educational reforms as cost recovery, privatization, and decentralization into the educational decision-making arenas of developing country governments (Carnoy, 1995; Jones, 1992; Moulton, Mundy, Welmond, & William, in press; Nelson, 1999; Samoff & Unesco, 1994; World Bank, 1995).

Other observers have noted that the Jomtien conference failed either to target, or later to mobilize sufficiently, OECD governments to deliver the resources necessary for a global expansion of access to public education. Indeed, at the level of resource mobilization, the EFA movement fell far short of raising the estimated additional $10 billion to $25 billion dollars required to meet World Conference goals (Bennell & Furlong, 1997; Colclough & Lewin, 1993). This failure led to the postponement of the original 2000 target for universal basic education proposed by the World Conference on EFA declaration; by the late 1990s the World Bank, UNESCO, and UNICEF had all agreed that a target date of 2015 would be more realistic.

The Rising Involvement of Nongovernmental Actors

One of the most interesting and perhaps unanticipated outcomes of the EFA initiative has been the rise of a transnational nongovernmental advocacy movement that is challenging the World Conference on EFA's framing of global educational needs. To get a sense of its novelty, keep in mind that the historical development of international nongovernmental actors interested in education has been slower, less coherent, and less prominent than that found in other fields such as gender equity and the environment. INGOs did not play prominent roles either as service providers or as advocates in the field of international education between 1950 and 1990, except in the area of adult education, project related training, and literacy. Nor until recently have INGOs been allowed a prominent place in the work of bilateral and multilateral development agencies (Chabbott, 1996; Hall, 1999; Mundy & Murphy, in press; Rauch, 1995; Thomas-Fontaine, 1993; White, 1951).

All of this began to change following the World Conference on EFA in 1990. On the one hand, the conference and subsequent basic educational programs of international and bilateral organizations officially promoted the idea of NGOs as flexible collaborators in the provision of educational services (Archer, 1994; Stromquist, 1998). In a remarkable departure from previous international meetings on educational development, 150 nongovernmental participants were invited to attend the World Conference. By the mid-1990s, driven in part by the new availability of project funding, many of the largest INGOs involved in development and relief (e.g., Care and Save the Children) had begun to expand programs in basic education and girls' education. These INGOs in turn also began to establish their own legitimacy as actors in national and international educational-policy arenas. Although multilateral and bilateral agencies continued to view INGOs primarily as service deliverers rather than active participants in inter-agency decision-making (e.g., NGOs were absent from the interagency EFA steering committee until 1997), there is considerable evidence that INGOs had begun to develop new levels of competency, legitimacy, and coherence in domestic educational policy arenas.

By the late 1990s, several NGOs and INGOs had also emerged as avid coalition builders and lobbyists for education at the global level (Mundy & Murphy, in press). Education became a prime theme amongst a new breed of "virtual" international NGO coalitions, who utilize new telecommunications technologies to build a common front for lobbying governments and the broader public about global governance issues (Gordenker & Weiss, 1996; Smillie, 1995). Thus, for example, both the Reality of Aid initiative, which brings together a coalition of NGOs to critique the delivery of official development assistance, and Social Watch, a coalition of southern NGOs that monitors the 10 commitments made by world governments at the World Summit for Social Development, have made basic education key targets for their work in the last several years (Eurostep/ICVA, 1998; Social Watch, 1999).

The Global Campaign for Education

The most extensive and striking of these new education-related advocacy initiatives is a jointly sponsored global advocacy campaign launched in October of 1999 by Oxfam International, Education International (the largest international association of teachers unions), the Global March against Child Labor, ActionAid, and a variety of smaller NGOs and networks. Clearly disgruntled by the policies and distribution of power within the bilateral and multilateral EFA initiatives, these organizations argue that the interagency and intergovernmental education efforts of the 1990s have been a failure. They plan to make the end-of-decade review of the interagency EFA efforts, including both the regional meetings and the World Education Forum meeting to be held in Senegal in April 2000, key targets for their campaign.

The Global Campaign for Education builds on the independent campaigns of three of its sponsoring partners. As illustrated in Table 13.1, each of these organizations brings specific repertoires of contention and distinctive ways of framing global educational issues. Oxfam International and the family of 11 national Oxfam chapters launched their Education Now campaign in March 1999. Their focus has been on the development and publicization of a Global Action Plan, which calls for specific, financial commitments from the international community for meeting EFA targets; the establishment of an independent facility for delivering resources to education; debt relief for impoverished countries; reform of the IMF, World Bank, and other intergovernmental organizations whose policies have impeded spending on basic education and other social services; increases in levels of bilateral foreign aid; and the use of debt relief and policy reforms to encourage Southern governments to spend more on education (Community Aid Abroad, 1999; Oxfam International, 1999).

Quality Public Education for All, the campaign of Education International, the recently formed coalition of international teachers unions, focuses on building an expansive agenda for international solidarity among teachers unions, not just around the traditional trade union rights of teachers but also around what its general secretary has described as a

Table 13.1. Global Campaign on Education: Partners, Repertoires and Mobilizing Frames

Partners	Core Mobilizing Frame	Distinctive Strategic Repertoires
Oxfam "Education Now"	The keys to global equity and development are debt relief and the provision of free, quality, public education to all. The world needs a coherent strategy which marries debt relief to educational improvement, and which brings about better coordination among international donors, increases global resources for education, and pressures Southern governments to make good on their promises of education for all.	Experience in aggressive global campaigning, lobbying and policy work through its debt and structural adjustment campaigns. Knows how to mobilize media and engage bilateral and international development organizations.
Education International "Quality Public Education for All"	Quality, free, and equal publicly provided education for all is a global priority, only possible if the working conditions and rights of teachers are protected globally and if teachers are engaged in policy decisions.	Union-like structure with access to wide geographic membership. Formal links to International Labor Organization, Unesco, UN, and other international trade union bodies. Solid resource base drawn from membership contributions. Potential to links Northern and Southern constituencies.
ActionAid "Elimu: Education for Life"	The achievement of quality public education for all depends on the involvement of local communities and NGOs in educational decision-making. Definitions of education must include the right to adult, and literacy education.	Distinctive record in community based literacy and adult education programs. Strong local NGO partnerships and commitment to giving poor and marginalized populations a voice in national policy making.

"battle with neo-liberalism," and the "international education crisis . . . [as marked] by austerity measures in the South and by neo-liberal schemes in the North, put forth to destroy free compulsory education and replace it with some form of fragmented semipublic or private system" (Education International, 1993, p. 30.) Education International brings into the international educational arena a nongovernmental actor with a large formal membership and extensive links to international organizations and other public sector unions. It also introduces a distinctive framing of educational issues, which includes the unequivocal commitment to the notion of publicly funded and provided free education and the right of teachers to participate in both national and international educational decision-making arenas.

The third INGO to launch an international advocacy campaign in 1999 was ActionAid, a large British NGO with affiliates in Ireland, France, Italy, and Greece and a distinctive pedigree in community-based adult literacy, and nonformal and nongovernmental educational initiatives in developing countries (Archer, 1994). ActionAid's Elimu: Education for Life campaign is focused on developing local level civil society capacities to participate in educational policy-making and planning at national levels (Jellema & Watt, 1999, p. 4). It has developed as a decentralized coalition of national campaigns and regional networks based in 14 Southern countries (Elimu, 1999).

The Global Campaign for Education brings together the strengths of each of these independent campaigns around the promise to mobilize "public pressure on governments to fulfil their promises to provide free quality education for all people, in particular for our children and for women," through the development of "a united South – North front of NGOs, unions and grassroots organizations similar in scale and impact to the anti-landmines and Jubilee 2000 campaigns" (Jellema & Watt, 1999). The campaign's specific demands fold in the interests of each of the sponsoring organizations, as shown in Table 13.2. The Campaign has also been joined by new organizational partners. The Global March against Child Labor and several southern NGOs and NGO coalitions, including the South Africa NGO Coalition, the Brazilian National Campaign for the Right to Education, CAMPE's Education Watch report in

Bangledesh, and the Citizen's Initiative on Elementary Education in India, are now members of the campaign effort.

Campaign organizers admit that the campaign is a work in progress. The draft strategy and action plans are not yet finalized and each organization continues to develop its own independent campaign program.

Table 13.2: Demands Made in the Mission Statement of the Global Campaign for Education

1. Free and compulsory, quality education for all children, for at least eight years, and a second chance for adults who missed out;
2. Increased provision of quality early childhood education and care;
3. Increased public expenditure on education to at least 6% of GNP, and new resources through aid and debt relief for the poorest countries;
4. An end to child labor;
5. Democratic participation of, and accountability to civil society, including teachers and their unions, in education decision making at all levels;
6. Reform of International Monetary Fund and World Bank structural adjustment policies to ensure they support rather than undermine free, quality education;
7. Fair and regular salaries for teachers, properly equipped classrooms and a supply of quality textbooks;
8. Inclusive and non-discriminatory provision of services for all;
9. A Global Action Plan for basic education to mobilize political will and new resources in support of national education plans to realize the 2015 targets.

Much of the campaign's coalition-building to date has happened around impressive efforts to get national NGOs and teachers unions to cooperate in preparing independent country assessments of the EFA goals set out at the World Conference in 1990. The campaign has been instrumental in organizing NGO parallel conferences at various regional EFA meetings planned to precede the EFA conference in Dakar. In addition, a

Global Week of Action is planned for April 2000, to engage NGOs around the world in advocacy activities the week prior to the EFA conference in Dakar.

Lobbying in the North has also seen significant progress. By mid-1999, Oxfam had been invited to join the EFA Forum, where (as one NGO representative told us) it had "raised the status and voice of NGOs with the campaign and made a clear illustration that NGOs can assert their political agenda." (Interview 12a, UNESCO-NGO Collective Consultation on Literacy and EFA Representative, Oxford, UK, July 7, 1999.)

Oxfam's Global Action Plan was endorsed by the World Bank, UNESCO, UNICEF and USAID--though not without modification. The multilateral development agencies ruled out Oxfam's idea of a special funding facility for education. Oxfam and its campaign partners nonetheless continued to advocate for the establishment of a single fund for global education that would eliminate the current fragmentation and confusion among donor EFA efforts. (Interview 16a, EFA Forum representative, Paris, France, July 28, 1999; Interview 12b, UNESCO-NGO Collective Consultation representative, Oxford, UK, July 13, 1999; Interview 14a, World Bank representative, Washington, D.C., July 13, 1999; Interview 13a, UNICEF representative, New York, New York, July 1, 1999.) In November 1999, the campaign sponsors sent a strongly worded letter to World Bank president James Wolfensohn, signaling their intention of making the end of decade review of EFA commitments their first target. They also issued a "Millenium appeal" letter to heads of states calling for high level participation in the EFA review, and began plans to lobby at the World Summit on Social Development Review in June 2000.

Conclusion: Assessing the Global Campaign

In this chapter, we have discussed the development of a new phenomenon in the international educational arena: The rise of an international coalition of nongovernmental actors focused on educational advocacy.

These organizations have moved into the international education arena not as service providers but rather as advocates mobilized around a well-developed action frame that links the problem of educational access to the wider issues of debt relief, human rights, and global equity. To realize these demands, these organizations employ a remarkable repertoire of strategies, drawn from the experience of other transnational advocacy initiatives. They work at both international and national levels, attempting to build strong national coalitions of NGOs and civil society actors who are capable of bringing grassroots demands home to Southern governments, while also attempting to generate international leverage capable of altering the resource allocations and assistance practices of Northern governments and their development aid organizations. Although it is too early to judge their success, our preliminary research suggests a density and coherence to these efforts that bodes well for the future.

Having said this, it seems important to turn back to the issue of global civil society and to consider the implications that the Global Campaign has for the wider development of world politics. What are its potential contributions to greater levels of global civility and democracy, so often stressed in liberal theories that emphasize the development of the capacity and habits of participation, reciprocity, and social pluralism? Equally important, how far can the Global Campaign go in contesting current global practices and formulations of human needs? Can it provide autonomous and forceful alternatives to the current structure of world order, including strategies aimed both at changing global decision-making structures and supporting local level struggles?

In our interim assessment, it seems clear that the Global Campaign has much to contribute to the development of civility and democracy, insofar as it is enlarging participation and reciprocity among nongovernmental actors around educational issues, and among nongovernmental actors, governments, and international organizations. It is less certain that these new levels of civility around educational issues can be sustained in the same ways as has occurred in the environmental and women's movements. For organizations like Oxfam, its is not clear whether education is simply a temporary venue for INGOs seeking enhanced legitimacy, or a part of a longer term commitment to the realization of a specific, global entitlement? Other potential threats to the Campaign's contributions to global civility and democracy include the likelihood of competition among the campaign sponsors, and the possibility of serious disputes over their various visions of education. For example, there would seem to be a likely tension between ActionAid's emphasis on local community control of education and the assumption by Education International and its teachers unions that educational decision-making is properly concentrated at the national level.

As for the contentious and transformative dimension of this campaign, our research suggests that the Global Campaign has departed significantly from the official framing of global educational needs that emerged at the World Conference on EFA in 1990. First, the Campaign demands the right of civil society actors to play a key role in national and international educational policy arenas, and rejects the notion that they are simply service providers. Second, it argues that Northern governments must expand the resources they provide for education in the poorest of countries. Finally (and perhaps somewhat surprisingly in light of NGO involvement in educational service provision at the national level), these actors have taken a strong stance against the erosion of governmental responsibility for the financing and provision of free public education. This is a direct challenge both to neoliberal policy approaches to educational reform and to the framing of educational rights suggested in the Jomtien World Conference on EFA declaration, where the right to free publicly provided education was not endorsed.

However, potential limitations to the Campaign's capacity for contention seem inherent in both its Northern origins and in its focus on the universalization of the Western model of formal, age-segregated public schooling (so often criticized by sociologists for reproducing social inequalities). Such a focus relies on a cadre of Western-trained experts, a technicist and increasingly neoliberal agenda for educational reform, and an interorganizational framing of global social problems that emphasizes the failure of the weakest states to meet their national responsibilities, but does not highlight the decline of global commitments and resources. Much of the future contentiousness of the Global Campaign for Education depends on how seriously these

tion depends on how seriously these organizations confront the official framing of global educational needs.

The Global Campaign promises to enhance global civil society by opening a political space for the development of what Edwards, Hulme, Wallace (1999) calls "new social contracts" between citizens and authorities at various levels. Meeting this promise would seem to require both the development of significant educational alternatives, and continued efforts to push beyond a narrow view of universal mass schooling as an end in itself toward a broader realization of social entitlements and redistributive justice at a global level.

Acknowledgments

The authors would like to acknowledge the assistance provided by the National Academy of Education and Spencer Foundation, through the postdoctoral fellowship awarded to Karen Mundy, 1998–1999. A more detailed treatment of this topic will appear in the Comparative Education Review, February 2001.

References

Archer, D. (1994). The changing roles of non-governmental organizations in the field of education. *International Journal of Educational Development 14*(3), 223–232.

Bennell, P., & Furlong, D. (1997). *Has Jomtien made any difference? Trends in donor funding for education and basic education since the late 1980s.* Brighton, UK: University of Sussex Institute for Development Studies.

Black, M. (1996). *Children first: The story of UNICEF, past and present.* New York: Oxford University Press.

Boli, J., & Thomas, G. (Eds.). (1999). *Constructing world culture, international nongovernmental organizations since 1875.* Stanford, CA: Stanford University Press.

Bhatnager, B., & Williams, A. (1992). *Participatory development and the World Bank.* Washington, DC: World Bank.

Carnoy, M. (1995). Structural adjustment and the changing face of education. *International Labour Review, 134*(6), 653–673.

Castells, M. (1997). *The power of identity, the information age: Economy, society and culture* (Vol. 2). Oxford, UK: Blackwell.

Chabbott, C. (1996). *Constructing educational development: International development organizations and the World Conference on Education for All.* Unpublished dissertation, Stanford University, Stanford, CA.

Clark, A., Friedman, E., & Hochstetler, K. (1998, October). The sovereign limits of global civil society: A comparison of NGO participation in UN World Conferences on the Environment, Human Rights, and Women. *World Politics, 51,* 1–35.

Colclough, C., & Lewin, K. (1993). *Educating all the children.* Oxford, UK: Clarendon Press.

Colclough, C., & Manor, J. (1993). *States or markets? Neo-liberalism and the development policy debate.* Oxford, UK: Clarendon.

Commission on Global Governance. (1995). *Our global neighborhood* . New York: Oxford University Press.

Community Aid Abroad. (1995). A new era of international advocacy. Oxfam International *Horizons.* Retrieved August 4, 1999, from the World Wide Web: http://www.caa.org.au/horizons/h12/forsyth.html

Cox, R. (1981). Social forces, states and world order: Beyond international relations theory. *Millenium, 10*(2), 126–155.

Cox, R. (1996). *Approaches to world order.* New York: Cambridge University Press.

Deacon, B., Hulse, M., & Stubbs, P. (1997). *Global social policy: International organizations and the future of welfare.* London and Thousand Oaks, CA: Sage.

Education International. (1993). *Congress highlights: Speeches from the Constituent Congress of Education International.* Morges, Switzerland: Education International.

Edwards, M., & Hulme, D. (Eds.). (1996). *Beyond the magic bullet.* West Hartford, CT: Kumarian Press.

Edwards, M., Hulme, D., & Wallace, T. (1999). NGOs in a global future: Marrying local delivery to world wide leverage: Conference background paper: Ford Foundation (mimeo).

ELIMU. (1999). *Newsletter of the Education if Life Campaign, Elimu Update Autumn/Winter 1999* . London: Elimu/ActionAid.

EUROSTEP & ICVA. (1998). *The reality of aid 1998/9: An independent review of poverty reduction and development assistance.* London: Earthscan.

Gordenker, L., & Weiss, T. (1996). NGOs, the United Nations and global governance. In L. Gordenker & T. Weiss (Eds.), *Pluralizing global governance: Analytical approaches and dimensions* (pp. 17–47). Colorado: Lynne Rienner.

Gummett, P. (1996). *Globalization and public policy.* Cheltenham, UK and Brookfield, VT: E. Elgar.

Hall, B. (1999). The International Council for Adult Education: Global civil society structure. In Hall, B. & Tandon, R. (Eds.), *Adult education, globalization and civil society.* London: Zed Books.

Held, D, McGrew, A., Goldblatt, D., & Perraton, J. (Eds.). (1999). *Global transformations: Politics, economics, culture.* Stanford, CA: Stanford University Press.

Held, D. (1998). *Democracy and the global order: From modern state to cosmopolitan governance.* Stanford, CA: Stanford University Press.

Hinchcliff, K. (1993). Neo-liberal prescriptions for education finance: Unfortunately necessary or inherently desirable? *International Journal of Education Development, 13*(2), 183–187.

Hodgson, D. (1998). *The human right to education.* Aldershot, U.K.: Ashgate Publishers.

Jellema, A., & Watt, P. (1999, September). *Confronting the global education crisis: Two NGO campaigns.* Paper presented at the Oxford International Conference on Education and Development: Poverty, Power and Partnership, Oxford, UK.

Jones, P. (1988). UNESCO and the politics of global literacy. *Comparative Education Review, 34*(1), 41–60.

Jones, P. (1992). Chapter 6: Project experience in education & Chapter 7: Setting priorities for educational financing. *World Bank financing of education.* New York: Routledge.

Jordan, L., & van Tuijil, P. (1998). *Political responsibility in NGO advocacy: Exploring emerging shapes of global democracy.* Novib. Retrieved July 12, 1999 from the World Wide Web: http://www.oneworld.org /euforic/novib/ novib1.htm

Jubilee 2000 Coalition. (1999). *Jubilee 2000: Details and interpretations of the Koln Debt Initiative.* Jubilee 2000. Retrieved June 29, 1999 from the World Wide Web http://www.jubilee2000uk.org/news/kolndebt.html

Keck, M., & Sikkink, K. (1998). *Activists beyond borders.* New York: Cornell University Press.

Lipschutz, R. (1996). Reconstructing world politics: The emergence of global civil society. In R. Fawn & J. Larkins, J. (Eds.), *International society after the Cold War.* New York: St. Martin's Press.

Lynch, C. (1998). Social movements and the problem of globalization. *Alternatives, 23,* 149–173.

McCarthy, J. (1997). The globalization of social movement theory. In J. Smith (Ed.), *Transnational social movements, Solidarity beyond the state* (pp. 243–257). New York: Syracuse University.

McNeely, C., & Cha, Y. K. (1994). Worldwide educational convergence through international organizations: Avenues for research. *Educational Policy Analysis Archives,* (electronic), *2*(14).

Meyer, J., Boli, J., Thomas, G., & Ramirez, F. (1997). World society and the nation-state. *American Journal of Sociology, 103*(1), 144–181.

Moulton, J., Mundy, K., Welmond, M., & William, J. (2000). *Paradigm lost: The implementation of systemic educational reforms in Africa in the 1990s.* Manuscript submitted for publication.

Mundy, K. (1998). Educational multilateralism and world (dis)order. *Comparative Education Review, 42*(4), 448–478.

Mundy, K. (1999). Unesco and the limits of the possible. *International Journal of Educational Development, 19*(1), 27–52.

Mundy, K., & Murphy, L. (in press). Transnational advocacy, global civil society: Emerging evidence from the field of education. *Comparative Education Review.*

Murphy, C., & Augelli, E. (1993) International institutions, decolonization, and development. *International Political Science Review. 14*(1), 71–76.

Murphy, C. (1994). *International Organization and Industrial Change: Global Governance Since 1850.* Cambridge, MA: Polity Press.

Nelson, J. (1999). *Reforming health and education: The World Bank, the IDB and complex institutional change.* Washington, DC: Overseas Development Council and John Hopkins University Press.

OECD. (1988). *Structural adjustment and economic performance.* Paris: OECD.

Offe, C. (1985, winter). New social movements: Challenging the boundaries of institutional politics. *Social Research, 52*(4), 817–868.

Otto, D. (1996). Nongovernmental organizations in the United Nations system: The emerging role of international civil society. *Human Rights Quarterly, 18*(1).

Oxfam International. (1999). *Education now .* Oxford: Oxfam International.

Putnam, R. (1993). *Making democracy work: Civic traditions in modern Italy.* Princeton, NJ: Princeton University Press.

Rauch, S. (1995). *The quest for universal literacy: Who got what from International Literacy Year, why and how.* Unpublished doctoral dissertation, University of Massachusetts, Amherst, Massachusetts.

Reimers, F., & Tiburcio, L. (1993). *Education, adjustment and reconstruction: Options for change.* Paris: UNESCO.

Rosenau, J. (1992). Governance, order and change in world politics. In J. Rosenau & E. O. Czempiel (Eds.), *Governance without government* (pp. 1–29). New York: Oxford University Press.

Rosenau, J. (1997). *Along the domestic-foreign frontier.* New York: Cambridge University Press.

Rutherford, B. (1998). Civil (dis)obedience and social development in the new policy agenda: Research priorities for analyzing the role of civil society organizations in social policy reform, with particular attention to Sub-Saharan Africa and Latin America. *International Development Research Center.*

Samoff, J., & UNESCO. (1994). *Coping with crisis: Austerity, adjustment and human resources.* London: Cassell [with] UNESCO.

Smillie, I. (1995). *The Alms bazaar: Altruism under fire. Non-profit organizations and international development: Act globally: the rise of the transnational NGO.* London: Intermediate Technologies.

Smith, J. (Ed.). (1997). *Transnational social movements, solidarity beyond the state.* New York: Syracuse University Press.

Smouts, M. (1999). Multilateralism from below: A prerequisite for global governance. In M. G. Schechter (Ed.), *Future multilateralism.* New York: St. Martin's Press.

Social Watch. (1999). *Social Watch, No. 3.* Montevideo: Instituto del Tercer Mundo-Social Watch.

Stromquist, N. (1998). NGOs in a new paradigm of civil society (1). *Current Issues in Comparative Education* [online]. Available: http://www.tc.columbia.edu/CICE/

Tarrow, S. (1998). Transnational contention. In S. Tarrow (Ed.), *Power in movement: Social movements and contentious politics.* Cambridge, UK: Cambridge University Press.

Thomas-Fontaine, J. (1993). *Collective consultation on literacy for all: Appraisal and prospects.* Paris: UNESCO (mimeo).

Tocqueville, A. (1969). *Democracy in America.* New York: Doubleday.

Tomasevski, K. (1999). *Economic and Social Rights: Preliminary Report of the Special Rapporteur on the Right to Education.* 55th Session of the ECOSAC Commission on Human Rights. New York: United Nations Economic and Social Council, E/CN.4/1999/4, January 13, 1999.

White, L. (1951). *International non-governmental organizations. Their purposes, methods and accomplishments.* New Brunswick, NJ: Rutgers University Press.

World Bank. (1988). *Education in Sub-Saharan Africa.* Washington, DC: World Bank.

World Bank. (1995). *Priorities and strategies for education.* Washington, DC: World Bank.

Contributors

William Lowe Boyd, Distinguished Professor of Education, College of Education, The Pennsylvania State University

Daniel J. Brown, Professor of Educational Administration, University of British Columbia, Vancouver, Canada

Bruce S. Cooper, Professor of Educational Administration, Graduate School of Education, Fordham University. New York

AnneBert Dijkstra, Senior Researcher, Department of Sociology, University of Groningen, Netherlands

Jaap Dronkers, Professor, Department of Sociology and Anthropology, University of Amsterdam, Netherlands

Jurgen Herbst, Professor of History and Education Policy (Emeritus), University of Wisconsin-Madison

Heinz-Dieter Meyer, Associate Professor, Department of Education Administration and Policy. State University of New York at Albany

Karen Mundy, Assistant Professor, International and Comparative Education, School of Education, Stanford University

Lynn Murphy, Doctoral Student, International and Comparative Education, School of Education, Stanford University

E. Vance Randall, Associate Professor and Chair, Department of Educational Leadership and Foundations, Brigham Young University

Ingo Richter, Professor of Law, Director of German Youth-Institute (DeutschesJugendinstitut), Munich, Germany

Kenneth A. Strike, Professor of Philosophy of Education, Cornell University

Geoffrey Walford, Professor in Education Policy, Department of Educational Studies, University of Oxford

Manfred Weiss, Professor of Educational Economics, German Institute for International Educational Research (DIPF), Frankfurt, Germany

Index